LETTERS FROM ROME ON THE COUNCIL BY QUIRINUS

A Da Capo Press Reprint Series

EUROPE 1815-1945

Board of Advisors

JOHANN JOSEPH IGNAZ VON DÖLLINGER

LETTERS FROM ROME ON THE COUNCIL BY QUIRINUS

VOLUME II

DA CAPO PRESS · NEW YORK · 1973

Library of Congress Cataloging in Publication Data

Döllinger, Johann Joseph Ignaz von, 1799-1890.
  Letters from Rome on the Council.

  (Europe, 1815-1945)
  Reprint of the 1870 ed.
  Translation of Römische Briefe vom Concil.
  1. Vatican Council, 1869-1870. 2. Popes—
Infallibility. I. Title. II. Series.
BX830 1869.D63   262.5'2   78-127193
ISBN 0-306-70040-9

Published by Da Capo Press, Inc.
A Subsidiary of Plenum Publishing Corporation
227 W. 17th Street, New York, New York 10011

Manufactured in the United States of America

Letters from Rome on the Council

THIRTY-SEVENTH LETTER.

Rome, April 15, 1870.—The *Constitutio Dogmatica de Ecclesiâ Christi* will receive its definitive form in the Congregation of Easter Tuesday, but the substance is already fixed. It received many significant alterations in the course of discussion, and the ready reception accorded to it as a whole is due to the many detailed amendments which have been conceded. These changes are so important that the spokesman of the Commission, Pie of Poitiers, said in his closing speech it was really the work of the whole Council, so that the Fathers might truly say, " *Visum est Spiritui Sancto et nobis.*" After the insertion of the word " Romana " before " Catholica Ecclesia," the three first chapters were accepted in their amended form. The fourth, on faith and knowledge, was debated only cursorily and by a few speakers on April 8. But this chapter contains a passage of the greatest practical importance. At the end occur these words : " Since it is not enough to avoid heretical pravity, unless those errors which more or less nearly approach it are shunned, we admonish all of the duty of observing the constitution and decrees where such evil opinions not expressly named here have been proscribed and prohibited by this Holy See."[1] The Bishops with good reason saw in this passage a confirmation of the judgments and increase of the authority of the Roman Congregations, *i.e.*, of the tribunals through which the Pope exercises his power. It seemed to them desirable to give due expression to their objections, and accordingly a request was made to the President to appoint a further day for this subject. But as nobody had inscribed his name to speak, the request was refused and the whole debate was closed on that day, Friday, April 8. But to avoid the danger of opposition at the last moment and secure the decrees being unanimous, a certain concession was made by announcing that the closing paragraph should not be voted on till the whole *Schema de Fide*, four chapters of

---

[1] " Quoniam vero satis non est, hæreticam pravitatem devitare, nisi ii quoque errores diligenter fugiantur, qui ad illam plus minusve accedunt : omnes officii monemus servandi etiam Constitutiones et Decreta quibus pravæ ejusmodi opiniones, quæ isthic diserte non enumerantur, ab hâc Sanctâ Sede proscriptæ et prohibitæ sunt."

which only were as yet ready, should be completed. Thus a great point was gained,—a decree on matters of faith was carried by moral unanimity and not by surprise, but after a serious though compressed debate, which helped to win for the views of the minority a very perceptible influence on the form of the decree.

But on the following day, April 9, a notice was communicated that, as the closing paragraph of the *Schema*—beginning with the words " Itaque supremi pastoralis," etc.[1]—had not been treated with sufficient particularity at the last general sitting, it must be again brought forward for deliberation before the whole fourth chapter came to be voted upon. The Fathers were thereby admonished that they might produce their amendments on the fourth chapter at the next sitting. This Congregation was held on April 12, when the final paragraph was put to the vote, and this roused them from the dream of unanimity. It was observed in the debate that if the voting on the paragraph were put off

---

[1] "Schematis de fide catholica conclusio, quæ incipit ab his verbis : *Itaque supremi Pastoralis*, etc., cum de eâ in ultimâ Congregatione generali non satis explicite actum fuerit, adhuc debet subjici Patrum suffragiis, antequam ad ferenda suffragia de toto Capite IV. procedatur. Ideo monentur Reverendissimi Patres, ut nunc in finem *Emendationes de capite quarto* hujus Schematis propositas etiam ad proximam Congregationem generalem secum deferre velint."

till the whole *Schema de Fide* was completed, this would be putting it off to the Greek Calends. But if the fixing of this *Schema* was undertaken directly after Easter, the more important subject of the *Schema de Ecclesiâ* must give place to it, and so it might easily happen that infallibility would not come on at all this spring. To withdraw the closing paragraph would be not only not to maintain but to lose that favourite form of authoritative papal utterance through the medium of the Roman Congregations, which especially required to be upheld. Pie of Poitiers insisted on the fact that the paragraph had been published in the *Allgemeine Zeitung*, and could not therefore without peril be withdrawn even for the moment only.

The Opposition were partly disposed themselves to treat the passage as unimportant. There were some who thought that in principle it was right for the Roman decisions to be respected and a certain authority attached to them, for this was necessary for the government of the Church ; and the very wording of the passage distinguished these decisions from matters defined under anathema. So the minority resolved not to make any collective resistance to it, and many well-known members of the Opposition accepted it without contradiction. Notwithstanding this, when the whole fourth chapter came to be voted on on Tuesday, April 12, the desired unanimity was not attained ; 83 Bishops gave a conditional *Placet* only. They handed in the grounds of their vote in writing, which seem to have been of various kinds, for even the Bishops of Moulins and Saluzzo, who are notorious infallibilists, were among them. Some, especially English Bishops, may well have demurred to the designation " *Romana* Catholica " before " Ecclesiâ ; " others may have thought it necessary to guard their rights as against majorities ; but far the greater number wanted to repudiate the concluding passage. The vote was understood here in this latter sense, and no stone was left unturned to induce the Opposition to yield on that point. The step they have taken makes the deeper impression, because it is known that they have not put forth their full strength.

It must be allowed that the final paragraph contained no actual doctrine which made the resistance of the Episcopate an absolute duty and required unanimous consent, but still it is obvious that the Council thereby sanctioned and strengthened what it ought to have reformed and limited, and therefore the carelessness manifested by a portion of the Opposition admits of no favourable explanation. For the chief cause of the weakness and corruption of the Church is to be found in those Roman Congregations,—in the principles of some and the defects of others. The Bishops who accept the paragraph give their approval, *e.g.*, to the Inquisition and the Index, and thereby prejudice not a little their moral influence and dignity. The vote of last Tuesday does not accordingly appear to me any proof of the firm organization or imposing power of the minority; it only shows what they might accomplish if they chose, but that they do not choose to do as much as they can. But the event will show whether the *Curia* holds to its policy of securing unanimity by prudent and well-timed concessions. The minority will be urged and entreated first to withdraw their objections. If that fails, the Court must either give up the hope of unanimity or accept a very sensible humiliation. For if the text remains unaltered, those who have now given a conditional *Placet* can give no simple *Placet* next time.[1] Rome will certainly exhaust all her arts to avert the scandal of an open opposition in a Solemn Session.

---

[1] [Conditional votes, as will be seen, are not allowed in Solemn Sessions, but only a simple *Placet* or *Non placet*.—Tr.]

I said in a former letter that the Opposition had taken up a position which no enemy from without could dislodge them from, but this did not imply at all that all internal dangers are overcome. These by no means consist in the decomposing influences of hope and fear which the *Curia* makes such use of, or the prospect of a Cardinal's Hat, or again in party divisions at home, which might have disturbed and divided the French, Austrian and North American Bishops. The latter danger might have made itself felt at the commencement of the Council, but constant intercourse and community of experiences during this winter have put an end to it. The real disease which has weakened the minority in the past and threatens it in the future lies deeper—the great internal differences of Catholicism, which are now being brought to a decisive issue, do not coincide with the antagonism of the rival parties in the Council, but divide the minority itself. The main question, exclusive of the immediate controversy and partly independent of it, which divides Catholics into two sections so sharply that no sympathy or confidence can bridge over the gulf, remains unsolved within the minority and constantly endangers their coherence. The common designation of Liberal Catholics tends rather to obscure than to express the principle of this division. By Liberal Catholics may be understood those who desiderate freedom not only *for* but *in* the Church, and would subject all arbitrary power of Church as well as State in matters of religion to law and tradition ; but that is the end they aim at, not their fundamental principle.   Such requirements concern the constitution rather than the doctrine of the Church, law rather than theology.   They are important, but they do not contain the crucial point of the present contest in the Church. The root of the matter lies not simply in the relation to be maintained towards the chief authority in the Church, but in the right relation to science ; it is not merely freedom but truth that is at stake.   It is mainly as an institution for the salvation of men and dispenser of the means of grace that the Church has to deal with the labouring, suffering and ignorant millions of mankind. And in order to guard them from the assaults of popular Protestantism, a popular Catholicism and fabulous representation of the Church has been gradually built up, which surrounds her past history with an ideal halo, and conceals by sophistries and virtual lies whatever is difficult or inconvenient or evil, whatever, in short, is "offensive to pious ears."

But such a transfigured Catholicism is a mere shadow Catholicism, not the Church but a phantom of the Church. Its upholders are compelled at every step to employ various weapons, to ward off any triumph of their enemies and avoid disturbing the faithful in a religious sentiment artificially compounded of error and truth combined. The more the notion of the supreme glory, and even infallibility, of the Pope was developed, the greater solidarity with the past became requisite, that the history of the Popes might not be suffered to bear witness too strongly against such views. To quote a significant phrase in constant use here during this winter, "the dogma must conquer history."[1] A contest has arisen, not of dogma but of a theological opinion against history, that is against truth ; the end sanctifies the means. It was held allowable in order to save the Church and for the interest of souls to commit what would in any other case have been acknowledged to be sin. Not only was history falsified, but the rules of Christian morality were no longer held applicable where the credit of the hierarchy was at stake. The very sense of truth and error, right and wrong,—in a word the conscience—was thrown into confusion. Thus, *e.g.,*

[1] [Cf. *supr.* p. 348.—Tr.]

when Pius v. demanded that the Huguenot prisoners should be put to death, he did right, for he was Pope and a Saint to boot.   Since Charles Borromeo approved the murdering of Protestants by private persons, it is better to approve it than to call his canonization in question. Or one moral aberration is got rid of by another. Many of the leading Catholic writers of this century deny that Gregory XIII. approved the massacre of St. Bartholomew,[1] or that heretics have ever been put to death at Rome.

This spirit, which falsifies history and corrupts morals, is the crying sin of modern Catholicism, and it reaches high enough.   Of the three men who are commonly held in France to stand at the head of the Catholic movement, one wrote a panegyric on Pius v., another under the name of *Religion et Liberté* attacked absolutism in France while defending the double absolutism in Rome, and a third vindicated the Syllabus—all three thus manifesting the influence of this deplorable spirit.

On the other hand the genuine Catholic, who wishes also to be a good Christian, cannot separate love for his

---

[1] [See an exhaustive article on the subject from a Catholic pen in the *North British Review* for October 1869.—Tr.]

Church from the love of goodness and truth. He shrinks from lies in history as much as from present adulation, and is divided by a deep moral gulf from those who deliberately seek to defend the Church by sin and religious truth by historical falsehood. This contrast is most conspicuously exhibited in the question of infallibility, as one example may suffice to prove. The principles of the Inquisition have been most solemnly proclaimed and sanctioned by the Popes. Whoever maintains papal infallibility must deny certain radical principles of Christian morality, and not merely excuse but accept as true the opposite views of the Popes. Thus the Roman element excludes the Catholic and Christian. Such differences obviously cut deep into men's ethical character, and divide them far more decisively than any striving for common practical ends or community of interest and feeling can unite them on the ground of prudence. In presence of so profound an internal division the question of the opportuneness of the definition of infallibility assumes a very subordinate place, and the mere inopportunist is immeasurably removed from the decided opponent of the dogma. Between Bishops who consider Popes fallible and those whose conscience is easy enough to swallow certain

2 G

doctrines of former Popes on faith and morals, and who do not see any deadly peril for souls in giving a higher sanction to these dogmas—between anti-infallibilists and mere inopportunists—the difference is far deeper than the union. The inopportunists stand nearer to the infallibilists than to those who oppose the dogma on principle. They are divided from the one party on a mere question of prudence, from the other on a question of faith and morality ; with the one they are united by an internal bond, with the other by an external bond only which circumstances may dissolve.

This is the true explanation of the halting policy so often observed in the Opposition. The honest opponents of infallibility wished to secure the support of those who do not properly speaking share their sentiments. But they should never for a moment have forgotten that they have to attack what Gratry has rightly described as an " école de mensonge." And the greatest honesty and outspokenness is necessary for defending the honour and truth of Catholicism against that school. Instead of that they exhibit themselves in a false light and obscure the situation.

Meanwhile Pius IX. by his letters to Guéranger and Cabrière has completely and publicly identified himself with that school, at the very moment when Gratry was so unmistakeably exposing its spirit, and he has made this still clearer by the distinctions bestowed on Margotti and Veuillot at the very moment when Newman characterized them as the leaders of " an aggressive and insolent faction." He said plainly to the French Bishop Ramadie of Perpignan that " only Protestants and infidels denied his infallibility." His official organ describes the Opposition as allies of the Freemasons, and he himself calls all who oppose his infallibility bad Catholics. It is true that the Opposition has gradually been brought to make very decided declarations of opinion, and has itself expressed doubts about the future recognition of the Council. But that has complicated its attitude still further. The other party may ask, " Why these doubts about Œcumenicity ? The Bishops of various countries are assembled in great numbers ; the Governments offer no hindrances, and the Council has united itself with the Pope in the greatest freedom in the capital city of the Church. Why then doubt the good results and œcumenical character of the Council and the validity and future recognition of its decrees ?" And the Opposition can only answer, " For the sole and single reason that the Pope destroys all freedom of action by his regulations, that he has already overthrown the ancient constitution of the Church and exercises a power over the Council incompatible with the rights of the Bishops and the freedom of the Church."

The French note is to be presented to-day to Antonelli and next week to the Pope, instead of to the Council. It is doubted whether Pius will communicate it to them.[1]

---

[1] [He refused to do so.—Tr.]

THIRTY-EIGHTH LETTER.

Rome, April 17, 1870.—It is a good sign that the minority have at length recognised the imperative necessity of grappling directly with the problem of papal infallibility, and examining in their own writings this question on which the future of the Church depends. It has been perceived now that it was an unfortunate notion to put forward only grounds of expediency, discretion, and regard for public opinion ; for no answer was left when Spanish, South American, Irish, Neapolitan and Sicilian Bishops said that no such public opinion existed with them, that some were apathetic and others had long held the doctrine, which would create not the slightest difficulty or inconvenience with them, and that they were the majority.

It was high time therefore to take firmer ground, and now this has been done by Cardinals Schwarzenberg and Rauscher and Bishop Hefele, three of the most influential prelates of the Church, or rather by four, for Bishop Ketteler too has either composed or got some one to compose a work on papal infallibility.[1]   But the whole edition had the ill luck to be seized in the Roman Post-office, so that not a single Bishop got a copy.   The authorities seem to know that the work opposes the dogma, on which all the thoughts and plans of the *Curia* now hinge, although Ketteler not long ago showed himself an adherent of the doctrine, and only assailed the opportuneness of defining it.

The *Univers,* as the official organ of the Court, now announces the principle on which the Papal Government acts.   One must distinguish, it says, between the Custom-house and Post-office.   The Custom-house gives the Bishops the missives and packets addressed to them unopened, for it assumes that they will only have proper books sent them.   It is different with the Post-office, which is bound not to favour the dissemination of error.[2]   So the conscientiousness of the officials of the Roman Post-office is a model for the rest of the world, and it is understood that the habitual opening of letters, so far from being immoral, is an expression of

---

[1] This proved to be a mistake.

[2] " Elle estime justement qu'elle a le devoir de ne pas favoriser la diffusion de l'erreur ou des attaques contre l'autorité des Vicaires de Jésus-Christ."

the purest and most delicate morality; for might not a letter contain some error or attack on the rights of the Vicar of Christ? And how could the officials answer to God and His earthly representative for even unconsciously co-operating in the spread of such error?

As I have not seen Ketteler's publication, I can only quote the judgment of a friend who has read it and thinks it will do good service. The other three works are before me. They must all have been printed at Naples, for the Roman police has to look after the consciences not only of the Post-office secretaries and letter-carriers, but of the compositors, printers, bookbinders and booksellers. It cannot allow that any breath of error should sully the pure mirror of their souls, even though concealed under the veil of the Latin tongue; and the corroding poison becomes worse when prepared, as in this case, by Bishops and Cardinals.[1]

I will speak first of Cardinal Rauscher's work, which is the most comprehensive of the three, and touches on many questions passed over in the other two. Written

[1] The infallibilists are of course luckier. Their writings are readily printed and circulated. At the same time with the writings mentioned above, Archbishop Spalding has published a letter to Dupanloup, emphatically denying that he had spoken against the opportuneness of the dogma in the paper he drew up with several other American Bishops, and declaring himself a zealous advocate for it.

in a calm and dignified tone, it carefully avoids every
word or phrase which could offend the *Curia,* and goes
to the utmost length in making concessions possible for
any one to accept without becoming an infallibilist;
but it will nevertheless pour much oil on the flame of
anger which has been blazing for weeks past, and singes
now one Bishop and now another.   Papal infallibility,
says the Archbishop of Vienna, must extend to everything ever decided by any Pope, and the whole Christian world must hold with Boniface VIII. and his Bull
Unam Sanctam that the Popes have received power
from Christ over the whole domain of the State.   That
will be welcome news to those who want to exclude
the Church altogether from civil society.   That the
Popes themselves in the ancient Church did not hold
themselves infallible, that the whole history and conduct of the ancient Church in doctrinal controversies
would be an inexplicable riddle on the infallibilist
hypothesis, and moreover that the Popes have often
fallen into open errors rejected by the Church—all this
is well established, though the author cites only some
particular facts from the abundant sources he has to
draw upon.   He then shows the sharp antithesis between the ancient doctrine of the Church and the Popes

on the relations of Church and State and the enuncia-
tions of Popes since Gregory VII. and Innocent III.
With papal infallibility the whole mediæval theory of
the unlimited power of Popes to depose kings, absolve
from oaths of allegiance, abrogate laws, and interfere
in all civil affairs at their will, must be declared to be
an immutable doctrine with which the Church stands
or falls. The Christian Emperors would have treated
such a doctrine as high treason, and even in the days of
Charles the Great it would have excited universal
astonishment. If this doctrine really had to be preached
now to the Christian people, it would be a triumph for
the enemies of religion, for the best men would soon be
convinced of the utter impossibility of paying any
regard to the precepts of the Christian religion in civil
matters. The Cardinal proceeds to dwell on the forgeries by which the great master of scholastic theology,
the favourite and oracle of all Jesuits and ultramontanes, Thomas Aquinas, was led to adopt the doctrine
of infallibility, and how again his influence shaped the
whole scholastic system and drew the great Religious
Orders, who were bound by oath to maintain his teaching, to adopt it. He concludes in these weighty
words :—" If the Pope is declared to be, alone and

without the Episcopate, infallible in faith and morals, the Œcumenical Councils are robbed of the authority recognised by Gregory the Great, when he said he honoured them equally with the four Gospels ; for they would be and would always have been, even at the time of the Nicene Council, superfluous for deciding on faith and morals.   This doctrine would be a declaration of war against the innermost convictions of the Church, and she would be robbed for the future of those aids supplied by the Council of Trent at her extremest need; even the See of Rome would lose the support the Bishops then assembled gave to it, for after the close of that Council, the power of the Popes became greater than it was before."

The remark of Cardinal Rauscher that, when the dogma of papal infallibility is defined the Church will be deprived of one of her most effective institutions, viz., General Councils, has made a great impression here, as far as I can see.   It is readily understood that an assemblage of men, educated to believe in the infallibility of one master, and to repeat mechanically without examination whatever he tells them, would have no influence among men and would be universally regarded as superfluous, a mere idle pageant rather than any real support to the Church. The Church would be impoverished by the loss of one member of its organism, and that very member would be paralysed which in moments of distress and danger had most effectually protected her.

Bishop Hefele's work is worthy of the man who is beyond question the most profound historical scholar among the members of the Council. One can only regret that a writer so pre-eminently qualified to pronounce a clear and weighty opinion on the whole controversy in all its bearings should have confined himself to the single question of the condemnation of Pope Honorius. Those who wish to know the history of Honorius and the Sixth Council in 681, and to see a flagrant example of the utterly crude and unscientific poverty of that modern scholasticism which is treated as theology in the Jesuit lecture-rooms, may be recommended a brief study of this question, which has already produced so many writings and hypotheses, simple and easily understood as it is in itself. A General Council, acknowledged by the whole Church in East and West, condemned a Pope for heresy after his death, and anathematized him on account of a dogmatic letter he issued. The sentence was without contradiction accepted throughout the whole Church, the Roman Church included, and even introduced into the profession of faith to which every new Pope had to swear at his election. It was repeatedly confirmed by subsequent Councils, and in short remained in full force for centuries, till the Popes were seized with a desire to become infallible. It is only since the fifteenth and sixteenth century, and especially since the Jesuits—beginning with Bellarmine—undertook to revise history according to the requirements of their new dogmatic system, that this extremely contradictory fact had to be submitted to a process of manipulation, and the rock on which all schemes of papal infallibility seemed to be wrecked had to be got out of the way. "Si plus minusve secuerit sine fraude esto," was said in the old Roman law which allowed a creditor to cut a pound of flesh from the body of his debtor, and so do the knives of the Jesuits and curialists cut right into the flesh of history. The Acts of the Sixth Council were said to have been corrupted through the perfidy of the Greeks, and the whole history and even the letters of Honorius to be forgeries. The Popes themselves, Rome, and the whole West had let themselves be fooled by the cunning Greeks into con-

demning an innocent and orthodox Pope as a heretic,
and the letters of Pope Leo II. must also be forgeries.
In short these reasoners were caught in the meshes of
their own net, and when in 1660 Lucas Holstein got the
Roman *Liber Diurnus* printed—an excellent edition of
which Rozière lately brought out in Paris—the whole
impression was suppressed, for it contained the old form
of oath which expressly attested the condemnation of
Honorius. But twenty years later the book appeared
to the great chagrin of Rome, and the infallibilist
school had to change their front. They now turned to
the letters of Honorius and tried to show that they
were perfectly orthodox. But that did not touch the
fact that a General Council had solemnly condemned
a Pope for heresy, and that the whole Church—the
Popes and the Roman Church included—had accepted
the sentence without demur. Hefele has shortly and
pointedly exposed the shifts and dishonesties of this
long controversy carried on in more than a hundred
polemical works ; and he has taken care, at the same
time, to establish conclusively the wide-reaching facts
and general results of the inquiry. He shows (page
11), how up to the eleventh century every Pope swore

to the truth that an Œcumenical Council had condemned a Pope·for heresy.[1]

Cardinal Schwarzenberg's work is chiefly directed
against Archbishop Manning.[2] Hitherto the infallibilists, to avoid pushing their theory into sheer absurdity, had appended the condition of *ex cathedrâ,* which
everybody could interpret more or less stringently
according to his own view, and theologians had actually
given twenty-five different explanations of what was
required for an *ex cathedrâ* decision. In order to
get out of this labyrinth, Manning has propounded
a simpler theory. Everything according to him depends on the Pope's intention ; whenever he " intends
to require the assent of the whole Church," he is
infallible.[3] Schwarzenberg points out with pungent
irony to what monstrous consequences this would lead.
He recalls the saying of Boniface VIII. that the Pope
holds all rights locked up in his breast. And thus it
must be assumed on Manning's theory that the Pope
holds in his own mind all doctrines present and future,

---

[1] [English readers may be referred to Renouf's *Case of Honorius Re-
considered.* Longmans, 1869.—Tr.]

[2] It is now understood to have been written by Dr. S. Mayer under his
direction.

[3] [See *Pastoral on Infallibility of Roman Pontiff.* Longmans, 1869.]

and draws from this internal treasure-house under divine inspiration what he wishes to reveal to the world, so that infallibility becomes inspiration. Has it occurred to the Cardinal that this is precisely the personal opinion of the very man who has now, for the sake of his own infallibility, resolved to plunge the Church into an internal conflict, of which no one can see the end?

It is then further pointed out that, if the new dogma with its consequences prevails, all Governments will put themselves in an attitude of self-defence against the Church. Bishops as well as Councils cease to be any necessary part of the *magisterium* of the Church, and there is no longer any need for the distinct assent of the Episcopate; the only office left them is to praise and accept with thanks every decision of the Pope's. Perhaps they may still be allowed to give their advice before he decides, but they have nothing to say to the decision itself or after it, but only to obey and promulgate the papal revelations.

THIRTY-NINTH LETTER.

Rome, April 23, 1870.—The four chapters of the *Constitutio Dogmatica de Fide* bear in their ultimate shape such evident marks of the influence of the minority, and so many concessions were made in them, that there is a danger of overlooking the greatness of their defeat and their change of mind, should they finally accept the supplemental paragraph mentioned in my last letter but one. Although it was determined that the minority should make no general opposition to this paragraph, there were not a few Bishops who saw clearly enough its importance and danger. They consoled themselves at first with the promise that the suspicious passage, which clothed the Roman Congregations and the mischief they work in the Church with conciliar sanction, would not be voted upon till the still incomplete portion of the *Schema de Fide* came on for final settlement. And when, in spite of this promise, it was announced to be the general wish of the Commission that the voting should take place at once, the opponents were quieted by a written assurance that no new power was thereby to be given to the Roman Congregations, and nothing to be altered about them, but all to remain as of old. Gasser, Bishop of Brixen, had the courage to say, in the name of the Deputation, that the passage did not refer to heresy, though it expressly binds the Bishops to the observance of the constitutions and decrees of the Holy See, not only in regard to heresy (*hæretica pravitas*), but also theological errors and controversies. It is incredible that any one could be deceived by such a ruse as this, and yet it is a fact that not even forty Bishops made the omission of this paragraph a condition of their *Placet*. As the Opposition seemed thereby to be shrunk to less than five per cent. of the Council, the *Curia* was persuaded that it could get rid of them altogether by acting with spirit.

On April 18 appeared an admonition with the following passage : " It must be remembered that according to the Apostolic Brief, *Multiplices inter* (of Nov. 27, 1869), prescribing the method of procedure in public Sessions, no other vote can be given in them than a simple

Placet or *Non placet.*"[1] The Fathers who had given
conditional votes in Congregation had to choose now
whether they would accept the chapter unconditionally
or reject it " sans phrase." It was foreseen that this
alternative would disclose the weakness of the Opposition, and that those of its number who shrank from a
decisive rejection would be won for the majority, for
the real test of an Opposition is not in words but acts.
Protests which are not answered, and speeches which
are not heard, may be patiently borne with, as long as
all goes well in the public voting.   The *Curia*
reckons that the minority will not now dare to show
itself, and thus the unanimity will not be disturbed;
and its consequent resolve might decide the whole
course and upshot of the Council.   If the minority
gives in here, it will have suffered a first defeat, and
must reconstitute itself on a new basis ; by taking part
in decrees carried under anathema, which are against
its own convictions, it breaks with its past, accepts the
responsibility and solidarity of the Council and com-

---

[1] " Animadvertendum quippe est, quod in publicâ Sessione juxta Litteras
Apostolicas *Multiplices inter* d. d. Novembris 1869 Num. VIII., quo modus
procedendi in Sessionibus publicis præscribitur, non liceat aliter suffragium
dare, nisi pure et simpliciter per verba : *Placet* aut *Non placet,* excluso
alio quovis modo."

plicity with the majority. This is to admit that all the petitions and protests it was thought necessary to present in the interests of the freedom of the Council were superfluous and aimless, and all the warnings offered of the threatened danger of its œcumenicity being questioned, etc., unmeaning. For the Council to publish anathemas implies the conviction that it is free, legitimate, and œcumenical, and that the order of business is acceptable. The minority thereby would themselves testify to everything they have hitherto assailed, and the only thing left for them would be to insist on their rights as guarded by the *consensus unanimis.* All other grounds for calling the Council in question would be abandoned, and it might fairly be doubted whether the Opposition would adhere to that after giving up so much; at the same time it is morally certain that the Court and the majority do not acknowledge that right.

During the General Congregation of the 19th, four Bishops, Latour d'Auvergne,. Dreux-Brézé, La Bouillerie, and Mermillod, went to the Pope and requested him to have the decree on infallibility brought forward directly after the Solemn Session of the 24th. They thought rightly enough the favourable moment had come and all was now ready. Pius received the Bishops, who came as deputies of the 400, with great distinction, and replied that he would discuss the matter with the Presidents.

As it is impossible to see how the Bishops or the Governments could get rid of the *regolamento* when once it is fairly established, the Opposition Bishops know that they will have to approach the great question in the position they take for themselves to-morrow in the first solemn voting, and with such power, unanimity, and influence as they thereby establish their claim to. It is still open to them up to to-night to use the present moment for a complete victory. They only need declare that their protests and warnings were not idle words but seriously meant, that the incongruities which endanger the freedom of the Council and suggest doubts of its legitimacy must be got rid of before any decrees are published under threat of everlasting damnation, and that until they are listened to on this point they refuse to take part in any solemn voting.

But, as far as I know of the Opposition, the majority of them have no ear or heart for such counsel; their grand object is to avoid any decisive conflict, and so to-morrow they will simply yield,—to consider quietly afterwards their future plan of campaign ! Some have thought they might save their honour and conscience by a written explanation of their vote. In the public international meeting of the Opposition these plans were rejected, but two rough drafts of the kind were proposed the day before yesterday, one by the Germans, one by the French. Both are too strong and dignified to find many supporters, and too weak to justify the Opposition in the eyes of the Christian world.

It is the sacred duty of the Bishops in Council to bear witness to the ancient doctrine of the Church, and to reform it when it has been obscured by abuses in practice and in the rule of the hierarchy. The more abuses there are, so much the more difficult, and so much the more indispensable also is this reform. What the Catholic world expect of the Council is not a fresh sanction, still less an increase, of these abuses, but the deliverance and purification of the Church from them. But to accept the paragraph which recommends obedience to the constitutions and decrees of Roman Congregations is to make the fulfilment of this serious duty, on which the fate of the Church hinges, impossible. For that paragraph will confirm and clothe with new authority decrees which are a disgrace to the

Church and an injury to civilisation, wherein the confused morality of dark centuries is taught and Christian morality denied; and that too without any examination or discussion, any limitation or exception. The Bishops will thereby degrade themselves to servants of the Roman *prelatura,* and sink into accomplices of the Inquisition. We are told indeed that the paragraph will not touch dogma, but for ethics and practice it is almost more important than infallibility itself. It gives full play beforehand for arbitrary caprice and paves the way for the infallibilist dogma.

If we look into the future, the questions come before us of unanimity in matters of faith, and of the confirmation and acceptance of the Council throughout the Church. As to the latter, the Bishops will make it far harder for the Governments to stand by them if to-morrow they virtually repudiate their own protests. The question of unanimity remains as weighty as before, and the gross errors of the *Civiltà* in its attack on Strossmayer's vindication of the principle of moral unanimity in decisions on faith has greatly lightened the task of two learned Bishops, who undertook to put in a clear light the true doctrine of the Church on the subject.

If the voting of to-morrow goes altogether in the sense

of the *Curia,* the inference will be that all the positions of the minority can be turned, and that as they are re-solved to avoid any collision, they may be brought by skilful manipulation not to trouble the moral unanimity any further. Many of them console themselves with the thought that they are only sacrificing everything to peace and harmony, and are not responsible for the undertaking they have been deluded into.

The propositions of the *Schema de Ecclesiâ* give abundant room for manœuvring. There are many opportunities for apparent concessions and for dividing and perplexing the Opposition, and finally driving them into a corner, so that in mutual distrust of one another they may abandon all hope of making any successful resistance, and satisfy themselves that as nearly everything has been given up already it is not worth while to risk a catastrophe by taking any further step.

FORTIETH LETTER.

Rome, April 24, 1870.—The final votes of *Placet* or *Non placet* on the four chapters of the *Schema de Fide* are to be taken in to-day's public Session. And thus after four months and a half a theological decree, or rather a batch of decrees and doctrinal decisions, will be brought to a successful issue, and the first ripe fruit plucked from the hitherto barren tree of the Council, so that there will be something in black and white to carry home. As these four chapters have been subjected to the pruning and toning down of the Opposition, they bear little resemblance to the original draft of the Jesuits, and the minority may lay claim to a victory which four months ago could scarcely have been hoped for. What has been gained for the future by these theological commonplaces and self-evident propositions is of course another question. The general view of the Bishops appears to be that there is no real gain for the Church in these propositions, which can only excite the wonder of believing Christians that it should be thought necessary to prohibit at this time of day such fundamental errors. The value of their labours they take to lie, not in what they have said, but in what they have with so much trouble expunged from the *Schema*.

Several Bishops attach great weight to the consent of the Deputation to substitute for "Romana Ecclesia" the words "Ecclesia Catholica et Apostolica Romana." Others think it a matter of indifference. Hefele's pamphlet on Honorius has created such a sensation that the Pope has commissioned the Jesuit Liberatore and Delegati, Professor at the Sapienza, to white-wash Honorius, and make away with everything in his history incompatible with the new dogma. Pius is persuaded, and his infallible "feeling" tells him, that everything must have happened quite differently from what is represented; how, he knows not, but he thinks that the Jesuit and the Roman professor have only to make the proper investigations and they will soon discover the requisite materials for refuting the German Bishop.

On Wednesday, April 20, Rome was illuminated to

celebrate the Pope's return from Gaëta. The Roman officials greatly dislike these illuminations on financial grounds, for they have to contribute to the cost out of their own pockets. A triumphal arch was erected for the Pope at the end of the narrow street leading to St. Peter's piazza, and the following inscription in letters of fire was conspicuous far and wide :—

> Popoli chinatevi innanzi al Vaticano,
> Ecco il Pontefice ch'io vi conservai nei giorni di pericolo,
> Esso è la pietra angolare della mia chiesa,
> Il refugio degli oppressi,
> Il sostegno del povero,
> Lo scudo della civiltà e della fede.

That is the witness Pius bears to himself. To theologians it may be a new idea that he personally is the corner-stone of the Church, but that is only one of the many predicates and prerogatives which may be deduced from infallibility. Two isolated voices cried " Evviva il Papa infallibile." It was clear the multitude was to be stimulated to swell the cry, but, as before, all remained quiet. The attempt has been sometimes made before, whether by amateurs or under official inspiration I know not, and then Veuillot asserts in the *Univers* that he has heard this shout of vast multitudes breaking forth spontaneously from the exuberance of their hearts. It is like the music of the spheres which only Pythagoras heard.

Ketteler's pamphlet was finally published on April 18, and the Bishop has begun to distribute it. It is really directed against the dogma itself, which for a long time people could not believe, and not merely against the opportuneness of defining it. How much better would it have been for the interests of the Church, if the necessity had been recognised long ago for looking this Medusa's head straight in the face, and defying its petrifying gaze, and if our Bishops had plainly and decisively announced their resolution last December to have no dealings with it. Now at least Cardinal Rauscher does not spare warnings ; he perceives the gravity of the danger and has had a new fly-leaf distributed, showing that the promulgation of papal infallibility will elevate the two Bulls *Unam Sanctam* (of Boniface VIII.) and *Cum ex Apostolatûs officio* (of Paul IV.) into rules of faith for the whole Catholic world, and thus it will be taught universally in Europe and America, henceforth, that the Pope is absolute master in temporal affairs also, that he can order war or peace, and that every monarch or bishop who does not submit to him or helps any one separated from him ought to be deprived of his throne if not of his life, besides the other wonderful doctrines in the second of these Bulls, which must reduce every theologian to despair.[1] All that is nothing to the majority, for whom the law of logical contradiction has no existence. It is their watchword that the dogma conquers logic as well as history. One of their German members gladly re-echoes the idea that the proper aim and office of the Council is to stop the mouth of arrogant professors ; if that is accomplished everything is gained, according to this pastor of a flock feeding on red earth. On the other hand I heard very different words fall to-day from the mouth of another German Bishop, who said he was constantly asking himself how long the German Bishops would look on and put up with everything.

The great and all-absorbing question now is what will next be brought before the Council after April 24. In the natural order the second part of the *Schema de Fide* would come on, which is comparatively innocuous though abundantly capable of improvement. But is it not time to fabricate the talisman of absolute power, the infallibilist dogma ? Then would the Council be in the fullest sense and for ever provided for and

---

[1] [Cf. *Janus*, pp. 382-4.—Tr.]

finished, and the master would praise his servants. Many will answer the question in the affirmative. The two modern Fathers, Veuillot and Margotti, strain every nerve daily for that end, and many of the most zealous French Bishops—as those of Moulins, Bourges, and Carcassonne, and the indefatigable Mermillod— have represented to the willing Pius, as I mentioned yesterday, that now is the nick of time, and that he may gratify the longing of his faithful adherents by placing infallibility in the order of the day. These Frenchmen consider that their Government, now occupied with the plébiscite, will not trouble itself with the acts and decisions of the Council, and moreover needs the help of the clergy. Amid the bustle of the plébiscite, they think the new dogma, and even the reproduction of the Syllabus in the twenty-one canons, will excite little stir or indignation, for the French can only embrace one idea at a time, and the Parisians only discuss one subject in their *salons*.

Banneville has at last actually presented the memorandum of his Government to the Pope, as President of the Council, and with the intimation that it should be communicated to the Fathers. That of course will not be done, for both Pius and Antonelli are irritated

at the paper.   Pius is annoyed at the innermost kernel
of the dogma being so openly exposed to view, when
Count Daru says, " You want to hand over all rights
and powers to the Church, and then by the infallibilist
dogma to concentrate this plenitude of temporal and
spiritual power in the one person of the Pope." That
is of course what the *Curia* does want, but it should be
uttered in pious and somewhat obscure phraseology,
as the *Civiltà* usually speaks, and not be called by its
right name in this bold and naked fashion.   Antonelli
again is much displeased, because his favourite distinction between the principles in which the Church
must be inexorable, and the practice in which Rome
will graciously concede the very opposite, is met here
by the inquiry whether the faithful are actually to be
taught henceforth that they must believe what they
need not carry out in practice, and accept as divinely
revealed rules which they may without hesitation
transgress ?   He had reckoned on a better understanding, on the part of the French Government, of the
favourite Roman theory of infinite and inexhaustible
papal indults and dispensations, and is glad that he need
make no reply to the note which throws so glaring a
light on the morality of the *Curia* and its notions of

duty and truth. He contents himself with telling the diplomatists that there would be some difficulty in the Pope's communicating the note to the Council. Clearly, for they must at the same time be directed to attempt a refutation, and that would lead to very awkward consequences. The French Government might indeed have sent their memorandum to each Bishop separately, but then they would have had the prospect of the non-French Bishops of the majority returning it unopened.

Count Trautmansdorff has also presented the memorandum of the Austrian Government to the Cardinal Secretary of State. It runs as follows :—

"Nous voulons seulement élever aussi notre voix pour dégager notre responsabilité et signaler les conséquences presqu'inévitables d'actes qui devraient être regardés comme une atteinte portée aux lois qui nous régissent. Comme le Gouvernement français, c'est à un devoir de conscience que nous pensons obéir, en avertissant la cour de Rome des périls de la voie dans laquelle des influences prepondérantes semblent vouloir pousser le Concile. Ce qui nous émeut, ce n'est pas le danger dont nos institutions sont menacées, mais bien celui que courent la paix des esprits et le maintien de la bonne harmonie dans les relations de l'état avec l'Église.   Le sentiment qui nous fait agir doit paraître d'autant moins suspect au St. Siége qu'il correspond à l'attitude d'une fraction importante des Pères du Concile, dont le dévouement aux intérêts du Catholicisme ne saurait être l'objet d'un doute.   Placés sur un tout autre terrain que cette fraction, puisque nous n'obéissons qu'à des considérations politiques, nous nous rencontrons toutefois aujourd'hui dans le désir commun d'écarter certaines éventualités.   Cette coïncidence de nos efforts nous permet de croire qu'en prenant la parole au nom des seuls intérêts de l'État nous ne méconnaissons pas ceux de l'Église.   Si la démarche du Gouvernement français, que nous dé-sirons seconder de tout notre pouvoir, vient en ce moment donner un appui à la minorité du Concile et l'aider à faire prévaloir des idées de modération ou de prudence, nous ne pourrons que nous féliciter d'un tel résultat, bien que, je le répète, notre action soit parfaitement indépendante et doive rester en tout cas indépendante de celle des membres du Concile."

Finally the observations of the French Government are urgently commended to the attention of the *Curia*.

FORTY-FIRST LETTER.

Rome, April 27, 1870.—We find ourselves in a remarkably critical position here. The great event so long expected of the first promulgation of dogmas is over, and the desired unanimity has been successfully attained for these four chapters of the *Schema de Fide,* notwithstanding the supplemental paragraph. Two Bishops who could not overcome their dislike to that paragraph preferred to stay away or leave Rome for the day. All the curialists are in high feather, and are congratulating each other on their victory, boasting that they have gained three most important points without any public opposition. First, the Pope, for the first time for 350 years,[1] and in contradiction to the practice of the first 1000 years of Church history, has defined and published the decrees in his own name as supreme legislator, just like those masters of

[1] [Since, that is, the Lateran synod of 1517 under Leo x.—Tr.]

the world, Innocent III., Innocent IV. and Leo X., merely with the addition that the Council also sanctions them. Secondly, the new order of business has now been virtually accepted by all, and the protest abandoned. Thirdly, the conclusion, which is meant to invest with conciliar authority the former dogmatic decrees of the Popes, has been accepted.

The excitement visible on the countenances of the majority, when Schwarzenberg, Darboy, Rauscher and Hefele were called up to vote, showed what had been expected. The mass of the majority say the same thing will happen when the *Schema* on the Church has to be voted on; the minority answer that it will not, and that they only want to avoid wasting their powder before the time; " la minorité se recueille," like Russia after the last war, and on the division day will be found fully equipped for the fight. We shall soon see, for that day is not far distant. But now what next ? The infallibilist party are afraid of this dogma being lost after all, like a ship wrecked in port. They reckon that the time is approaching when the Council must inevitably be prorogued, and therefore urge the Pope to break through the regular order of the *Schemata*, and bring forward at once either the whole *Schema de*

Ecclesiâ or the article on papal infallibility which has been interpolated into it. The four French Bishops assured him that they spoke in the name of the 400. Pius would not of course feel any very constraining influence in their wishes *per se*, for he knows well enough that the 400 are composed mainly of his foster-sons and of the Bishops of the States of the Church and the Neapolitans, who all speak or hold their peace and sit or stand as they are bidden. But it would be an unspeakably bitter sacrifice for him to refuse to his trusty adherents what he so earnestly desires himself, and to let these 400 or at least many of them say, " Your own organ, the *Civiltà*, the Jesuits, Veuillot, Margotti— have forced this question upon us ; we have agitated for it and staked our name and theological credit on it, and now it is all to be labour lost !"

But now the writings of the German Bishops have appeared and the notes of the Governments have been delivered. To the French note is added a more urgent one from Austria, as well as a Prussian, a Portuguese and now also a Bavarian note, and all breathe the same spirit. All give warning that they shall regard the threatened decrees on the power and infallibility of the Pope as a declaration of war against the order and authority of

the State.   Even the English Government leaves no
room for doubt about its mind, and if the Pope—as I
know—fears above all things any manifestation of
feeling there, he might learn from Manning that the
strongest antipathy is felt among all classes, high and
low, to the proposed dogmas, and that English statesmen see in them nothing less than a suicidal infatua-
tion.   Manning has thoroughly authentic proofs of
that in his hands, but of course he won't produce
them.

Pius is in a chronic state of extreme irritation.   He
sees with pleasure his two favourite journals—the
Univers and *Unita*—abuse the Opposition Bishops in
the most contemptuous language, and he indulges
himself in outbreaks of bitterness against those who
question his infallibility, which pass from mouth to
mouth here but which one dares not write down.
Even Cardinal Bilio is alarmed at such ebullitions, and
affirms that he is constantly urging moderation and
forbearance on the Pope, and has already warded off a
great deal of mischief.

What strikes us foreigners is the evident indifference to the Council and its acts manifested by the
inhabitants of the eternal city of every class.   It is

seldom spoken of in society, and what absorbs the
attention of the world north of the Alps seems hardly
to have the least interest for the Romans, what is there
heard of with astonishment they hardly think worth a
passing mention. And if ever the Council is spoken of,
it is in hurried, mysterious, abrupt sentences, for every
one says the espionage system has never been in such
force here as since the opening of the Council, and a
large staff lives by the trade. I know persons here
whose doors are constantly watched by spies, who do
not even conceal themselves, and if the Roman theologians had such rich materials for their investigations
as is possessed by the Roman police, they would not
have their equals in the world.

The Romans as a rule are fully aware of the financial
value of the infallibilist doctrine, and know right well
that a large increase of revenue as well as power from
all countries is looked for as its product. That in
their eyes is already an accomplished fact. They
know for certain that the dogma will be at once proclaimed, and there is hardly a Roman here who has
not an uncle or brother or nephew in orders and may
not hope to share the anticipated profits in his own
person or in the person of his relatives. The curialists

here say, " We have lost so much by the diminution of
the States of the Church, and so many payments, bene-
fices and lucrative posts have passed out of our hands,
that we absolutely require to be indemnified in some
other way, and this the new dogma is intended to do
and must do for us." If ever the Pope is acknowledged
thoughout Christendom as an infallible authority, it is
inevitable that ecclesiastical centralization should take
much larger dimensions than before. Not only doctrine, but everything concerning Church life will be
drawn to Rome and there finally settled. Theologians
may undertake to distinguish between matters to which
the Pope's infallible authority extends or does not
extend, but in practice everything signed with his
name will be held to be an utterance of divine truth,
and nothing which is not attested with that signature
will be held valid. There is a proverb here—

> Quei consigli son prezzati
> Che son chiesti e ben pagati.

And who would not gladly pay a handsome sum to be
armed with an infallible decision, which will at once
crush all opposition and put down all adversaries?
The golden age of papal chanceries and clerks lies
not in the past, in the fourteenth and fifteenth cen-

turies when, as a court prelate of the day tells us, the papal officials were daily employed in counting up gold pieces; it will first dawn on the day this truly golden doctrine of infallibility is promulgated. Were Cicero to re-appear in Rome now, he might repeat what he said in the Oration *Pro Sextio,* "Jucunda res plebi Romanæ, victus enim suppeditabatur large sine labore;" only he could no longer add, "Repugnabant boni, quod ab industriâ plebem ad desidiam avocari putabant." For such "boni" no longer exist at Rome; rather is the account of Tacitus completely verified, "Securi omnes aliena subsidia expectant, sibi ignavi, aliis graves."[1] Another thing is the large and incurable deficit in the Roman finances, which must increase every year. There is an annual expenditure of thirty million francs to cover, and the Peter's pence, which came to fourteen millions in 1861, have sunk to about eleven millions, notwithstanding the collections ordered to be made everywhere twice a year. No further help can be obtained from loans. M. de Corcelles, who has exposed this uncomfortable state of things with the best intentions, has no other remedy to propose but a great increase of Peter's pence.

[1] Tac. *Annal.* II.

It is hoped in Rome that the different nations will contribute larger sums than before to the Pope, now he is become infallible and thus more closely united to Deity. But they reckon much more on the enormous centralization and all-embracing monopoly of all possible dispensations, indulgences, consultations, canonizations, and decisions on moral, liturgical, political, dogmatic and disciplinary questions. They remember the treasures amassed in the temple of Delphi in ancient days, and expect the new oracle to be erected on the Tiber to attract, like a vast magnet, not iron but gold and silver.

Neither Pius nor the Monsignori and other curialists think it conceivable that the minority will hold out to the last in their opposition. They reckon securely on this fraction of the Council being broken up by fear and discouragement, and that few if any of them will let matters come to a *non placet* in the next public Session, and thus openly confess themselves unwillingly subdued. To those Roman clerics, who are accustomed to look at religious questions only as the ladder by which to mount to an agreeable life and good income, courage and steadfastness in the confession of ascertained truth is something strange and inconceivable. Fear and hope, calculations of loss and gain, will finally decide the Bishops' votes—that is the firm persuasion of every Italian member of the *Curia.* So much is certain : if on the very eve of the Solemn Session, when the new dogma is to be promulgated, it was certainly known that eighty Bishops would say *Non placet* next day, the Session would be countermanded and the Church saved. The first question for us Germans is of course whether we can trust our Bishops ? Will they abide steadfast ? Or will they at last sacrifice themselves and the truth, their clergy and their flocks ? As to what immediately concerns the clergy, this is not strictly a question of doctrine belonging to the sphere of religious faith and mystery, where one might make a willing submission of mind to a decree held to be the voice of divine revelation ; it is a pure question of historical facts to be determined by historical evidence, of points on which every educated man capable of judging evidence, whether a Catholic or not, can form an independent judgment. Every one with eyes to see can answer with absolute certainty these three questions, on which the whole matter hinges—

1. Is it true that the admonition to Peter to confirm

his brethren has always and in the whole Church been understood of an infallibility promised to all Bishops of Rome ?

2. Is it true that this infallibility of all Popes has been taught and witnessed to in the whole Church through all ages down to our own day ?

3. Is it true that no Pope has ever taught a doctrine rejected by the Church, and that no Pope has ever been condemned by the Church for his doctrine ?

It is absolutely impossible for any one, who feels compelled by his own investigation of history to answer these three questions in the negative, to submit inwardly to the opposite decision of the Council, whatever external homage he may pay to it.   Ten Councils will not be able to shake him for a moment in his conviction ; he will only say, " pur si muove."   His doubts will be turned, not against what is historically certain but against the Council; he will call in question the real freedom, the intrinsic claims and authority of this Council, and—to go no further—the two successive regulations for conducting business supply in this case abundant materials for the question.   And it is just as impossible for a man who has a notion of historical certainty to believe in any one else's mind being changed by the decree of an assembly of Bishops. If a well-educated man told me he had just come to the conclusion that Julius Cæsar never lived, I should not believe in his conviction but in some disorder of his mental faculties, and should advise him to undergo medical treatment. And so, if the new dogma is proclaimed and the clergy submit either tacitly or expressly, no cultivated man in all Germany will believe that the thousands of scientifically trained men who have had a German education have suddenly changed their convictions, because some hundreds of Italians and Spaniards have chosen to decree away the testimony of history. " Facts are stubborn things." Public opinion will recognise only two alternatives in the case of those who submit, ignorance or dissimulation and falsehood. And the effect will ·be an immeasurable moral degradation of the Catholic clergy and a corresponding decay of their influence.

This consideration will not of course make the slightest impression on the majority of the Council, or even on those Germans who belong to it. We have psychological riddles to deal with here. How, *e.g.*, are we to explain the fact that a man, who has taught the very opposite doctrine in a manual of instruction for the higher class of colleges published seventeen years ago, and has let it pass through eleven or twelve editions without a word being altered, is now in Rome one of the most zealous promoters of the definition, and is constantly affirming that all the clergy except a few professors will readily submit?

FORTY-SECOND LETTER.

Rome, April 29, 1870.—What I mentioned in my last letter as a pamphlet of Cardinal Rauscher's, is a printed memorial addressed to the Presidents of the Council, bearing the title of *Petitio a pluribus Galliæ, Austriæ et Hungariæ, Italiæ, Angliæ et Hiberniæ et Americæ Septentrionalis Præsidibus exhibita,* and dated April 20th. It states that papal infallibility is beset by many objections and difficulties, which require an examination such as is impossible in a General Congregation. Among them is one of supreme importance, bearing directly on the instruction to be given to the faithful on the divine commandments and the relation of the Catholic religion to civil society.

" The Popes have deposed Emperors and Kings, and Boniface VIII. in the Bull *Unam Sanctam* has established the corresponding theory, which the Popes openly taught down to the seventeenth century under anathema, that God has committed to them power over temporal things. But we, and almost all Bishops of the Catholic world, teach another doctrine. We teach that the ecclesiastical power is indeed higher than the civil, but that each is independent of the other, and that while sovereigns are subject to the spiritual penalties of the Church, she has no power to depose them or absolve their subjects from their oaths of allegiance. And this is the ancient doctrine, taught by all the Fathers and by the Popes before Gregory VII. But if the Pope, according to the Bull *Unam Sanctam*, possessed both swords—if, according to Paul IV.'s Bull *Cum ex Apostolatûs officio,* he had absolute dominion by divine right over nations and kingdoms,—the Church could not conceal this from her people, nor is the subterfuge admissible,[1] that this power exists only in the abstract and has no bearing on public affairs, and that Pius has no intention of deposing rulers and princes; for the objectors would at once scornfully reply, ' We have no fear of papal decrees, but after many and various dissimulations it has at last become evident that every Catholic, who acts according to his professed belief, is a born enemy of the State, for he holds him-

[1] Antonelli's, notoriously.

self bound in conscience to do all in his power to reduce all kingdoms and nations into subjection to the Pope.' We need not define more precisely the manifold accusations the enemies of the Church might deduce from this.

" This difficulty then must be most carefully sifted before papal infallibility is dealt with. The Conference we demanded on March 11 may do much towards clearing it up. But the question, whether Christ really committed to Peter and his successors supreme power over kings and kingdoms is, especially in this day, one of such grave importance that it must be directly brought before the Council, and examined on all sides. It would be inexcusable for the Fathers to be seduced into deciding, without thorough knowledge and sifting, on a question which has such wide consequences and affects so deeply the relations of the Church to human society. This question therefore must necessarily be brought before them, before the eleventh chapter of the *Schema de Ecclesiâ* can be taken in hand. It might, if you please, be separately treated. But, as it cannot be adequately judged of without a thorough examination of the relations of the ecclesiastical to the civil power, it appears to us very desirable that the thirteenth and fourteenth chapters of the *Schema* should be discussed before the eleventh."

What first strikes one about this remarkable document is, that the German Bishops belonging to the minority—Martin, Stahl, Senestrey and the Tyrolese are of course out of the reckoning—are not represented here. Does this indicate a real divergence of view or only a difference of tactics ? The former notion seems to me inconceivable. It is impossible that men like Hefele, Ketteler, Eberhard and the rest should have any doctrinal predilection for the system of papal absolutism extended over sovereigns and the whole political and civil domain. Certainly they too are so strongly opposed to the infallibilist dogma because it involves the mediatizing of all kings and governments. I can therefore at present discover no explanation of this phenomenon, and cannot allow any room for the suspicion that the persistently active curialistic influences have succeeded in dividing the German Bishops from the rest of the minority.

What will the Presidents do with a document so serious, so moderate and so incisive ? What have they done already ? So far as I know, nothing. It is a principle, and has now become an habitual practice with hem, to leave all representations and petitions of the minority unnoticed and unanswered. The directing Deputation, which is intrusted with the entire control of the Council, feels quite justified in adopting this line by the papal ordinances.

The policy hitherto pursued by the Jesuits and the *Curia* was, first to extend to the utmost the comprehensive office of the Church, as legislator for the nations and guardian of faith and morals; and then, by making the Pope absolute master and dictator of the Church, to assign to him all that had been claimed for the Church, so that he—acting of course in the interests of religion and morality, but simply according to his own good pleasure—should have every office, person and institution subject to him, and that the final appeal in every cause should lie to his tribunal. Since all this can only be secured and guaranteed by the infallibilist dogma, the inferences on the relations of Church and State drawn by the opposing Bishops form precisely the chief recommendation of that dogma in the eyes of the Legates, the Italian Cardinals, the Spanish and Italian Bishops and those of the French who are ultramontanes. They all say among themselves, if not aloud before the world, "That is just what we want; our very object is

2 K

to get the doctrine on the relations of Church and State changed, the independence of civil society and the civil power abolished, and the complete temporal supremacy of the Church—*i.e.*, the Pope—at least gradually established." It is not indeed advisable to say this as yet in such explicit and unreserved terms, but the reason why the infallibilist dogma is so opportune and indispensable is exactly because it implies jurisdiction over the temporal sphere, which the Pope can according to circumstances either leave unused and say nothing about it, or suddenly draw forth for use like a weapon concealed under a mantle. He has dealt thus with the Austrian Constitution; while he let alone other countries, whose constitutional systems must have been partly at least a scandal on Roman principles, he pronounced the Austrian Constitution abominable (*nefanda*). And any one, who wishes to examine the practical significance of this infallible judgment, need only go to the Tyrol and observe how it has been already explained there to the inhabitants by their enthusiastic clergy.

At the audience, when he presented the French note to the Pope, Banneville expressed the wish of his Government that the discussion of the *Schema de Ecclesiâ* (with the chapter on infallibility) might at least not be taken before its time—which was equivalent to saying, " At least give us time, for the matter is not yet ripe for discussion." Hitherto delay has been for the interest of the *Curia,* for it was expected that the minority would wither away and finally be extinguished ; they trusted to the power so often proved of the Roman solvents. The article of the *Civiltà* which told the prelates, " We care nothing for your talk about moral unanimity in matters of dogma, and shall make the new dogma in spite of your opposition," was written *in terrorem,* and was meant to hold up before the refractory the terrible perspective of a contest emerging in the abortion of an impotent schism. The article has not in the main produced the desired effect, for the Bishops still hold together and bind themselves by writings and public declarations, and the number of those who can no longer with any decency desert to the majority threatens to increase. Now therefore it is the interest of the *Curia* to allow no further delay, but to bring forward the *Schema* at once.

The Bavarian ambassador has presented the note of his Government, which appeals emphatically to the attitude of the German Bishops who represent in the Council sound principles on the relations of Church and

State.[1]   It cannot indeed appeal to its own Bishops,
for three of them are active and fiery supporters of
infallibilism and the supremacy of the Pope over Kings
and States.   It was previously thought impossible for a
German Bishop to desire to see the day when the Popes
could again grasp the reins of temporal dominion which
had dropped from their hands, depose monarchs, give
away countries, abolish constitutions, annul laws and
dispense oaths of allegiance.   But this spectacle we
now enjoy !   For the pastors of souls must be assumed
to intend to make dogmas, not for a mere pastime or
for the enrichment of theological commentaries and
text-books, but in order to reduce the theory to practice.

Pius did not say, when receiving the French memorandum, whether he would communicate it to the Council.
But Antonelli has now stated that the Pope, though
President of the Council, will not find it at all advisable
to do so.   That is only consistent, for every curialist

---

[1] " Animés d'un profond respect pour l'autorité *légitime* du S. Siége,
nous sommes obligés d'autre part de préserver de toute atteinte présente ou
future les rapports entre l'église et l'état (as lately settled by the Concordat and the Constitution).   Nous joignons nos instances aux remon-
strances du Gouvernement français et nous nous croyons appelés à le faire
d'autant plus, que dans le sein du concile lui-même une grande partie des
représentants de l'Église d'Allemagne, dont le dévouement religieux est
bien connu, atteste par son attitude que nos craintes sont loin d'être
vaines."

regards the Council as under strict tutelage, and in fact only existing by the will of the Pope and living by the breath of his mouth. It is simply from care for their health that he withholds so unsound a document from his Bishops. Antonelli says he will not reply to it, as it contains nothing new, and merely repeats the note of Feb. 20, which is not strictly true. He adheres to his favourite distinction, " In theory we are inexorable, grasping, high-flying, as Gregory VII. or Innocent III., but in practice full of forbearance and compassion. We take account of human weakness and blindness, and, if the Northern nations do not acknowledge the prerogatives of our priestly absolutism, and desire to retain their political and religious liberties in spite of our theoretical condemnation of them, we shall not force matters to an open breach and shall make no use of the old methods of compulsion."

Now are the Governments agreed or not in reference to the Council? They are no doubt all agreed in their aversion to the new dogma and the renewal of the Syllabus, but there is a great difference in their practical attitude. The rulers in some States mean to utilize the occasion for bringing about the entire separation of Church and State, *i.e.*, for gradually extruding the Church and the clergy from all the positions of public trust they still hold, and reducing the Church to the level of a sect tolerated and as far as possible ignored by the State, and secularizing education, marriage and family life. This is the attitude of Belgium, Italy and Spain towards the Council. Out of Belgium there is no country so remarkably indifferent about the Council and its decrees, whatever they may be, as Italy, *i.e.*, the Italian Government and many millions of Italians. The statesmen there say, " We have no Concordats to defend, for they have fallen with the old Governments ; the State has no longer any concern with religion and the Church, which are mere private affairs of the individual. And thus the separation of Church and State is already in principle accomplished." I can vouch for the following saying of a high public official there : " There are hundreds of us who do not know whether we are among those excommunicated on political grounds or not. In a dangerous illness we may send for a confessor, and then we shall find out."

The number of those who desire and aim at this complete divorce of Church and State is legion. Their view predominates in the French cabinet since Daru's retirement, and most of them view what is going on in

Rome with satisfaction and hope. The more frantic and insolent is the conduct of the Papalists, so much the better in their opinion, for so much easier and more painless will the separation be for civil society. To make papal infallibility and the Syllabus into dogmas is in their eyes a step which, far from hindering, one should wish to see thoroughly effected. When the Church is caught in this net, she must assume the full responsibility of all doctrines and principles established by any of the Popes, and she has herself pronounced judgment on their utter incompatibility with the whole existing order of society. The State can then no longer go hand in hand with her anywhere, and will dismiss her. It is impossible to be ignorant that this view is widely prevalent, and is rapidly and powerfully increasing.

FORTY-THIRD LETTER.

Rome, April 30, 1870.—Now that the matter has gone so far, those about the Pope no longer make any secret of the fact that for many years—indeed from the beginning of his pontificate—he has formed the design of making papal infallibility an article of faith. A work has lately been distributed here, *Riflessioni d'un Teologo sopra la Riposta di Mgr. Dupanloup a Mgr. Arcivescovo di Malines*, Torino 1870. The writer says, "Could the Bishop of Orleans be ignorant that Pius IX. has always intended to define this dogma and condemn Gallicanism ? All the acts of his pontificate have been directed to this end. Nay, we affirm distinctly that he believed himself to have received a special mission to define the two dogmas of papal infallibility and the Immaculate Conception.[1] And as

[1] "Si, diciamolo altamente, Pio IX. credette aver ricevuto speciale missione di definire la Immacolata Concezione e la infallibilita pontificia."

he is under the special guidance of the Holy Ghost, his will sufficiently establishes the opportuneness of this definition."

This was obviously written for the eyes of the Pontiff, whose whole life is surrounded as with a rose-garland of miraculous deliverances, illuminations and divine inspirations. And thus the veil is now dropped, and the time come for speaking openly. Up to the end of last summer, and even till December, the answer given from Rome to all inquiries and anxieties of Bishops or Governments was, that there was no intention of bringing infallibility before the Council and that the *Civiltà* was mistaken ; the Court of Rome was not responsible for what an individual Jesuit might write. Antonelli gave the most quieting assurances on all sides. But meanwhile the Committee of Theologians employed in preparing the materials for the Council had already voted this new dogma, under direction of the highest authority, and Archbishop Cardoni had sent in his report upon it, which was received by all against the single vote of Alzog. The subjects to be brought before the Council were carefully concealed from the Bishops, and an oath of silence imposed on the theologians who were summoned, in order that they might come to Rome unprepared and without the necessary books, and might simply indorse the elaborations of the Jesuits as voting-machines in the prison-house of the Council.

It is merely repeating what is notorious in Rome to say that Pius IX. is beneath comparison with any one of his predecessors for the last 350 years in theological knowledge and intellectual cultivation generally. One must go back to Innocent VIII. and Julius II. to find Popes of similar theological and scientific attainments. It is known here that, small as are the intellectual requisites for ordination in the Roman States, it was only out of special regard to his family that Giovanni Maria Mastai could get ordained priest. His subsequent career offered no opportunity or means for supplying this neglect, and thus he became Pope with the feeling of his entire deficiency in the necessary acquirements. This unpleasant consciousness naturally produced the idea that the defect would be remedied without effort on his part by enlightenment from above, and divine inspiration would supply the absence of human knowledge. This illusion has been and will be so common, that we need not have troubled ourselves about it, did it not threaten now to become a destructive firebrand.

The public letters which have passed of late between the assembled Fathers on the absorbing question of the day deserve attention. They show the deep gulf which divides the members of the Episcopate. There is Spalding, Archbishop of Baltimore, who first wanted to help the Pope to get his infallibility acknowledged indirectly by his now famous *postulatum*, where the real point was kept in the background, when he proposed a decree that every papal decision was to be received with unconditional inward assent. But now, in his letter to Dupanloup, he has changed his mind, and wants infallibility to be openly and explicitly defined. So again in the *postulatum* he had declared moral unanimity to be necessary for a dogma, but now on the contrary he considers a mere majority of votes to be sufficient. Two other American Archbishops have come forward in opposition to him, Kenrick of St. Louis and Purcell of Cincinnati. They say that Spalding's letter has fallen among them like a bomb-shell; it has hitherto been their custom for such matters to be discussed in an assembly of the American Bishops, but that has not been done in the present case, and he has written his letter alone and without any communication with his colleagues. Indeed he had previously advised them to oppose the definition of infallibility, as sure to produce nothing but difficulties, but now he has taken up just the opposite view, on what grounds they know not. The two prelates add that American Catholics have very special reasons for disliking the definition, for the notion of the Pope having the right to depose monarchs, dispense oaths of allegiance, and give away countries and nations at his will, is equally strange to Protestants and Catholics in their country. They think that Archbishop Spalding will find himself greatly embarrassed in America with his infallibilist doctrine, as has already been the case for some years with regard to the condemnation of religious freedom by the Syllabus. The two Archbishops, as one sees, tread lightly and cautiously. They are in Rome,—" incedunt per ignes suppositos cineri doloso." Still they assert with American freedom of speech, " We, and several more of us, believe that the dogma contradicts the history and tradition of the Church."

The citizens of the United States, whether Protestant or Catholic, will certainly be astonished when the new dogma comes into full force among them and its con-sequences are brought to light, suddenly recalling a long series of papal decisions into active life ;—when, for instance, the recent Bull (*Apostolicæ Sedis*), with its many and various excommunications reserved to the Pope alone becomes known, and again the decision of the infallible Urban II. that it is no murder to kill an excommunicated man out of zeal for the Church, a decision which to this day stands on record in 200 copies of the canon law. And as a commentary on this the work of the present Jesuit theologian of the Court of Rome, Schrader (*De Unitate Romanâ*), will be put into their hands, from which they will learn that the contents of all papal decrees are infallible, for they always contain some " doctrina veritatis "—whether moral, juridical, or rational—and the Pope is always infallible " in ordine veritatis et doctrinæ." Yet that is but one flower from the dogmatic garden, into which Archbishop Spalding will introduce the citizens of the United States after infallibility is happily proclaimed. They will then also hear, among other interesting truths, that according to the irrefragable decision of Leo X. every priest is absolutely free by divine and human law from all secular authority, and no layman has any right over him.[1] And they must be reminded, in order to

[1] " Jure tam divino quam humano laicis nulla potestas in ecclesiasticas personas attributa est."

make them more submissive, that in 1493 Pope Alexander VI. gave over their country with all its inhabitants, " in virtue of the plenitude of his apostolic power," to the kings of Spain in the infallible Bull *Inter cœtera,*[1] and then drew the famous line from the North to the South Pole, which included whole provinces of the present United States in his great and generous gift. By virtue of papal infallibility they are subjects of the Spanish Government, and who knows if right and fact may not some day again coincide? " Res clamat ad dominum."

[1] See Raynald. *Annal.* xix. ann. 1493, 22.

FORTY-FOURTH LETTER.

Rome, May 13, 1870.—The time for the most eventful decisions is come : to-morrow the debate on infallibility commences. The opponents of the dogma have taken every means to put off this decision, and now that they are foiled, enter upon the question with the greatest repugnance and a sense of being defeated by anticipation in the perilous contest. The diplomatists too, who had presented notes from their Governments to the Vatican or had been instructed to support the notes presented, made urgent representations that the existing order of business should not be departed from, so as to get the discussion of infallibility deferred. And then some Bishops made an attempt to move the Pope's conscience. They told him that by this undertaking he was sowing divisions among the faithful, shaking faith, preparing for the closing days of his life a terrible disillusionizing and bitter reproaches, and kindling a fire which after blazing up in various parts of the Catholic world would turn into a frightful conflagration. He was urgently entreated to listen to some of the Bishops, who were in a position to inform him of the real state of things in different countries.

There has unquestionably for some time past been a certain vacillation among the Pope's counsellors, but never for a moment did they think of giving up the whole enterprise, and confessing themselves defeated. And as it was clear that, if the *Schemata* preceding the infallibility question were discussed in their regular order, the hot season would set in with its miasmas, and the inevitable prorogation of the Council would most seriously imperil the dogma, the resolve to proceed at once with the matter, regardless of consequences, prevailed in the *Curia*. The Opposition tried to hinder this intention by a solemn act. A deputation, consisting of several Bishops of different nations—a German, a Hungarian, and a Bohemian Bishop for Germany—was to be sent to the Pope, with Archbishop Purcell of Cincinnati for its spokesman, to make the most earnest and direct representations to him. From fear of this demonstration, and in order at once to cut off all hopes placed upon it, the *Curia* had the *Synopsis Animad-versionum* distributed in great haste, *i.e.* a selection from the Opinions of the Bishops, partly in favour of the dogma, partly against it. The opinions are about equally divided, but some represent more than one author. Thus *e.g.* 4 Hungarians and 16 Dominicans, in one case 24 Bishops, gave in the same Opinion. They are all printed without the names, but some of the writers are easily recognised, as *e.g.* Rauscher, Schwarzenberg, Fürstenberg, Krementz, Dupanloup, Clifford, Kenrick, etc. It is to be observed that some of these opinions are printed word for word, while others—of the Opposition Bishops—are cunningly tampered with, to the great disgust of their authors. But in most cases the reader cannot tell whether he has the opinion of a man of high position or of a nobody before him.

In consequence of this rapid manœuvre of distributing the Synopsis, the Opposition did not think it well to send their deputation, which accordingly fell through. The dogmatic constitution on infallibility was known here on the 1st of May, but was not published for eight days afterwards. The *Curia* was evidently not yet quite clear about its tactics ; perhaps the season might not appear sufficiently advanced, and they might feel more secure of carrying their point when the heat had driven the foreign Bishops away and the Council was left to the Italian and Spanish rump.

The minority however did not cease to labour for the postponement of the infallibilist discussion.   The certainty that the *Curia* would be in earnest about it gave them somewhat more energy than they had shown in the debate on the Little Catechism.   The voting on it on May 4 had been quite unexpected.   For it had been resolved that the amendments modifying the text should first be voted on, and the whole text be decided afterwards, when printed and brought forward in the definitive form it had received through the voting on the amendments.   But instead of that, amendments and text were voted upon on the same day, so that many Bishops—including Darboy and Kenrick—were absent, and the whole number of *non-placets* and conditional votes together did not reach 100.   This voting on May 4 was however provisional; the definitive voting takes place to-day, Friday, May 13.   The *Curia* of course does not wish to have so considerable an Opposition left, and has therefore somewhat altered the text, but not in their sense.   All the German Bishops of the minority, amounting to about 40, will vote *Non placet*, as I hear, and the French also, with a single exception, making some 30 more. Several others will join them, so that the previous 56 *Non-placets* will be augmented by most of the 44 prelates who voted *juxta modum*. The opposition to the Little Catechism may thus reach 100 votes, and will certainly exceed 80.

One might be tempted to ask why the Opposition, when it is so numerous, has no confidence of victory and is alway shrinking from decisive measures. It is idle to suppose that the cancerous ulcer of infallibilism can ever be once for all cut out of the body of the Church, except by a scientific demonstration of its falsehood, or its adherents subdued without a decisive contest. This uneasy attitude of the minority arises from the want of sympathy and confidence among its various elements. The inopportunists are afraid of their allies not only hindering the definition but undermining belief in the doctrine and upsetting the whole Jesuitical system and school of lies, and thus exposing the contrast between the primacy as Christ founded it and as it has since been perverted. And the others judge from what they themselves say that their resistance will not be firm and persevering, and that they already think of yielding sooner or later. And even for those who hold the doctrine to be thoroughly false and unecclesiastical, it is much more convenient not to proclaim their conviction so roundly and maintain the opposition at all hazards, after the Pope has solemnly and formally committed himself and done all in his power to get the dogma defined and all condemned who reject it. For all who openly declared the doctrine to be an error would be declaring the Pope to be an innovator; and he must appear to every decided opponent of infallibilism no common innovator either, like any "doctor privatus," but the most fearful and dangerous enemy of revealed truth and the pure doctrine of the Church, since he abuses his supreme authority to impose a false doctrine on consciences by terrorism, anathema and excommunication. But it is too much to demand of the Bishops to express such judgments, or give occasion for such conclusions and alternatives. While they wish to hold aloof from so tremendous a conflict, it is their interest to avoid a collision which must involve such considerations. The more many of them are ensnared in the delusion of the present papal system, the more vivid is their desire not to be forced into so public and decisive an announcement.

It is exactly those Bishops who are not the strongest

dogmatically who display the most zeal in hindering the discussion on infallibility, and they have done a good deal to rehabilitate a force capable of resistance even after the abject surrender of April 24. This fact shows how little the astute and practised Roman Court has succeeded in gaining over the Fathers separately. The Hungarian primate notoriously signed the *postulatum* against infallibility with reluctance, and he has since openly adhered to the majority as spokesman of the Deputation *de Fide*, after he had previously retired from the assembly of German Opposition Bishops. He has a good right to reckon confidently on a Cardinal's Hat; and yet it is known that he, like almost all the Hungarians, will come forward to oppose the definition, and will probably speak against it to-morrow. Ginoulhiac, Bishop of Grenoble, who is perhaps the most learned Bishop in France, after Maret, though his learning is of a somewhat narrow and old-fashioned kind, is by nature and education one of those who are anxious to find some middle way, by which they may at once bow to authority and escape the consequences of an inexorable logic. The *Curia* has long believed his theologian's heart could be won by well-selected citations, but other means have been also

employed. After he had been named to the Arch-
bishopric of Lyons, the Pope refused him the desired
audience and also the preconisation, so that the diocese
will have to remain many months without a chief pastor.
But he continued firm, and took part in the compilation
of a document, which might well become the most
important in its results of all the declarations of the
Opposition. The Bishop of Mayence was predisposed
by all his sympathies and antipathies to support the
cause of Rome in this Council, and he has often, as well
at Fulda as here, repudiated the notion that the Pope's
claim to infallibility is an encroachment on the divine
prerogatives. For a time he was a drag on his colleagues, but the policy of the Court and its treatment
of the Opposition has more and more alienated him
from the curialists; so that from seeming at first in
Roman eyes to be divided by an immeasurable gulf
from men like Dupanloup, he has become a powerful
influence in the minority. The pamphlet on infallibility, written at his suggestion, and addressed from
Solothurn to the Bishops, showed his changed attitude.
This publication is well known to have been for a time
kept back, and it was only after a contest of some
weeks with the authorities that he succeeded in getting

it issued. As the contemporaneous writings of Rauscher, Schwarzenberg and Hefele met with no particular opposition, this hostile treatment of Ketteler was ascribed to the belief that the greater sharpness of the German protest against the order of business, as compared with the French, was due to him. Where the French text speaks of the Bishops as representing the Churches, the Germans added the remark that this was the more important to insist upon in the case of the Vatican Council, where so many Bishops were admitted to vote, whose claim to vote by divine right was doubtful.[1] This historical consideration has since been urged with great effect by Kenrick, whose decisive weight in fixing the value of the Vatican Council will only be known later. It was universally believed that Ketteler had co-operated in getting this passage inserted in the German Protest, and so one is not surprised that he should have taken a leading part in the last move of the Opposition. To-day a declaration, signed by 77 Fathers, has been presented to the Presidents, protesting energetically against the inversion of the established

---

[1] " Hæc conditio pro Concilio Vaticano eo magis urgenda esse videtur, cum ad ferenda suffragia tot Patres admissi sunt, de quibus non constat evidenter, utrum jure tantum ecclesiastico an etiam Jure divino ipsis votum decisivum competat."

order in the interests of infallibility.   It contains the severe remark that they well know no answer can be expected, but they are unwilling to let any doubts be cast on the freedom of the Council, and to have the Bishops made a public laughing-stock.

They cannot take much by this move.   The arguments against inverting the purely arbitrary order of business, previously introduced, are weak in comparison with the objections to the definition on principle, and to insist on them is simply beating the air.   The majority only see proofs of their weakness and grounds for increased confidence in the obstinate holding aloof of the Opposition from the main question, and in the fact that men who are not real assailants of the dogma play a prominent part in its proceedings.   Wherever there has been any talk of hesitation, it has been only in the Vatican and the Commission *de Fide*, never among the mass of the party.   Pius may for a moment have shared the scruples suggested to him by two of the Legates, and the Deputation may have believed that the dogma could be established without any violent precipitation, and regretted the indecent zeal of the French, but the ardent infallibilists—French, English, Belgian, Swiss, etc.—have never slackened in their confidence or their assiduity. They still affirm, as they ever have done, that infallibility has no real opponents or hardly any, and that the leading members of the Opposition privately hold the view or at least have never openly rejected it; there are but few even among the *Animadversiones* which deny the admissibility of the definition. So they think that there is a bait for every one of these troublers of peace, and that they can all either be won over by concessions or frightened into submission. The example of the Prince Bishop of Breslau, who is known to have suspended a priest for attacking the doctrines of the Syllabus, is very interesting in this point of view. If the Pope were to issue a Bull condemning the opponents of his infallibility, and to deal in the same way or—as he easily might—more solemnly and harshly with other doctrines than the Encyclical of 1864, Prince Bishop Förster would at least punish all malcontents as severely as he punished the contemner of the Syllabus.[1] Yet in spite of all this, he is a member of the Opposition, and the majority believe it would probably soon melt away, if the Pope could resolve on adopting this policy. Moreover their leaders

---

[1] It appears from a passage in Letter LII. that this severe judgment on the Prince Bishop was based on an erroneous report of his conduct in the papers.

speak as though the Opposition had already incurred censures. They expect to make short work with the German Bishops who signed the Fulda Pastoral. In that document it is said, " The Holy Father is accused of acting under the influence of a party, and desiring to use the Council simply as a means of unduly exalting the power of the Apostolic See, changing the ancient and genuine constitution of the Church, and setting up a spiritual domination incompatible with Christian liberty. Men do not scruple to apply party names to the head of the Church and to the Episcopate, which hitherto we have been accustomed to hear only from the lips of professed enemies of the Church. And they plainly avow their suspicion that the Bishops will not be allowed full freedom of deliberation, and will themselves be deficient in the knowledge and straightforwardness requisite for the discharge of their duties in Council. And they accordingly call in question the validity of the Council and its decrees."

Here in Rome the Bishops have to listen to these and similar observations *usque ad nauseam,* which their adversaries use only to remind them of this Pastoral. While denying before the world that the definition of infallibility was the object of the Council, or was intended at all by the holy Father, they at the same time wrote to Rome to deprecate it, being perfectly well acquainted with the designs of the *Curia*, and corresponded with friendly prelates on the means of averting it. And thus the other party may now say to them, "You acknowledge yourselves that the unity and strength of the Church is to be preferred to strict veracity, and that in so sacred a cause some measure of deception is allowable. Don't choose then to be better than your neighbours. You have already abandoned the ground of objective truth, and you may as well come over to us altogether." But the chief means of breaking the Opposition consists in the Pope's making the Bishops feel the full weight of his authority and compromising himself yet more deeply.

The *Curia* has succeeded in setting aside the attempted intervention of the Governments, and the battle will have to be fought out, as is fitting, by the Bishops themselves. In the mind of the majority it is already over; the Deputation has issued a reply to the objections of the minority, which deserves the most careful attention of the theological world. It contains a flat denial of the force of historical evidence, and closes with a repudiation of the necessity of moral unanimity.[1] This points out the road which the loyal Bishops of the Opposition must follow.

Postscript.—I have just heard that the definitive voting on the Little Catechism, which was announced for to-day's sitting, has not taken place. The *Curia* had discovered that the German and French Opposition Bishops would vote *en masse* against it. No regard had been paid to the representations and objections of those who voted *juxta modum* on May 4, and accordingly this stronger resistance was foreseen, and the *Curia* shrank from appealing to a new vote. Matters remain as the voting of May 4 left them, and it is hoped that before the next Solemn Session the minority will be split up by a more important controversy.

---

[1] "Jamvero infallibilitatem S. Ap. Sedis et Romani Pontificis ad doctrinam fidei pertinere ex allatis fidei documentis constat, et contrariæ illi sententiæ a magisterio Ecclesiæ non semel fuerunt improbatæ. Cujuscunque ergo scientiæ etiam historiæ ecclesiasticæ conclusiones Rom. Pontificum infallibilitati adversantes, quo manifestius hæc ex revelationis fontibus infertur, eo certius veluti totidem errores habendas esse consequitur."

FORTY-FIFTH LETTER.

Rome, May 14, 1870.—The sitting of May 4 requires a more particular mention which shall be added here. The reporter on the scheme of the Catechism was Zwerger, Bishop of Seckau, who is a special favourite of the *Curia*,—forming as he does with the Tyrolese Rudigier and Fessler the little party of Austrian in-fallibilists,—a youthful and elegant prelate, whose Latin is seasoned with such terms as *portraitus, præcautionibus,* etc. He gave the consoling assurance that the new Catechism should be compiled by a Commission of Bishops named by the Pope, so that it might be " omnibus numeris absolutus." He added that unfortunately he could not introduce this masterpiece into his own diocese, but he would in principle vote for it.

The question of the Catechism is of course closely connected with that of infallibilism. For first the

Catechism will quickly and strongly inoculate the rising generation with the dogma, and secondly, as being a papal text-book, it will familiarize all the young from an early age with the notion, that in religion everything emanates from the Pope, depends on him and refers to him. Thus every one will be taught that not only all rights, as Boniface VIII. said, but all religious and moral truths, are drawn forth by the Pope from the recesses of his own breast.

The notion is excellent, and does infinite honour to the Jesuits who invented it. It is like the egg of Columbus. One cannot think at first how it did not occur centuries ago to the astute members of the *Curia*. But to begin with, it would have been impossible earlier to fit this catechetical strait-waistcoat on such a Church as was the French ; and then again a sufficient motive was wanting, for it is four centuries since any Pope thought of introducing new dogmas into the Church. The whole history of the Church offers but three examples of it. The first was the attempt of Gregory VII. and Innocent III. to alter the doctrine hitherto prevalent on the relations of Church and State, and to substitute the new doctrine of the Pope's divine right to exercise temporal sovereignty over princes and peoples. This did not succeed. The second instance was the attempt made from the thirteenth century downwards by the *Curia*, and especially by the Jesuits, —for which a long series of forgeries and fictions paved the way,—to replace the primacy of the ancient Church by something totally different, viz., an absolute monarchy, so as to destroy the power and authority of the Episcopate, reduce the Bishops to mere delegates or commissioners of the Pope, and erect him into the irresponsible master of the whole Church and all its members, the sole source of all ecclesiastical jurisdiction. This scheme too was wrecked on the opposition, first of the great Councils, and afterwards of the French Church. The third attempt, to make all Popes infallible and thus establish the sole and universal monarchy of the Pope, is now going on. And as the teaching of the Church has to be altered and enriched with new dogmas, the Jesuits who inspire the Pope have quite rightly perceived that a Catechism clothed with supreme authority, such as never previously existed, must be introduced throughout the whole Catholic world. This undertaking promises special advantages to the Jesuit Order, and so it has been brought before the Council, and forced rapidly and unexpectedly to the vote.   So little had it been anticipated, that over 100 of the Bishops in Rome were absent.   Another attempt was made in this *Schema* to get papal infallibility accepted by a side-wind, by inserting a statement that the whole teaching office of the Church resided in the primacy, to the exclusion of the Bishops.   It was felt at once that this would give the Pope a position and authority incompatible with any other, even that of the Church herself, and that the Bishops would entirely lose their judicial office in matters of doctrine.   Partly on account of this passage, and partly on general grounds, 57 Bishops voted *Non placet*, among whom were Cardinals Schwarzenberg and Rauscher, Archbishops Scherr and Deinlein, and Bishops Dinkel and Hefele.   It created a great sensation that Cardinal Mathieu, Archbishop of Besançon, also voted against it. He has only lately returned from his Easter visit to France, and is said now to belong decidedly to the minority.   Among the 24 Bishops who voted *juxta modum*, were the Archbishops of Cologne and Salzburg, and the Bishop of Mayence.   An interval of two days was given them to put into shape the condition on which they wanted to make their vote dependent. But we have already seen that, when the time was come, the Legates preferred not calling for any definitive vote.

Are we to infer from the collapse of so weighty and pregnant a question as this of the Catechism that henceforth everything will be settled much quicker? I cannot say. But as early as January 22 the Pope declared, in a Brief addressed to M. de Ségur, that the delay in the proceedings of the Council was due to the powers of Hell, for as it was to inflict on them their inevitable death-blow, they wished to protract it as long as they could. Pius is persuaded that, as soon as the Council produces its fruits, all faults and vices will at once disappear from human society, and all who are in error be led into the truth. That is expressly stated in the Brief; and these are no mere phrases, such as the *Curia* frequently indulges in, but are uttered in sober earnest. Pius really holds his infallibility to be the divinely ordained panacea for effecting a thorough cure of mankind, who are now sick unto death. He is convinced that the fount of unerring inspiration, which will henceforth flow incessantly from the holy Father at Rome, will fructify all Christian lands like a supernatural Nile stream, and overflow all human science for its purification or its destruction. The Jesuits make the decrees, who are not indeed themselves infallible, but whose compositions, directly the Pope has signed his name to them, become inspired and free from every breath of error.

The psychological enigma presented by Pius can only be solved by looking steadily at the two root-ideas, which interpenetrate and supplement one another in his mind.   There is first his belief in the objective infallibility of his 256 predecessors, and next his belief that he, Mastai, has through continual invocation and worship of the Madonna attained to an inspiration and divine illumination of which she is the medium.   This last privilege is in his eyes, as all about him know and occasionally say, a purely personal one, which his predecessors did not all experience.   But it strengthens his faith in infallibilism, and—which is the main point—he is certain by virtue of this infused illumination that he is God's chosen instrument for introducing the dogma.   And this higher certainty naturally leads him to regard the opposing Bishops as unhappy men snared in the meshes of a fatal error, who rebel in their sinful blindness against the counsel of God, and will be dragged at the chariot-wheels of the triumphal car of the infallible Papacy in its resistless progress, like boys hanging on behind, in spite of their efforts to pull it back. And therefore sharp rebukes—*verbera verborum*— must not be spared these episcopal opponents. Pius knows that the German and American members of the party are infected by the atmosphere of Protestantism, and the French by that of infidelity, so that they are suffering at least under a violent heterodox influenza, and require drastic remedies. But no one had imagined that all regard for decency would be so completely laid aside, and that the Pope would so far forget his high position as to actually descend into the arena, deal blows with his own hand, and assail all disputants with bitter and insulting words, as he has in fact done. He might have waited quietly till his unconditional majority of 500 had voted the dogma, and then have fulminated to his heart's content the plenitude of anathemas and curses at the still unbelieving " filii perditionis " and " iniquitatis alumni," in the forms that are stored up ready for use in the Roman Chancery. But he is too impatient to wait for the decision, and exhausts all the weapons in his quiver by anticipation. When the Bishops of the minority presented their first remon- strance against the new dogma, he had it announced in his journals that it was only from the lofty impartiality which became him that he had not received their memorial, as neither had he received those of the other party. But now this mask is dropped, and no means are omitted for overreaching or intimidating the minority. It is confidently expected that fear and discouragement will soon do their work in splitting up the Opposition. Many of its members recoil in alarm from the position they will be placed in by persevering to the last. It needs more than ordinary episcopal courage, it needs a deep conscientiousness and faith firm as a rock in the ultimate victory of the true doctrine of the ancient Church, to confront in open fight the triple host of the *Curia*, the Jesuits and the ultramontanes.

And now for the first time the excellence of the Council Hall is proved, and the wise foresight of the *Curia* in choosing it and adhering to it with the firmness of old Romans in spite of all entreaties and representations to the contrary. It is precisely adapted to the present tactics of the majority. The Bishops will occupy a number of sittings with speeches, generally read, seldom spoken, which four-fifths of their auditors, as before, neither understand nor wish to understand. For the majority know everything already ; they are armed with a triple breastplate, and have their short and powerful watchword, which renders them invincible. Those who frequent infallibilist circles here may hear St. Augustine's saying quoted ten times a day, "Roma locuta est, causa finita est," or St. Ambrose's "Ubi Petrus, ibi Ecclesia," or that St. Irenæus said every one must necessarily agree with the Roman Church. These are mere fables; Augustine and Irenæus said nothing of the kind, but something quite different; and while Ambrose did indeed use the words, it was without the remotest reference to the Pope and his infallibility. But the words are quoted in a hundred books and pamphlets, and are used like theological revolvers which never miss fire. And then Mermillod will repeat in the Council what he lately said in a sermon here about the threefold manifestation of God in the crib of Bethlehem, in the Sacrament of the Altar, and—in the Vatican. Pie of Poitiers will utter some of those bold Oriental metaphors, which all France laughs at but which are gravely received in the Council Hall. Manning will commend infallibility as the one plank of safety for mankind who are sinking in the shipwreck of scepticism, while he sings a pæan over the triumph of the dogma over history. There will be room even for some

flashes of genius from the German infallibilists, the
Tyrolese and the three Bavarians, if they can resolve on
opening their lips hitherto so firmly closed.　And then
the African heat and sultry atmosphere, drying up the
brain, which have already begun to press on Rome like
a leaden pall, will come in to expedite the close.　The
majority will avail themselves of the right the Pope
has conferred on them to break off abruptly the discussion, in which nothing has been discussed, and the
Pope will appear in a Solemn Session, in the full pomp
of the earthly representative of Christ, to proclaim with
infallible certainty his own infallibility and that of all
his predecessors and successors, "approbante Concilio."
And thus will he enter on his new empire of the world;
for he will then for the first time be the acknowledged
master and sole teacher of mankind; before, he was
only a pretender.　The Bishops will bow their heads
reverently under a profound sense of their own fallibility
before the one divinely enlightened man, and the world
will go to sleep to wake next morning enriched and
blessed with the new and fundamental article of faith.
The day of the promulgation will be a great day of
creation.　"God said, Let there be light, and there
was light, and the evening and the morning were the

first day" of the new Church, after the old Church for 1869 years had been unable to ascertain and formulize its chief article of faith. For the Popes were always infallible; "the light appeared in the darkness, and the darkness comprehended it not." From the Pentecost of the blessed year 1870, as Manning has prophesied, dates the age of the Holy Ghost, and the Church is for the first time really complete. As the Pentecost of the year 33 was the birthday of the ancient Church, so will the Pentecost of 1870 be the birthday of the new and infinitely more enlightened Church. Nearly all commentators now assume that the seven days of creation in Genesis are not seven ordinary days, but signify a great period of the world's history. It cannot then be taken ill if the Church, instead of distinctly putting forward her principal dogma on the first Pentecost, which would certainly have been the most natural course, should have waited nineteen centuries in the vain attempt to ascertain and formulate it, and have only now hatched the egg in the year 1870.

FORTY-SIXTH LETTER.

Rome, May 15, 1870.—Yesterday the discussion of the *Schema* on the Primacy began, *i.e.*, speeches were delivered for and against infallibility, for any regular discussion is of course impossible in the Council Hall. The Hall is really more patient than the proverbially patient paper, as long as the majority do not get excited. Things can be said there which would not be allowed to be written, still less printed. The names of 69 Bishops are inscribed to speak. Bishop Pie of Poitiers had already the day before, as reporter of the Deputation, exceeded the expectations generally formed of him. He had discovered a wholly new argument, to which he gave utterance with evident self-complacency. The Pope, he said, must be infallible, because Peter was crucified head downwards. As the head bears the whole weight of the body, so the Pope, as head, bears the whole Church ; but he is infallible who bears, not

5

he who is borne.—*Q.E.D.* The Italians and Spaniards applauded enthusiastically. On the 14th Cardinal Patrizzi spoke. The Pope, he observed, certainly claims personal infallibility, but he does not therefore wish nor is he obliged to separate himself from the Episcopate. Certainly not, thought the minority, since we must all assent to that claim of the infallible, so that he cannot separate himself from us Bishops or shake us off if he wished it. Bishop Rivet of Dijon carried off the honours of the day among the Opposition. Bishop Ranolder of Vesprim referred briefly but forcibly to the dangers into which the new dogma would plunge the Hungarian Church. Dreux Brézé, who followed worthily in the footsteps of Pie, was this time eclipsed by a Sicilian prelate, who said that the Sicilians had a reason peculiar to themselves for believing the infallibility of all the Popes. It is well known that Peter preached in that island, where he found a number of Christians ; but when he told them that he was infallible, they thought this article of faith, which they had never been taught, a strange one. In order to get at the truth about it, they sent an embassy to the Virgin Mary, to ask if she had heard of Peter's infallibility, to which she replied that she certainly remembered being present, when her Son conferred this special prerogative on him. This testimony fully satisfied the Sicilians, who have ever since preserved in their hearts faith in infallibility. This speech was really delivered in the Council Hall on May 14. The Opposition Bishops see a proof of the insolent contempt of the majority in their putting up such men as Pie and this Sicilian to speak against them.

Sicily is truly the land where faith removes mountains, and Pius would find himself among his most genuine spiritual children if he went to Messina. There the letter is still preserved, which the Virgin Mary addressed to the inhabitants and let fall from heaven, and the feast of the *Sacra Lettera* is annually observed with the full approval of the Roman Congregation of Rites, when the excited populace shout in the streets " Viva la Sacra Lettera." The Jesuit Inchover has written a book to prove its authenticity to demonstration.

A great many copies of the remarkable pamphlet *Ce qui se passe au Concile* have been secretly disseminated—the Government naturally wants to suppress it— and it is eagerly read. I have learnt from a Frenchman that Pius himself has read some pages, on which

he observed, " C'est mal, c'est très-mal, excessivement
mal." It is clear that the author has himself collected
his notices in Rome. If its revelations show how every
usage of former Councils has been reversed and all true
freedom carefully destroyed, a further evidence of this
is supplied by the statement of the official *Giornale di
Roma* about the departure of the Americans, where the
Bishops are plainly reminded that they are liable to
arrest, and that any of them who quit Rome without
leave incur heavy censures. A German Archbishop,
who had an audience of the Pope to-day, took the
opportunity of speaking to him about the universal
aversion and resistance of the Germans to the infallibilist dogma. It made not the slightest impression.
Pius answered : " I know these Germans of old, who
choose to know best about everything; every one
wants to be Bishop and Pope." Yet it is notorious
that he does not understand a word of German, and
has never been in Germany or read a German book,
even in a translation. But he reads Veuillot and Margotti, and hears the Jesuits at least three times a week.
Meanwhile the Protest drawn up by Ketteler against
the arbitrary change of the order of business was presented on the 12th of March with 72 signatures. It

contains, as I said before, the words : " We know well
that we shall receive no answer to this any more than
to our former memorials."

All German Catholics count here for half Protestants.
A German must here give special evidence of his
orthodoxy, I do not say before he is trusted, but
before he is reckoned a Catholic at all by the side of
Spaniards and Italians.   Above all is German theology
in ill repute, and the mere word "history" in the
mouth of a German acts like a red handkerchief on
certain animals.   The good times are gone by when
Germany was considered the classical land of obedience
in comparison with France, so copious was the influx
of Peter's pence ; the Jesuits, on whom the chief hopes
are centred, have effected very little here except in
Westphalia and the Tyrol.

It is hard for the Bishops, even after a five months'
experience, to comprehend the rôle assigned them, and
to understand that they have only been summoned to
receive commands, to obey, and to do service.   It is a
saying current among the Monsignori that the Bishops
are nothing but servants of the Pope.   " Just consider
the monstrosity," said one of the youngest but most
actively employed of the Cardinals to a French priest,

when the famous letter of censure addressed by the
Pope to the Archbishop of Paris appeared in the newspapers, " this Archbishop dares to speak of rights
which belong to him !   What would you say if one of
your lackeys were to talk of his rights, when you gave
him your orders ?"

FORTY-SEVENTH LETTER.

Rome, May 16, 1870.—The Bishops of the minority want to bind themselves by subscribing an agreement to vote for no formula which contains the personal infallibility of the Pope. A calculation emanating from them has been shown me, according to which the strength of the Opposition is undiminished, or rather increased. It enumerates 43 Germans and Hungarians, 40 North Americans, 29 French, 4 Portuguese, and 10 Italians. The number of Bishops from the United States who are considered to be trustworthy is especially worthy of notice. They have been greatly influenced by the recent publications of the Bishops, and particularly by the excellent work of Archbishop Kenrick of St. Louis. When they first came to Rome they were nearly all inclined to the new dogma, but here their eyes have been gradually opened. The insolent and

despotic treatment of the Bishops, the spectacle of adulation exhibited by persons who call themselves successors
of the Apostles, and the lamentable sophistry employed in torturing historical facts—as *e.g.* the case of
Honorius—all this has gradually filled these Republi-
cans with disgust and aversion, and driven them to the
opposite side. But clearly what has chiefly influenced
them has been the conviction produced by the controversy that, if they take home with them the new dogma
of the Pope's political supremacy over all States, they
will be exposed to the contempt and hatred of all
educated America. And as many of them are Irishmen
by birth, they have been reminded that, as Alexander
VI. gave the American peoples to Spain, so Adrian IV.
gave Ireland to the King of England and thereby
brought misery on the emerald isle.

The Bishops of the Opposition know how to appreciate the strength and numerical preponderance of their
rivals; they know too that, besides a cool calculation
and passive subjection to the commands of their
"lord," a certain enthusiasm and confidence also prevail
among their ranks. There are first the numerous
missionary Bishops and Vicars-Apostolic, who must
certainly vote as they are told, for they are entirely in

the power of the Propaganda, and Cardinal Barnabo is an inexorably strict master : the Orientals have experienced that. And moreover the Bishops engaged in converting the heathen say, "How conveniently the new dogma will simplify and facilitate our work with Negroes, Kaffirs, New-Zealanders, etc.! We have hitherto had to refer them to the Church, of whose nature and authority we could only impress a dim conception on their minds with much time and trouble. Henceforth we shall tell them that God inspires one man in Rome with all truth, from whom all others receive it. That is short, simple, and what a child can understand."

But the main strength of the papal army consists in the 120 Bishops from the kingdom of Italy with the the exception of 10, the 143 from the States of the Church, and the 120 titular Bishops without subjects or dioceses, most of them created by the present Pope, who represent nobody but themselves, or rather him who has raised them from the dust and set mitres on their heads. That makes altogether 373 Italians. This chosen band will remain here patiently through the heat so unendurable to the Northern Bishops, and the question has been already mooted in the Vatican, as I hear from the mouth of one who is in its confidence, whether it would not be best to protract the affair and defer the final voting till these recalcitrant Northerners have obtained the permission which will be readily accorded them to flee from the heat and fevers, after which the Italian and Spanish prelates would vote the darling dogma with conspicuous unanimity. The idea deserves to be preferred to another, which is also under consideration. The Pope might issue a Bull defining that the moral unanimity, which has been so much talked of, is not necessary for Councils in voting articles of faith, and that a simple majority is sufficient. For it is thought that most of the minority Bishops, especially the in-opportunists, would not dare to resist the new papal definition, and would thus be compelled at last to succumb to the infallibilist decree. We shall soon see. You may gather what the leaders of the minority think of the situation from a remark of Cardinal Mathieu's, " On veut jeter l'Église dans l'abîme, nous y jeterons plutôt nos cadavres."

The two Bavarian Bishops, Stahl and Leonrod, have thought fit after two months to make a public demon-stration of their assent to Bishop Räss's condemnation of Gratry. The explanation accepted here is that, after

2 N

the Bavarian note had been presented, the authorities wished the Bavarian Bishops to make an adverse move on the conciliar chess-board; and as these two prelates would not openly contradict their King, the expedient of a very late adhesion to the effusions of the Bishop of Strasburg was chosen.

It is commonly assumed that all the Cardinals are infallibilists as a matter of course, and the more so as this is at bottom the only doctrine which may be said to have been exclusively invented and built up by men who either were already or were soon about to become Cardinals. Still this is not quite the case. Apart from the non-resident Cardinals, Rauscher, Schwarzenberg and Mathieu, there are some among the residents who would gladly be dispensed from voting for the new foundation article of faith on which the whole edifice is henceforth to rest. But one of them said to-day, "We shall ruin our position, lose all influence, and become the mark of endless attacks. And as every one here has some weak and vulnerable point in his past life, he dare not expose himself to these fatal assaults on his character and honour from which there would be no escape." At the same time the Cardinal admitted that the whole College has so lost its influence and become so insignificant, that for six months the Pope has not once assembled them. Antonelli and a few favourites, with the Jesuits of the *Civiltà,* are the people who now construct the history of the world and the Church.

FORTY-EIGHTH LETTER.

Rome, May 20, 1870.—The first week of the great debate is drawing to a close. The Archbishops of Vienna, Prague, Gran, Paris, Antioch and Tuam have spoken against the infallibilist definition. So much is gained; the Catholic world knows that it is represented in Council, while the Court party is robbed of some illusions about the strength of the resistance to be looked for. The only fruit of its better knowledge as yet observable is seen in an increased obstinacy and a greater insolence of tone. The Commission has already declared by anticipation, in its reply to the remarks of the Bishops against the dogma, that the denial of infallibility is condemned under pain of censure, and scientific arguments are no longer available. The giving out of this watchword does excellent service to the majority, who are very shy of theological arguments and treat their opponents as heretics. That

far-famed courtesy, which has hitherto been an ornament if not exactly a real excellence of Rome, has
greatly diminished, and the hypocrisy so long spun out
has disappeared ; it has become necessary to recognise
the broad gulf which divides parties. And this has
produced a tendency on the side of the Court and the
majority to push their claims to the extremest point, to
play for high stakes, and hold out no prospect of concessions beforehand. The minority is in their eyes not
a power to be negotiated with but a gang of insolent
mutineers to be put down. The mass of the majority
have carried their leaders with them, and only passion
now prevails in that camp. But the harshness and
roughness the *Curia* has thought it necessary to display
has done more to strengthen the Opposition than the
changes and concessions already pre-arranged will do
to dissolve it. They have been suffered in this way to
gain a position which they might never have won if the
Curia had exercised more foresight. Whether all the
elements of the Opposition will be found reliable, pure
in their aims and loyal in their hearts, the future will
show. At present I only record the audacious policy of
the majority based on cunning calculations, as it has
been evinced in the early days of the discussion. But

the majority naturally includes men of different minds ; there are some who would like to be well rid of the affair, and others who would gladly discover a formula not looking like a positive innovation which might satisfy opponents, while the great mass of them want the blow to be struck so that, after crushing the Opposition within the Council, they may annihilate it without the Council also. These last have the upper hand in the majority, and will probably retain it till the general debate is over and the doctrine itself and its definition come to be discussed. They are led by cool, calculating heads, but consist for the most part of the uneducated and unlearned mass of the episcopate who have no independence, the people who during Strossmayer's speech presented the spectacle of a rabble of conspirators rather than an ordered assembly. To keep them in the requisite state of exaltation the speeches must be adapted to their intellectual level. And as they are more easily excited than controlled they do not of course exhibit the majority in a favourable light, and one may be prepared at any moment for the Council being disgraced by an outbreak of their frenzy. Nothing more of the kind however has happened yet.

At the head of the extreme party stands the close ally of the Jesuits, the Archbishop of Westminster. He was the first to say out with the utmost distinct-ness that infallibility belongs to the Pope alone and independently of the Episcopate. The ultramontane speakers, Pie, Patrizzi and Deschamps, have vied with one another in their endeavours to get this ex-treme view of Manning's accepted, which they them-selves did not all share before. The emancipation of the Pope from the entire Episcopate is the very turning-point of the whole controversy, the object for which the Council was put on the stage; infallibility tied to the consent of the united or dispersed Episcopate nearly all the Bishops would accept, for very few indeed clearly understand that even Councils depend on another con-sent than that of the Episcopate. But such a defini-tion of infallibility would cost Rome the very thing she has laboured so much and sinned so much to gain. It is a great advantage for the Opposition that in this matter there are no formulas of compromise possible but such as are manifestly perfidious and insincere.

On the 17th Deschamps, Archbishop of Mechlin, made perhaps the most important, certainly the most remarkable, speech delivered in favour of the *Constitutio*. He is considered the ablest speaker of his party, which notoriously has no superabundance of good speakers, and is said to be a superficial man who takes things easily. He not only committed himself to the extremest section of the party, but denounced his opponents as bad Christians not walking in the fear of God. The change of tone was much remarked in him, as in the Bishop of Poitiers. Manning exhibits the same change, who now maintains that all who do not submit to the majority might well be excommunicated directly after the promulgation of the decree. Two German Bishops, Greith and Hefele, spoke on the same day; and indeed in this debate many weighty voices will be raised from every land where the contest about the Church is being fought, to point to the practical dangers involved in the circumstances of the case—a kind of argument Pius is wont to put aside with a "Noli timere." Greith of St. Gallen spoke for Switzerland; as a learned theologian he declared himself against the definition on scientific grounds, and as a Swiss Bishop on account of the pre-sent circumstances of his country; for he is persuaded that his Swiss brother bishops, with their zeal for the infallibilist decree, are simply forging weapons against the Church for the Radicals. Bishop Hefele of Rotten-burg touched in the course of his speech on the affair of Honorius, which must later on come into the discus-sion. Next day Hefele read Cardinal Rauscher's speech. But Cardinal Schwarzenberg's address exceeded all expectations and left a profound impression. Cardinal Donnet and the Archbishop of Saragossa, who spoke in the name of the Deputation, did not bring the defence any further or develop any new points of history, and —which is more important—gave no further informa-tion about the plans and hopes of the *Curia* and the majority.

On Thursday the 19th Cardinal Cullen, Archbishop of Dublin, spoke, who for twenty years has been the protagonist of Romanism in the British isles. With sound tact he chose the most learned Bishop of the minority, Hefele, for attack, and assailed not his speech but his publications. Yet he did not attempt to refute him, but only to prove that he had contradicted him-self, since the account of Honorius given in his History of Councils is different from that in his latest work. It is true that in the History, where no doctrinal in-ferences were to be drawn, the theological significance of the condemnation of Honorius does not receive the same exhaustive appreciation and exposition as in the little tractate on the question whether he was justly condemned for heresy. But there is no difference of principle between the two works; in both Hefele says plainly that Honorius was justly pronounced a heretic, even if he was no heretic at heart. But when the two passages are separated from each other, it can be made to look as though he had maintained in the former that Honorius was really orthodox whereas he now declares that he was a heretic. But the process could with equal reason be reversed, and the heresy of Honorius shown to be affirmed in the History and his orthodoxy in the pamphlet. But what use would even an ortho-dox Pope be for upholding the purity of the Church's doctrinal deposit, if he used heretical formulas to express his own really true opinion?

None the less however was Cullen's attack received with great satisfaction, for the ruling powers know well enough on what the Bishop of Rottenburg's opposition is based, and think to subdue German science—*i.e.*, the devil himself—in his person. On the same day the Patriarch Jussuf uttered words that deserve to be laid to heart on the consequences such a dogmatic blunder would entail in the East—a significant indication that the Orientals are not prepared to bend obediently under the yoke of a decree aimed at their ritual and their rights as well as their tradition. The Archbishop of Corfu answered him next day. There is very little that can be properly called debating, for the order of proceedings is better suited for academical addresses than for real discussion ; the practice of making prelates speak in their order of precedence makes any honest interchange of blows impossible. But the Greek coming forward to speak looked like a preconcerted answer to the Armenian. The Archbishop of Corfu insisted that, so far from the dogma rendering the reunion of the Greek Church more difficult, such a result was inconceivable without it, nor could the dogma excite any suspicion, because the Greeks found it in their tradition as well as their Fathers and Councils, and envied the Latin Church her infallible Pope. In evidence of this he cited the passages where the Pope's primacy is recognised. The great body of the Fathers listened to this with grave faces : it was only following the style of their own theologians.

But three more important speakers had been heard before the Corfiote. The first was Simor, primate of Hungary, who was chosen, as is well known, into the

Deputation on Faith and has shown himself a more zealous advocate of its proposals and adherent of the *Curia* than ever. The majority believed that it possessed in him a master of Latin who could rival the eloquent leader of the Opposition, and Simor justified his reputation as an accomplished Latinist. But he spoke—assuredly to the no small disgust and amazement of the majority—as an unequivocal opponent of the proposed decree. And this implied that the whole Hungarian Episcopate would vote against it. He was followed by a feeble old man whose speech fell flat after that of the eloquent primate, and who could only be known to a few of his hearers, though he holds an important place in the history of the last generation. This was John MacHale, for the last thirty-five years Archbishop of Tuam and formerly the most powerful prelate in Ireland, a famous name in the days of O'Connell ; but his political rôle has long been played out, and he belongs to a bygone age and an obsolete school. For the twenty years during which Cullen has been introducing Roman absolutism into Ireland his influence has been on the decline, and while he was expounding his antagonism to the definition to-day in a long and complicated address, men said to themselves, " magni nominis umbra." It was the accumulated debt of twenty years he paid off to Cardinal Cullen. But he can hardly be expected to have gained over any of his countrymen to the Opposition besides the three or four of them who already belong to it.

MacHale was succeeded by the Archbishop of Paris, the most accomplished and skilful, and therefore the most feared, of all the Opposition prelates. Darboy was lately the most influential advocate of that system of dallying and postponement which has so grievously injured the minority, and was involved through his intimate alliance with the Tuileries in the unhappy policy of his Government, so that he had become somewhat less trusted and influential. So much greater was the impression produced by his speech to-day, wherein he declared distinctly and repeatedly that a dogmatic decree not accepted by the whole Episcopate could not have any binding force. A suppressed murmur which ran through the ranks of the majority as he spoke seems to herald coming storms.

So far the Opposition has made its voice clearly heard. That it has on its side reason, Scripture and history signifies nothing for the moment; what is important is that it makes its strength felt, that it has won over waverers or doubters to its ranks, and that it has at last spoken plainly.   The position of parties and the question itself will take many new shapes, when the separate chapters of the Constitution come on for discussion.

FORTY-NINTH LETTER.

Rome, May 26, 1870.—The intellectual superiority of the Opposition has made itself so sensibly felt in the course of the debate on infallibility that they have visibly won in spirit and confidence, while a decrease of the assurance of victory hitherto manifested by the majority is observable. There is no sign yet of the breaking up of the Opposition or the desertion of its members to the infallibilist camp. The Court party had confidently reckoned on a considerable number of mere inopportunists giving in and separating from the opponents of the actual doctrine of infallibility, as soon as the dogma came to be discussed. The latter was said to be a mere tiny fraction, who would eventually take fright at their own impotence and come over. But as yet this hope has not been realized, and there are many indications that it is not likely to be realized, for the course of events and their experiences in Rome, as well as the discussions, both oral and written, have converted inopportunists into decided fallibilists. Cardinal Schwarzenberg has spoken with great power and dignity, and even the most zealous adherents of the Roman dogma must have been somewhat impressed by his declaration that its effect in Bohemia would be to make the nation first schismatic and then gradually Protestant. It at the same time illustrated the conduct of the Jesuits in a way that will not be forgotten. When the Archbishop of Paris affirmed that the much desired infallibilist decree was not one of the causes of the Council, but its sole cause, every one felt what a bitter truth had been uttered, and that the veil would thereby be torn away from that web of untruths and dishonest reticences about the object of the synod, by which the Bishops had been deceived and enticed as it were into a trap to Rome. Veuillot indeed had openly said in his official organ at the end of April, that to decree the new dogma was the principal and at bottom the sole office of the Council. That was at the very time when about eighty Bishops put out their strong protestation that they had come to Rome under the erroneous impression, deliberately suggested by the *Curia*, that the question of infallibility would not be brought before the Council ; while yet Cardoni had many months before, in the Commission on Faith, presented by command of the Pope the report which has lately been printed, and the whole Commission had agreed with him that papal infallibility should be defined. That same Commission, with the Jesuit Perrone and Dr. Schwetz of Vienna at its head, has now presented an address to the Pope urging the definition of the new article of faith, without which those worthies think they cannot exist any longer.

The infallibilist speaker who created most sensation was Cardinal Cullen, Archbishop of Dublin. He gained the warm applause of his party by the aggressive tone of his speech, in which he attacked especially Hefele and Kenrick. He appealed to the testimony of MacHale to show that the mind of Ireland has always been infallibilist—a glaring falsehood, as is proved by the famous Declaration of the Irish Catholics in 1757 formally repudiating the doctrine. And it made no slight impression, when the grey-haired MacHale rose to repudiate the pretended belief in infallibility not merely for himself but for Ireland. But it is certainly true that in former times for more than a century the Irish people, like the Spanish, was victimized to papal infallibility.   Every Irishman or Spaniard, who knew the history of his country, would recoil with horror from a theory which has borne such poisonous fruit for both nations in the past and may be equally injurious in the future.   To acquaint the Catholic tenants in Ireland with the infallible decisions of Popes about heresy and heretics would be enough at once to increase tenfold the agrarian crimes prevalent there, and would be the surest means for reproducing such a massacre as occurred there in 1641.

When Cullen replied to the Archbishop of St. Louis, "non est verum," the aged prelate requested leave of the Legates to defend himself briefly.   It was refused. Hefele was as little free to answer Cullen's attack, and has therefore had a pamphlet in his justification printed at Naples.   A new work by one of the most illustrious of the French Bishops is also expected from Naples, designed to prove against the Jesuits of the *Civiltà* the necessity of moral unanimity for dogmatic decrees. Another Irishman, Leahy, Archbishop of Cashel, said such absurd things in favour of the Court dogma that his speech was considered a clear gain for the minority.

There are 89 speakers inscribed for the general debate, and not a third of them have yet spoken.   This opens out a prospect of the debate being spun out to a great length, oppressive as the tropical heat is now become. The *Curia* still relies on the Northerners being tamed down. If only a good many of them would emulate the example of the Bishop of Hildesheim, and go away! The plan has often succeeded with English and Irish juries, of locking them up, when they could not agree, till they found a true verdict. But that won't answer here. On the contrary the longer the debate lasts, the more numerous the Opposition party becomes. At first many Bishops thought they might fairly gratify the good and amiable Pius, who won all hearts, even by making a new dogma, and give him the present he so greatly longed for. But Pius has completely cured his former worshippers of this disposition to make an article of faith " pour les beaux yeux du Pape." It has no doubt happened before that Italian Bishops have been treated by the Pope like servants, hired for the day's work and dismissed again if they did not obey the orders of the *Curia*. One need only refer to that parody on a synod, the fifth Lateran assembly, when Leo x. propounded downright forgeries and untruths to his Italian Bishops, who had to call themselves an Œcumenical Council, and dictated their votes. But even there no one ventured to treat Transalpine Bishops—Germans, French and Hungarians —with the insolent contempt now shown, to refuse even a reply to their urgent petitions and representations, and to make them drain the cup of humiliations and grievances to the very dregs. But the great task to be achieved in the first months of the Council was the kneading and manipulating the Bishops in all possible ways, so as to make them feel the immeasurable gulf between the master and the servants, that they might be more ready at last to sacrifice their episcopal dignity and ancient rights on the altar of Roman supremacy. When once they have assented to the infallibilist dogma, they neither can nor ought to be or desire to be anything else but passive and unintelligent promulgators and executors of papal commands and decrees on faith. That what is really required of them is to abdicate their office as a teaching body and themselves abolish their authority, Ketteler has lately declared without reserve in the Congregation; and he is a man who has profited much by his Roman schooling, though in a quite different sense from what his master intended. The Roman system of drill does not succeed with Germans, Hungarians and Americans.

A note received a fortnight ago from Paris by M. de Banneville, to be communicated or read to Cardinal Antonelli, has created great excitement here, owing to his studiously concealing it from his diplomatic colleagues. Its substance is as follows : France renounces any further interference with what is going on here, and contents herself henceforth with taking note of the decisions of the Pope and the Council. The Government has done its duty, as a friendly Catholic power, in seeking to withdraw the Court of Rome from the perilous path on which it has entered. The attempt has proved fruitless. The *Curia* seems resolved to ruin itself. France will maintain the attitude of a passive spectator, but accepts the altered condition of things introduced by this declaration of war on the part of the Roman Court. On the day of the definition the Concordat ceases to be in force and the previous relation of Church and State expires. The State separates itself from the Church and the French troops leave Rome. Separation of Church and State means in France and elsewhere that the budget of worship will be dropped, and the clergy must be supported by the faithful. And here I may mention a fact which has come to my knowledge on the best authority. When

Count Daru was going to despatch his famous memorial to the Holy See, he wished for an interpolation in the Chamber on the attitude of the Government towards the occurrences in Rome, and a friend of his applied on the subject to one of the most celebrated orators of the Left, who declined, saying, "Rome fait trop bien nos affaires pour qu'il soit de notre intérêt de lui créer des embarras." The contents of the note mentioned above are confirmed by the words of a leading statesman at Paris, quoted by a Bishop who has lately returned from thence, that for his own part he considered the separation of Church and State in France inevitable. He had however assented to the well-meant attempt of Count Daru to warn the Pope, and if possible deter him from his short-sighted enterprise ; but as that attempt had proved futile, it remained to take advantage of the blunders of the *Curia.* So enormous a spiritual power as the Court of Rome was aiming at was incompatible with the possession of secular power, and accordingly the French troops must be withdrawn from Rome, and matters left to take their course.

Even now there is a wish discernible among Cardinals like di Pietro, Corsi and Bilio, to discover some

intermediate formula, while the party men, like Manning, Pie, Cullen, and all who have been concerned in the
agitation and have staked their credit on its result, hold
to the most uncompromising form, as laid down in the
existing programme. The latter reckon on their overpowering preponderance of numbers, on the power of
the Pope, and the dread of ecclesiastical methods of
coercion, such as excommunication and the like, whereby all resistance will be certainly put down. On the
other hand, the Cardinals and members of the Papal
Cabinet just referred to prefer to set their hopes on the
hazy views and yielding temper of many Bishops of
the minority, and think that an ambiguous formula
might serve at once to delude and divide them. Their
watchword is " conciliazione, un partito di conciliazione."
But all their ingenuity is expended in the elaboration
of a phrase which may contain in a somewhat alle-
gorical and obscure form the infallibility and universal
monarchy of the Pope. To this conciliatory section
also belongs a man who understands the greatness of the
danger clearly enough, and who so lately uttered words
which have become notorious here : " This Pope begun
by destroying the State, and now will close his career
by destroying the Church too." Yet the speaker of

these words does not scruple to use his high ꞏposition and influence for actively furthering the undertakings which must lead to the catastrophe.

It is impossible for outsiders to form anything like an adequate conception of the complication of views and plans and the multifarious activity of the Roman *prela-tura.* Things happen which must appear incredible to every one who has heard of the proverbial skill and gift of accurate calculation possessed by the ruling clergy here. Thus a member of a powerful Order is sentenced to six years' imprisonment by the Holy Office on account of an occurrence in a nunnery here, the convent being at the same time broken up and the nuns distributed over other convents.   Yet after scarcely two years' imprison-ment this man, who is unhappily a German, is brought back here, and intrusted with the preparation of the draft decrees for the Council, and now the Court trusts to its favourite " segreto del S. Ufficio " for the cause of his sentence and of the dissolution of the convent not coming to the ears of the Bishops, but in vain.   The matter has created too great a sensation, and the culprit is too well known.

Meanwhile the minority are being plied with reasons, which are only mentioned cursorily, or not at all, in

the printed documents of the Court and the majority.
They are·told that all their own interests depend on
the papal authority being preserved intact, and that
the evils they fear from the proclamation of the dogma
cannot come into comparison with this common interest. They are bidden to remember how far the
Pope has already committed himself in this matter ;
since John XXII.—more than 600 years ago—no Pope
has thrown the Brennus sword of his authority into the
scale to decide a question of doctrine, but Pius has cut
himself off from all possibility of retreat by his *Schema*,
his conversations with many Bishops, and his letters of
encouragement and commendation to infallibilist writers.
He has declared, not once or twice but a hundred times,
that he knows and *feels* his infallibility, and wills the
Catholic world to believe it. He might simply by a
Bull condemn all who oppose it as heretics, and how
many of the Bishops would summon courage to resist
the Bull ?

As yet these reasons, practical as they appear, have
not produced much effect. The Opposition grows
visibly, and the speeches of its members have produced
an impression quite unexpected by themselves. The
words of the Melchite Patriarch, Jussuf, have kindled

a flame among the Orientals too, and there are Bishops who tell me they had not thought it possible for a discourse in the Council Hall to produce so great a revolution of feeling. But I will not conceal from you that you may find in Margotti's *Unita*, which draws its information from the highest authority, news in comparison to which my statements must appear pure fables. He writes from here on the 18th of May, "The action of the Holy Ghost is beginning to be felt; the Opposition diminishes daily. Cardoni has just issued his masterly work on papal infallibility, and now every one comprehends that it is the sole remedy and defence against the dominant pest of journalism and a free press. We must have a Pope who, being himself infallible, can *daily* teach, condemn and define, and whose utterances no Catholic ever dares to doubt."[1] So runs the statement in the *Unita* of May 24. Inconceivable blindness of past generations, who allowed whole centuries to pass without needing or asking for a single papal definition! Henceforth the definition wheel, which the Pope is to turn, is never to remain still for a day—because of journalism.

[1] " Al male dominante della licenza dei tipi, per cui il giornalismo nega e bestemmia ogni giorno, bisogna contrapporre il salutare rimedio del Papa infallibile, che ogni giorno può insegnare, condannare, definire, senza che mai sia licito ai cattolici dubitare de' suoi oraculi."

Thus does civilisation increase the wants of men. Our forefathers had to lead a joyless life without sugar, coffee, tea, alcohol and cigars, and stood on so low a level of cultivation that they fancied they got on very well without any infallible papal definition. But we, who are so gloriously advanced, require besides bodily enjoyments many—if possible very many—daily infallible definitions, and the Pope, out of sheer inexhaustible goodness, is on the point of acceding to the earnest prayers of 180 millions and opening the definition machine. Veuillot lately declared it was high time that the fact of the Pope's permanent divine inspiration should be universally acknowledged ; Margotti says that we want not only this, but daily definitions.[1] In this noble rivalry of the two Court journalists the Italian has evidently stolen a march on the Frenchman.

In my former statistics the number of Americans was put too high and of French too low. Only 23 Americans were lately calculated to belong to the Opposition, to whom must be added 10 Orientals, 4 Portuguese, 10 Italians and 5 Spaniards, making the whole minority over 120.

[1] [The English Jesuit, Father Gallwey, says they will be like " the daily provision of manna" to the Israelites.—TR.]

FIFTIETH LETTER.

Rome, May 27, 1870.—New speakers are continually inscribing their names for the debate on infallibility. And as only four can usually speak in one sitting, it is impossible to foresee the end of the general debate, after which the detailed discussion of the separate chapters is to follow. The minority seem resolved at this second discussion to enter thoroughly for the first time on the numerous separate points, exegetical, dogmatic and historical, which offer themselves for consideration. If the majority and the Legates allow this, the end will not be near reached by June 29; and after that date residence in Rome is held to be intolerable and the continuation of the Council impracticable. This last assumption I conceive to be mistaken. The Pope can very easily go to Castel Gandolfo for his summer holidays, while he leaves the Council to go on here. That it

should consist of hundreds of Bishops is quite unneces-
sary; former Popes have known how to manage in such
cases. Eugenius IV. had his Florentine Council nominally continued, after the Bishops were all gone except
a handful of Italians; Leo X. was content with about
sixty Italians at his so-called fifth Lateran Council.
What is to hinder Pius IX. from keeping on the Council,
after the Northern and distant Bishops are departed,
with the Bishops of his own States and the titular
episcopate resident in Rome, together with a host of
Neapolitans and Sicilians? Some too would be sure
to remain of the leaders and zealots of the majority.
But the Court party can cut short the discussion and
push matters to a vote whenever they like. The order
of business enables them to do so, but of course this
imperial policy will only be applied when the Pope
gives the signal.

Nearly the whole sitting of May 25 was taken up by
a speech of Manning's, who justified the expectations
formed of him by assuring the Opposition that they
were all heretics *en masse*. But he left the question
undecided, whether they had already incurred the
penalties of heresy prescribed in the canon law. Ketteler's speech made a precisely opposite impression.

Men were in a state of eager suspense as to what he would say, for he was known to have passed through a mental conflict. Ten months ago, in his publication on the Council which was then convoked, he had come forward of his own accord as the advocate of papal infallibility; he had come to Rome full of burning zeal and devotion for the Pope, though at Fulda he had declared the new dogma to be inopportune. I omit the intermediate steps of the process of disillusionizing and sobering he has gone through. His speech has shown that, like many others, he has become from an inopportunist a decided opponent of the dogma itself.

Such a change of mind based on a conscientious weighing of testimonies and facts is inconceivable and incredible to a regular Roman. When some of the Vicars Apostolic who are supported at the Pope's cost signed the representation against the definition, the indignation was universal among the Monsignori and in the clerical world here. " Questi Vicari, che mangiano il pane del Santo Padre!" they exclaimed in virtuous disgust. That a poor Bishop, and one too who is maintained by the Pope, should yet have a conscience and dare to follow it, is thought out of the question here; and this view comes out with a certain *naïveté.*

The anxiety of the German Bishops about the new dogma perplexing so many Christians and shaking or destroying the faith and adherence to the Church of many thousands can hardly be mentioned here, so impatient are the Monsignori and Cardinals at hearing of it. People here say, "That does not trouble us the least; the Germans at best are but half Catholics, all deeply infected with Protestantism; they have no Holy Office and have little respect for the Index. Pure and firm faith is to be looked for among the Sicilians, Neapolitans and Spaniards; and they are infallibilists to a man. And even in Germany your women and rustics are sound. Why do you have so many schools, and think every one must learn to read? Take example from us where only one in ten can read, and all believe the more readily in the infallible living book, the Pope. If thousands do really become unbelievers, that is not worth speaking of in comparison with the brilliant triumph of the Papacy now rendered infallible, and the inestimable gain of putting an end to all controversy and uncertainty in the Church for the future." When I look at the careless security of the majority, I could often fancy myself living in the year 1517. The view about foreign countries and Churches prevalent here is just what Molière's Sganarelli expresses about physicians and patients : " Les veuves ne sont jamais pour nous, et c'est toujours la faute de celui qui meurt."

The finance minister has had the bad condition of the papal treasury communicated to the Bishops ; a standing annual deficit of 30 million francs, and the Peter's pence decreasing ! Some new means of supply must be discovered, and the extremest extension of ecclesiastical centralization and papal absolutism has always been recognised at Rome as the most productive source of revenue. Every one here believes that the new dogma will prove very lucrative and draw money to Rome by a magnetic attraction. It will make the Pope *de jure* supreme lord and master of all Christian lands and their resources. The ultramontane jurists and theologians have long maintained that he can compel States as well as individuals to pay in to him such sums as are required for Church purposes. And there is no more urgent need for the Church now, than that an end should be put to the deficit of the Roman Government. And if it should be impossible or unadvisable to put in force these supreme monetary rights of the Papacy at once, still, when the temporal supremacy of the Pope is made an article of faith, Rome possesses the key which may be used at the right moment for opening the coffers and money-bags. And therefore the opponents of the dogma are regarded as enemies of the Roman State economy and the wealth of the Roman clergy; and the variance between the two parties is embittered.

Meanwhile the Pope is never weary of carrying on his personal solicitations for the votes of the Bishops; he has the right of being a persevering beggar. But one hears less of conversions to the majority than of men going over to the Opposition; and the effluences from the Tomb of the Apostles close to the Council Hall, of which such great expectations were formed, seem to act in the opposite direction.

A new system of tactics has been for some time adopted, in France principally, and is now to be introduced into Germany. The clergy in the dioceses of Opposition Bishops are to be seduced into signing addresses expressing strongly their belief in papal infallibility and desire for its speedy promulgation. This device has been pursued with great success through means of the Paris nunciature and the *Univers*. The French parish priests who, since the Concordat, have been removeable at the will of the Bishops and have suffered sufficiently from their arbitrary caprice in transferring or depriving them, see their only resource in the *Curia*, and the notion has lately been disseminated among them that the infallibilist dogma will procure their complete emancipation from episcopal authority. Accordingly almost every number of the *Univers* contains enthusiastic addresses, which might be tripled by making all the nuns subscribe, as they would do with the greatest pleasure.

The plan which has proved so successful in France is to be adopted now in Germany also. The nuncio at Munich reports that there is a swarm of red-hot infallibilists there, and that the clergy are eagerly awaiting the news of the definition; the diocesan organs of Munich and Augsburg, together with the clerico-political daily papers, are quoted as indubitable testimonies, and the Bishops of Cologne, Augsburg, Munich, Mayence, etc., are told on high authority that they have nobody behind them, and that their claim to represent the faith of their dioceses is in contradiction with facts. There are indeed no numerously signed addresses to show in Rome, but the daily papers give weighty evidence. Silence, it is thought here, implies consent, the women and the rustics are certainly for the Pope.

The Pope says in his supreme self-satisfaction, "Scio omnia." He knows the true state of things beyond the Alps far better than the Bishops; the Jesuits and their pupils and the nuncios take care of that. Hugo Grotius says, with reference to Richelieu, "Butillerius Pater et Josephus Capucinus negotia cruda accipiunt, cocta ad Cardinalem deferunt." So it is here; the Jesuits do what the Fathers Boutillier and Joseph did in Paris. Pius receives only what is "cooked," and twice cooked, first in the Cologne and Munich kitchen and then in the Roman. The German Bishops remember with some discomfort that they themselves sharply rejected and censured every declaration of adhesion, and violently suppressed the movement only just beginning.

The Cardinal General-Vicar has ordered public prayers for a fortnight by the Pope's command: the faithful are to invoke the Holy Ghost for the Council, since the whole world presents so wretched an appearance (*miserabile aspetto dell' orbe*), and the longer the conflict (of the Council) with the world increases, the more glorious will be the victory, and then, it is said, will all nations behold miracles—which appears from the context to mean that, considering the opposition of the world (and of so many Bishops), the erection of the new article of faith must be regarded as a miracle of divine omnipotence, but a miracle which will certainly be wrought.   Many interpret this to mean that people must be prepared for a conciliar *coup d'état*.   But as matters stand, it can hardly be supposed that the Court party will let matters come to a *non placet* of at least 120 Bishops, nor would anything be gained by cutting short the debate.   In the last analysis the main ground of the dogma with the majority always resolves itself into this—that the present Pope and his predecessors for many years past have held themselves infallible. That is the only ground on which the Dominicans, Jesuits and Cardinals have interpolated it into the theology of the schools.   Pius might certainly define it in a Bull to the entire satisfaction of the majority, and thereby put an end to the contention of the Bishops. An end? it may be asked.   Well, yes—the end of the beginning.

FIFTY-FIRST LETTER.

Rome, June 2, 1870.—The debate drags on its weary length without any turning. Of real discussion there is none, for very few of the prelates can speak in Latin without preparation. As I have said before, academical discourses are delivered, almost always without any reference to what has immediately preceded. Only the majority have the right of reply allowed them. If a Bishop is attacked or calumniated, he cannot answer till his turn comes, which is often not for some weeks, as was Kenrick's case; and if he has spoken already, he cannot speak again in the same debate, and cannot therefore defend himself at all, as occurred with Hefele. But the members of the Deputation can speak whenever they choose; they interrupt the order and interpose as often as seems necessary to them for defending their proposals or weakening the force of an important speech on the other side. Very often they break in on the course of proceedings quite arbitrarily and without any connection with previous speakers. They have the stenographic reports before their eyes, and thus know the exact words of the speaker and can answer them while their opponents have no similar advantage. That all this implies an iniquitous injustice and want of freedom never occurs to the dominant party, who are on the contrary astonished at the kindness and patience of the Pope in allowing an opponent of his omnipotence and advocate of doctrines long since condemned to use St. Peter's as the theatre, and his Council as the occasion, of a persevering attack on his dearest wishes, ideas and acts. They ask themselves how long he will tolerate so strange a reversal of his plans and views. It is certain that his excitement has reached fever heat, but it has not yet been resolved to break off the debate, which is so far remarkable, inasmuch as according to the opinion of the Court it can neither have any practical results nor any character of sober reality. As they did not regard it from the first as a means for establishing the truth, it must now appear to them simply a hindrance in the way of the truth already ascertained. For those who attack infallibility, and thus utter error and blasphemy over the tomb of the Apostles, freedom of speech can be no right in the opinion of the majority, but simply a favour dependent on the pleasure of the deeply injured and offended chief. It is characteristic of the present stage of the affair, that during this debate there has been no disposition shown to interrupt the speakers of the minority. Signs of discontent have been frequent enough, but no further attempt to stop a speech by force.

There is still an immense and unprofitable number of speakers enrolled. Above a hundred have sent in their names since the beginning, who might easily have been debarred from doing so, and the tediousness of the discussion is aggravated by the members of the Deputation, who lengthen it out still further by their frequent and usually prolix interpositions.

The chief events of the last fortnight have been the speeches of Manning and Valerga for the dogma, and of Ketteler, Conolly and Strossmayer against it. The Bishop of Mayence spoke on Monday, May 23, when he expressed his opinion more forcibly and gave more offence than any previous speaker. He defended the constitution of the Church against the Roman conspiracy, citing the arguments contained in the pamphlet he had before distributed, and denounced against ecclesiastical centralization the same penalty of revolution, incident to a centralized State, which, he said, is already knocking at the doors. He gave his decisive adhesion to those who demand unanimous consent, and declared that he had always held the personal infallibility to be " opinio probabilissima," but could find no necessary certainty in it, neither " certitudo dogmatica" nor " veritas dogmatizanda."

One might think that a man who is so unclear about the logic of history and the principles of morals belongs to the majority. However the impression produced by Ketteler's speech was favourable to the minority, and all who have watched his attitude before the last four months, especially at Fulda, must have recognised the decided advance in the line taken by the Opposition. Many think the conversion is complete, and the great wound of the Opposition—its containing members ready sooner or later to turn renegades—finally closed. The Bishop of Mayence was at first believed to be the author of the pamphlet he has distributed, but it was not composed under his eye or under his influence, nor even at his suggestion, and bears no trace of his mind. The general line is Maret's, but his leading idea, that in case of a conflict a Council is superior to a Pope, does not occur in it. Ketteler must have acquired a great deal of Roman experience and non-Roman development before he would denounce a papal decree to his country and his diocese as uncatholic. But the advance which he, like others, and more than many others, has already made, is unquestionably a gain, and gives a peculiar force to his words. But it has damaged and discredited the minority that so many Bishops are more careful about the position and influence of the Church than about the purity of doctrine.

I must return once more to Manning's speech of May 25, as it was very interesting and important. He asserted roundly that infallibility was already really a doctrine of the Church, which could not be denied without sin (*sine publico peccato mortali*) or proximate heresy (*proximâ hœresi*), and therefore they did not want to make a new dogma but simply to proclaim an existing one. In these bold but highly significant words Manning pointed to what many better men choose to be blind to. He no longer acknowledges the opponents of the doctrine as brothers in faith, as members of one and the same Church, since they do not satisfy his conditions of orthodoxy; his faith and theirs are not the same. He has been the first to proclaim this great truth in Council, and it is time for the minority to ask themselves, whether unity still really survives in the sense hitherto maintained against Protestants, whether the foe is really still outside and has not penetrated into the inmost sanctuary of the Church, for the temple must be cleansed before the nations are converted. The minority can no longer live in peace with Manning and his like, or imagine that the contest does not threaten the very existence of the Church. Manning has indeed said that he does not think the decree strong enough. The Spaniards agree with him, and an open difference on this point has arisen in the Deputation. The great majority would be glad to find a formula less offensive to the Opposition, but Manning has the Pope on his side, and gets him worked upon by certain sacristan-like natures, like the Bishops of Carcassonne and Belley, who have won the special confidence of Pius IX. through having a certain mental affinity with him. Manning's whole speech was an attempt to hinder concessions, and keep the *Curia* to the point of forcibly suppressing the minority. And it counts also for a sign that the Pope is resolved to go all lengths. The fanatics would prefer the Church

being exposed to the danger of schism to modifying
their theory in the least particular, for the latter would
be a humiliation for themselves, while the other kindles
a contest the end of which they feel no doubt about.
It is reckoned certain that of the Bishops who will
vote against the dogma, not all have the courage for a
protest, and that of those who do protest some will
rather resign their sees than undertake the contest
with the *Curia* under excommunication.

Manning's argument for infallibility from the condition of England was remarkable. It is unquestionably his chief motive, and what gives the stamp of
sincerity to his position, to make Catholicism more
compact and closely united in Protestant England. He
hopes by means of the dogma to suppress those differences of opinion which are a source of disturbance and
weakness, so that all will re-echo his words, uphold
his theology in the face of a disintegrating Protestantism, and his policy in the face of political parties with
the combined strength of five million men. He conceives
that the Christian element is more and more disappear-
ing from the Established Church and the sects of England, and sees a general dissolution of belief which
offers a future to Catholicism as the one definite

authority. But he maintained in the Council that the English Catholics were in favour of infallibility, and that even Protestants testified that it would strengthen his hands. That the leading English theologian, Newman, has spoken so strongly against the definition he of course did not say. It was only consistent with the bitter enmity between the two to ignore it. Nor did he say that the English Bishops present at the Council are equally divided—himself, Ullathorne, Chadwick and Cornthwaite being infallibilists, against Errington, Clifford, Amherst, and Vaughan, who are fallibilists. He read extracts from Protestant papers, stating that papal infallibility is the logical outcome of Catholicism ; to such miserable weapons was he driven for defending his cause. Clifford, who followed him, had an easy task in exposing these misrepresentations and false-hoods. One point in his speech his hearers missed : he said that the mischief the definition threatened the Church and the mischief it had already done to the interests of religion in England, might be gathered from the letter of an illustrious English statesman, for the authority of which he could appeal to an Arch-bishop there present. This Archbishop was Manning himself, and the allusion was to a letter addressed to him by an English minister, saying in substance that in England it was the most vehement Protestants, and those most notorious for their hostility to the Catholic Church, who eagerly desired to see infallibility and the Syllabus made into dogmas, and that the present policy of Rome had so greatly increased the anti-Catholic feeling of the country that every step taken by the Government to extend the rights of Catholics and improve the social condition of Catholic Ireland met with the most persistent opposition.

The Italian Valerga, titular Patriarch of Jerusalem, delivered on Tuesday, May 31, a more spirited, piquant and insolent speech, which I will give a report of in my next letter.

The great debate may last till the middle of June, when it is hoped that the chapter on the primacy may be carried without difficulty, and the special debate on infallibility be brought to a successful end before the middle of July. But there is sure to be a lively and protracted discussion on the primacy, which may easily exhaust the patience of the majority, for the continuance of the present situation is a deep humiliation for the Pope and *Curia*. The Opposition, whose existence at first was so boldly denied, and of which there was originally only a germ in the Episcopate, subsequently developed in Council through the clumsy tactics of Rome, places the Roman See in an unwonted and what is thought an intolerable light.   What Pius IX. and the Jesuits reckoned on accomplishing, first in three weeks, then in four months, at Easter, at Pentecost, on the feast of St. Peter and St. Paul, by acclamation, by unanimous consent, is not done yet and seems to recede further and further.   The Roman people are losing their reverence for the Pope, though they await the doctrine with equanimity.   They say, " Si cambia la Religione," and laugh good-humouredly.   But I heard the words from the mouth of a Roman priest, " L'idola restera al Vaticano, ma l'altare serà deserto."

It is certain attempts will soon be made either to cut short the debate or adjourn it and overcome the opposition by some compromise.   Such an attempt was made before by a Cardinal, but the Bishop of the minority to whom he applied would not even look at the formula. Then the Dominicans conceived a similar idea, but were answered that there were strong reasons not only against the wording of particular forms, but against any reference to the question.   Such proposals are sure to be repeated in spite of Manning and the fanatics.   But the Opposition Bishops cannot entertain them separately without breach of word to their colleagues, though it is always possible that some formula or other may find friends and advocates among them.

The rupture with France is a decisive one. In the first place a Bishop from the North of France has repeated here a conversation he had with a leading statesman in Paris, who said that the attitude of Rome was equivalent to a declaration of war against France, and that the Government had done everything to withhold the *Curia* from its perilous course, but in vain. He himself opposed Count Daru's policy, as he did not wish to prevent what might lead to the separation of Church and State, but now he thought they were free to carry out the separation, as Rome had made it inevitable. The reciprocal obligations of the two Courts would cease, and therefore the occupation of the Roman States by French troops, for the spiritual power the Pope was aiming at was incompatible with secular power. At the same time the French ambassador uttered similar warnings here, and informed the Cardinal Secretary of State that he was ordered to do nothing more to restrain the course of events. Antonelli is said to have replied that he took the same view, but had not influence enough to do anything. It is of course believed here that the present administration in Paris is not strong or firm enough to carry out a policy which would be more after the mind of Prince Napoleon than of the Emperor. But the *Curia* underrates the offence given to France by the quiet contempt with which both Daru's notes were treated.

Meanwhile the incense is being constantly swung before Pius, so that the clouds of homage conceal the abyss to which he is drawing on the Church. There is great agitation going on among the French as well as the Italian clergy, with a view to securing their votes for infallibility and also presents of money. Their expressions not seldom exceed in devotion to Pius everything of the kind ever heard of before; and it seems as if the old canon law sycophants had come back to life, who made no scruple of designating the Pope God and Vice-God. Let us give two examples. One of these true sons of the Church in Italy submits by anticipation to whatever Pius chooses to define, whether with the approval of the Council or by his own sole authority. Seven priests from Cuneo bring these verses—

Parla, O Gran Pio,
Cio che sona il tuo labbro,
Non è voce mortal, voce è di Dio.

The international Committee of the minority thought it necessary that a treatise should be expressly composed to discuss the weighty question of moral unanimity being required for dogmatic decrees, and Dupanloup has undertaken the task.   He had a pamphlet on the subject printed at Naples and laid before the Fathers. He first proves from history that this condition was never wanting in any Councils which count as œcumenical, and was distinctly recognised and maintained at Trent by the Pope himself.   He then examines the opinions of the chief theologians of all ages, including St. Vincent of Lerins and St. Augustine, and Popes Leo I., Vigilius and Gregory the Great, who all agree in making moral unanimity an indispensable condition for a decree on faith.   He proceeds to observe that in matters of discipline and canon law a numerical majority is enough, as decisions of that kind may be altered afterwards, but for a dogma there must be moral unanimity of the Council and the Churches to whose faith it bears witness, or else Catholicism would be annihilated. But great theologians and theological schools of former ages opposed papal infallibility, and it is opposed now by a large number of Bishops at the Vatican Council representing great Churches and Catholic nations.   A

Council is only then infallible when the assembled
Bishops of the whole Church bear witness to the faith
inherited from the beginning.   The majority must
therefore either convert the minority to their views by
free discussion or give up their design; were they to
suppress the minority by mere brute force of numbers,
that would be unconciliar and unprecedented in Church
history.   It is not mere probability but unquestionable
certainty that is required for defining a dogma, and a
considerable number of distinguished members of the
Council have no such firm belief in papal infallibility.
To define it in spite of this would be to act as judges
and masters of faith, not as its depositaries and witnesses.   A minority denying a dogma which had been
the perpetual belief of the Church would be in the
wrong, but not a minority repudiating the definition of
a doctrine which had never been held an article of
faith.   Even the Pope cannot by his authority raise
the decision of a mere majority to the dignity of a
dogma, for he only promulgates decrees on faith " sacro
approbante Concilio," and without moral unanimity the
Council has not approved.   The words of the Bishop of
Orleans are directed principally against the *Civiltà*,
which has notoriously laboured to establish the opposite

hypothesis, and he asks, " Are we at a Council or not ? If we are, the rules of Councils must be observed, or else a great assembly of Bishops is reduced simply to playing the part of a theatrical exhibition."

Dupanloup goes on to remark on the storms and incalculable evils which the definition of papal infallibility would bring on the Church and the Papacy. He concludes with these words : " If ever moral unanimity was requisite for a dogmatic decision, it is so at a Council like the Vatican, where there are 276 Italian Bishops, of whom 143 belong to the States of the Church ; 43 Cardinals, of whom 23 are not Bishops or have no Sees ; 120 Archbishops or Bishops *in partibus*, and 51 Abbots or Generals of Orders—while the Bishops present from all Catholic countries of Europe, exclusive of Italy, only number 265, so that the Patriarchs, Primates, Archbishops, and diocesan Bishops of the whole world are outnumbered by the diocesan Bishops of Italy alone.[1] At a Council so composed a mere majority can never decide ; and the less so when the personal intervention of the Pope makes itself felt, when the freedom of the Bishops is so seriously hampered, and in so many ways, when the question of infallibility has been so

[1] He should have said "the Italian prelates."

unscrupulously and violently brought forward for discussion by a mere sovereign act—a sort of *coup d'état*—when consciences are tormented and a number of writings are issued which have created a great sensation and give evidence of the anxiety of the faithful, and when lastly the Bishops themselves let a cry escape from their tortured hearts which the whole press re-echoes. Under such circumstances it is impossible to settle the matter by a mere *coup* of the majority; and if it is done all kinds of mischief must be feared. Nor is it I alone who say so; there are 100 Bishops who say, " An intolerable burden would be laid on our consciences. We should fear that the œcumenical character of the Council would be called in question, and abundant materials supplied to the enemies of religion for assailing the Holy See and the Council, and that it would be without authority in the eyes of the Christian world, as having been no true and no free Council. And in these troubled times no greater evil can well be conceived."

FIFTY-SECOND LETTER.

Rome, June 3, 1870.—Valerga attacked the "Galli-cans," drawing a parallel between the Pope and Christ, and between the Fallibilists and Monothelites. As in Christ the human will co-existed with the divine, so in the Pope may personal infallibility co-exist with moral sinfulness, and to conclude from the former against the latter—to draw an argument from scandals in papal history against the *privilegium inerrantiæ*—is analo-gous to the error of the Monothelites, who denied the possibility of a human will subject to sin co-existing with the divine will in the same person. Never has the well-known spirit of the Roman *Curia* shown itself so openly and with such technical adroitness as in this carefully elaborated and minute accusation against the Opposition. As Archbishop Purcell of Cincinnati expressed it, it was "exemplum sophismatum artis ad instar congestorum," and great expectations might be formed of its salutary effect on the French. Purcell answered shortly and pointedly that the charge applied equally to the Council of Trent and the sixth, seventh, and eighth Œcumenical Councils, and that he and his colleagues were content to endure the patriarch's anathema in such good company. Even Bellarmine quotes a whole cloud of witnesses against infallibilism, and neither he nor later writers had refuted them. It is matter of thankfulness to God that he has never suffered this opinion to gain dogmatic authority. Purcell then cited clenching proofs of the public erroneous teaching of Popes, and among them the history of the ordinations and reordinations of Formosus and Sergius. The standpoint which he took as a republican was interesting. He said that the Church was the freest society in the world, and was loved as such by its American sons, for the Americans abhorred every doctrine opposed to civil and spiritual freedom. As kings existed for the good of the peoples, so Popes for the good of the Church, and not *vice versâ*. Perhaps he was thinking of the words of the absolutist Louis XIV., "La nation ne fait pas corps en France, elle réside tout entière dans la personne du roi." For "nation" put "Église," and the words describe precisely the papal system, as it is now intended to be made exclusively dominant by means of the Council.

The most important speech in this sitting, and one of the most remarkable theologically since the opening of the Council, was that of Conolly, Archbishop of Halifax. Formerly an unhesitating adherent of personal infallibility he had come here without having specially studied the question, and under the full belief that the *Allgemeine Zeitung* had calumniated the Roman See in representing this dogma as the real object of the Council. But when he found what was expected of him here, he instituted a searching examination, and thoroughly sifted, as he said, what the classical Roman theologians cite for their favourite doctrine. He now frankly submitted to the Council the result of his studies,—that the whole of Christian antiquity explains the stock passages of Scripture alleged for papal infallibility in a different sense from the *Schema*, and bears witness against the theory that the Pope alone, without the Bishops or even in opposition to them (*etiam omnibus invitis et contradicentibus*), is infallible. But what our Lord has not spoken, even though it was certain metaphysically or physically, can never become the basis of an article of faith, for faith comes by hearing, and hearing is not by science, but by the words of Christ. It is the speciality of Catholicism not to interpret passages of Scripture singly and by mere critical exegesis, but in the light of tradition and in harmony with the Fathers. To found a dogma on the rejection of the traditional interpretation would be pure Protestantism. It is not therefore the words of Scripture simply but the true sense, as revealed by God and attested by the perpetual and unanimous consent of the Fathers, which all are pledged by oath to follow, that must be called the real revelation of God. To cite modern theologians, as Bellarmine does, is nothing to the purpose. I will have nothing, he said, but the indubitable word of God made into a dogma. The opinions of 10,000 theologians do not suffice me. And no theologian should be quoted who lived after the Isidorian forgeries. But no single passage of Fathers or Councils can be quoted from that earlier time of genuine tradition, which affirms the Pope's dogmatic independence of the rest of the Episcopate. If there be any such, let it be shown; but there is none, and innumerable and conclusive testimonies can be cited on the other side. Even at the Apostolic Council at Jerusalem St. James proved the teaching of Peter by the Prophets, and appealed to it because it agreed with theirs and not on account of his authority. Conolly was ready for his part to believe that no Pope could wilfully and knowingly become heretical,—*i.e.*, persistently hold out against all the rest of the Church ; but that did not prove papal infallibility, and to define it would be to bring the Vatican Council into contradiction with the three Councils which condemned Honorius, to narrow the gates of heaven, repel the East, and proclaim not peace but war. To those who said, " Pereant populi sed promulgetur dogma," Conolly replied that the loss of one soul was serious enough to outweigh all the advantages looked for from the new dogma. He declared, against Manning, that no one was justified in calling an opinion "proximate heresy" which the Church had not condemned as such ; for it was a duty to follow and not to anticipate her sentence. A Pope had said that no one should censure a doctrine before the Holy See had spoken, and the Penitentiary had declared in 1831 that the Gallican Articles were not under any censure. He had worked thirty-three years among Protestants, and could testify that what Manning affirmed was the reverse of the truth.

Conolly is a man who is on the whole in tolerable

harmony with Roman views, but who is therefore all the more resolved to vote against infallibility. While he forbids the Gallican doctrine being taught in his diocese, he protests here against the Roman. There is evidently a process going on in his mind, which in so cultivated a theologian can have but one result. He ended by declaring that he would accept the definition if the Council proclaimed it, for he was convinced that God was among them. But that merely meant that he was convinced the dogma would never be proclaimed. On the strength of that conviction he was almost the first speaker who briefly but decisively maintained the doctrine to be untenable.

Yesterday, Thursday, Vancsa, Bishop of Fogarasch, of the Greek Rite, quoted the testimonies of Greek Fathers against infallibility, and his speech was thought a remarkable one. Dreux-Brézé of Moulins followed him, and again had the misfortune immediately to precede Strossmayer. He contended that, as the Pope is supreme teacher, and the French call him " Souverain Pontife," and he is the highest judge, he must be infallible. As Vicar of Christ, he is also king, for Christ said to Pilate, " Thou rightly callest me king," and the royal title was affixed to the cross. But if Christ was

infallible as king, so is the Pope.   He supported all this
by texts of Scripture, and spoke against the Fathers
who accused the Pope of despotism or maintained that
the new dogma would be the formal introduction of the
grossest despotism.   Without the Pope, who is " Epi-
scopus universalis," and can seldom exercise his office on
account of the number of the faithful and of his labours,
the Bishops have no jurisdiction, and cannot even
absolve without powers derived from him.   " Let us
therefore go on," he concluded, " to unity and agreement,
and give Cæsar what belongs to Cæsar, and the Pope
what belongs to the Pope."

Strossmayer followed him, and declared that papal
infallibility was against the constitution of the Church,
the rights of the Bishops and Councils, and the immutable rule of faith.   He explained the constitution of
the Church according to the holy Fathers and especially
St. Cyprian (*De Unitate Ecclesiæ*), who did not hold
their jurisdiction to be limited to their dioceses, since
by virtue of their character they often had to exercise
authority in the concerns of the universal Church, and
were obliged to do so, as, *e.g.*, in Councils.   This sharing
of authority and rights between the Pope and the Episcopate was evident from the controversy between Pope

Stephen and Cyprian in the third century about the rebaptism of heretics, in which the latter did not the least admit any personal and absolute infallibility bestowed on the Pope by our Lord. And St. Augustine defended him on the ground that the question had not yet been decided by a General Council, which shows that the sole authority in matters of faith and morals was in his opinion a General Council, united with its head.

Strossmayer took this opportunity of vindicating the French Church admirably from the calumnies and attacks of the Patriarch of Jerusalem. He complained indignantly of a Church which had come forth pure and victorious from the bitterest persecution, and which boasted such great martyrs and confessors, being slandered by the comparison of so-called Gallicanism to Monothelitism, and of those great men being libelled who during life had rendered such conspicuous services to the Church of God, as well as their successors who had made wonderful and exceptional sacrifices for the Church and the Holy See. Strossmayer blamed the Patriarch's vague and general statements about the constitution of the Church, and advised him to bring arguments from positive tradition, which were alone of any decisive force. He proceeded to insist on the power and necessity of General Councils, especially in our days, and he proved the necessity of their being frequently held from the conduct of the Apostles, from the holy Fathers, and from the Councils of Constance and Trent. But if once the personal infallibility of the Pope were defined, Councils would become superfluous and useless, and the Bishops would be robbed of their authority as witnesses and judges of faith. In the one way the greatest injury would be done to the prosperity of the Church, and in the other the rights of Bishops would be reduced to a mere assent, so that they would hardly any longer be consultors and theologians; but this would be clearly against the unchangeable constitution of the Church and the usage of Councils, as for instance that of Chalcedon, where the Bishops most unmistakeably exercised the office of judges as regarded the Letter of Pope Leo. The Bishops could make no such concession without betraying their authority, and casting a slur on their predecessors at the Council of Trent, who are well known to have so emphatically vindicated their freedom and rights, when the two words " proponentibus Legatis " were inserted by the Legates against their will. And the speaker praised the wisdom of the Council of Trent in resolving to abstain from deciding any questions which might give occasion for discord or for prejudicing the rights and freedom of the Bishops.

In the last part of his speech Strossmayer discussed the Catholic rule of faith, which had been completely changed and violated by the comments of the members of the Deputation of Faith on the *Schema*. The principle of at least moral unanimity was, he said, a sacred one, corresponding to precedent and pleasing to the faithful. There were whole volumes of the holy Fathers extant on this principle, as of Irenæus, Tertullian, Augustine and Vincent of Lerins, who in common with all others maintained that there are three essential conditions for proving a divine tradition and propounding an article of faith, antiquity, universality and agreement. They all thought the tradition of the Roman Church a principal river, whereby the whole earth was watered, but they regarded the traditions of the other Churches also as tributaries by which the river must be constantly fed, or it would in course of time be dried up. They all ascribed the first authority to the witness of St. Peter's successor, but that authority was only manifested clearly to the Catholic world after being reinforced by

the consent of all the other Churches. This divine
rule would be completely overset by the personal infallibility of the Pope, to the great injury of faith. If it
is said that the definition is earnestly desired by many,
it must be replied that it is also desired by the worst
enemies of the Church, who openly say in writing and
by word of mouth that it is the best means for destroying
the infallibility of the Church. That fact alone would
explain the alarm and anxiety of so many of the most
learned Fathers of the Council. Strossmayer dwelt in
conclusion on the danger that would result from the
definition for the Southern Sclaves and Catholic Croats,
who lived side by side with eight million persons out of
the unity of the Church. Not only would the return
of these separated brethren be barred, but it might be
feared that the Catholic Croats would be driven out of the
Church. He therefore always hoped, and entreated the
holy Father, that he would emulate the example of the
humility of St. Peter in his martyrdom, and of Christ
who was exalted by his Father because He had humbled
Himself to the death of the Cross, and magnanimously
have the subject withdrawn.

The speech was listened to with great attention, and
became the topic of conversation in all circles at Rome,

and even Bishops of the other party paid a high tribute to it. As yet 24 Bishops have spoken against the dogma and 35 for it,—most of the latter having no real dioceses.

Two interesting episodes have intervened. Last week the police refused the Prince Bishop of Breslau his *visa* for Naples, because he could show no permission from the Presidents of the Council to go there. This implied that the Fathers are civil as well as spiritual subjects of the Pope. The Bishop, who was wearied out with the objectless proceedings in the Council Hall, sent to Fessler, the Secretary of the Council, for the requisite permission; Fessler replied that he could not give it, and referred him to the President de Angelis, who tried to represent the whole affair as a mistake. It had not been so ill meant, and at most only the departure of the Orientals was intended to be prevented, he said, and he authorized Fessler to instruct the police to give the permission. But that was the most complete indorsing of what they had done, and proved that the Pope meant to use his temporal power for managing the Council and controlling the actions of the Fathers. On that account the departure of the Prince Bishop had been hindered, and the whole affair involves the question of ecclesiastical freedom and international right. Does a member of the Council thereby lose or prejudice his rights as the subject of a foreign state, or is the freedom of individual Bishops suspended while taking part in it? So anxious is the Pope to give up nothing which may serve for dominating the Council, that he restricts the Bishops in the most harmless exercise of personal freedom, which at other times he would never have thought of. I will not dwell on the insult in this procedure to the King of Prussia, whose safe-conduct was no more respected than the Emperor Sigismund's at Constance, for a graver question is at stake,—that of international right and freedom of the Council. Meanwhile they reckon on Prussia taking no further notice of the affair, and the Prince Bishop has given up his journey after these difficulties. France, too, has quietly endured a series of insults, and so they hope not to have to abolish the regulation or disavow the police.

Rome cannot admit the principle of international right in this case, without giving up one of her own principles, the Inquisition, according to whose laws foreigners can be arrested, imprisoned, and put to the question. No secular tribunal limits its power, and

2 R

every Bishop therefore could in theory be brought
before it. By papal law the Pope might at any moment
have Cardinal Schwarzenberg arrested, and if the right
has become inapplicable, that is due to the influence of
foreign states and the modern spirit, whose restraints
on the full exercise of Church authority it is the office
of the Council to remove, as the Syllabus, Bull of
Censures, *Schema de Ecclesiâ,* etc., prove. According
to Roman canon law, freedom at the Council is inconceivable.

In a former letter I gave an inaccurate account of the
Prince Bishop's conduct towards the priest Jentsch, at
Liegnitz, being misled by statements in the Roman
newspapers.[1] The text of the explanation accepted by
the Bishop shows that no principle was conceded or
denied, and he said himself that he agreed in substance
with Jentsch.

The arrival of Father Hötzl in Rome seemed for a
time likely to produce still more serious conflicts, for
his affair looked as if it would oblige the minority to
give expression to their view of Döllinger's teaching on
the necessity of general consent for the œcumenicity
of a Council. Those who had undertaken the in-

[1] Cf. *supr.* p. 517.

struction of Hötzl cared less for converting him than for using the opportunity to provoke dissension among the minority. He was told that an explanation, not a retractation, was all that was demanded of him, and when the explanation he offered was found unsatisfactory another was proposed to him on May 31. The crucial passage in it was read and examined by leading bishops of the minority, whose names were calculated to inspire complete confidence. Hötzl had some cause to think he had saved honour and conscience, and responsibility to man and God, when he sought the judgment of liberal German Bishops and resolved to abide by it. But though they disliked the passage, they thought it difficult to know how to save a man who had come to Rome in such childish confidence, and did not feel justified under the circumstances in urging him to go to extremities and sacrifice himself to their interests. It was not their place to drive him to a breach with his Order or a loss of personal liberty, at a time when they had not themselves publicly, solemnly and decisively repudiated the doctrine imposed on him. Still less did they want to compromise themselves or break up their harmony before the time. And their hesitation may have led Father Hötzl into his mistake;

he was acting in concert with the minority when he signed.

I give only a brief preliminary notice of the most important points in to-day's sitting. After Dinkel, who spoke very well, and Domenec, Bishop of Pittsburg, who was much interrupted, Maret made a longer speech, which he delivered in a very loud voice, as deaf persons are apt to do. In the course of it he declared that it would be called a vicious circle for the less to give power to the greater, as would be done if the Council, which was said to possess a lower authority, were to confer on the Pope—a higher authority—the prerogative of infallibility. Thereupon Bilio struck in very excitedly, crying out " Concilium nihil dat Papæ nec dare potest, sed solummodo recognoscit, suffragia dat, et Sanctus Pater quod in Spiritu Sancto ipsi placet decidit."

In yesterday's sitting a *postulatum* for the close of the general debate was prepared, which is said to have received 150 signatures. After Maret's speech it was at once produced and the close voted. Little more than 60 prelates have spoken, and above 40 were waiting their turn, amongst whom were Haynald and other considerable persons. The continuation of the debate had been reckoned upon and much was hoped from it; but now that the example has once been set of using the well-known clause in the order of business in the interests of one party, the step may be repeated in every succeeding debate. The Opposition will be driven into greater firmness by this occurrence, which they had foreshadowed in the half-threatening formula at the end of their great Protest. The question is now forced upon them, whether they were in earnest in what they then said.

FIFTY-THIRD LETTER.

Rome, June 4, 1870.—The first impression made on the minority by the violent closing of the general debate led many of them, in discussing it directly after the sitting, to say they would take no further part in the debates. A great meeting was arranged for to-day at Cardinal Rauscher's to decide the question. It was the largest international gathering of the Opposition yet held, including nearly 80 Bishops, but was for that very reason difficult to manage. Two possible courses were discussed—to remain in Rome but take no further part in the debates, as not being free, and vote at the end *non placet* against the infallibilist *Schema*, or simply to issue a protest against the injustice they had suffered, and continue to take part in the proceedings. The former view was supported principally by the Hungarians, North Americans, the leading French Bishops, and men like Strossmayer, Simor, Haynald, Darboy,

Dupanloup, Clifford, Conolly (represented by proxy), and others. They insisted that words were of no further avail, and they should show their sense of the want of freedom by acts, so that, as far as in them lay, no decree should be carried which had not been thoroughly discussed. In this way the œcumenicity of the Council would be denied without coming as yet to a breach in Council or a disturbance in the Church; for they could no longer recognise the Council as legitimate, nor yet retire, for to retire would precipitate the most extravagant decisions and lead to an open conflict. There were many reasons why it could no longer be held legitimate, such as its composition, the order of business, the pressure exercised on the Bishops by the Pope personally or through his officials, the notorious design of getting dogmas promulgated by a majority, etc. It would be simply a degradation to give in any longer to such a farce. In Parliaments speeches were not altogether useless, for if they could not influence votes they enlightened public opinion, but at this so-called Council most of their hearers were quite incapable from their standard of cultivation of appreciating theological arguments, not to add that the moral standard of many among them was such that, even if

they were convinced, they would not act on their convictions. And speeches, which were not made public,
could produce no effect out of doors. To debate under
these circumstances would only be to incur a large
responsibility for the entire conduct of the Council.
But if the Opposition refrained from discussion and
left the field free to the majority, the differences among
them would soon be made manifest. The *Curia* could
hardly hold out against so serious a demonstration, but
if it remained obstinate, no further doubt would be
possible in the Church as to the opinion of the minority
about the Council.

On the other side it was urged that all which could
be gained by such a demonstration would be gained
equally by a declaration showing how the forcible closing of the general debate had undermined the founda-
tions and future authority of the Council. They owed
it to the world to do more than merely give reasons
against the legitimacy of the Council; they must
debate and bring forward the objections to the infallibilist doctrine itself, and thus give public testimony of
their convictions. Most of the Germans took this view,
which many French Bishops readily acceded to, when
they observed that the Hungarian phalanx had been

broken up: Perhaps other and more subordinate motives helped to establish this opinion, but many of its advocates are men of no decided resolution, and men who in reality want only a semblance of resistance and are already secretly prepared to yield at the last moment. It was thought strange that at this assembly, which had been summoned to consult on the means of meeting the violent *coup* of the majority, a German Archbishop was present who had joined the enemies of his party in subscribing the proposal for closing the debate the day before.

The draft of the Protest finally adopted against this act of violence had been brought to the meeting by Cardinal Rauscher, and bears marks of the antagonistic elements it combines. Yet it contains one passage, which may perhaps be appealed to hereafter, " Protestamur contra violationem nostri juris."[1]

---

[1] It will be seen from the protest afterwards published that this passage was greatly toned down.

FIFTY-FOURTH LETTER.

Rome, June 6, 1870.—There have been indications for some time past that the *dénouement* was likely to be precipitated. The Pope himself declared that it was impossible to keep the Bishops here in July. The great debate, with 106 speakers inscribed, wearied every one, and the tropical heat increases the exhaustion and disgust. But the minority maintained their resolve to carry on the general debate to the end, while the majority counted on its absorbing the discussion of the separate chapters of the *Schema*, and accordingly Fessler announced that the speakers were at liberty to treat of points which belonged properly to the special debate. His party considered that, if the general and special debate were mixed up in this way, they might insist at the end that the separate chapters required no further discussion, since everything had been said already, and so they might come sooner to the decision they so earnestly desired. Very few speakers have attempted

any theological argument—perhaps only Conolly, Dinkel and Maret; and this made it easier to mix up the
general and special discussion, which again has helped
to give a vague and rambling character to the debate.
It was clear that after 106 or more speeches on the
preliminary question, there were still five weary debates
to come on the preamble and each of the four chapters,
so that, unless the discussion was to be forcibly closed,
it must either last on through the whole summer, or a
prorogation be allowed while the main question was
still unsettled. The first expedient seemed hardly practicable, and could only be held out *in terrorem,* so that
the Court really had to choose between an act of arbitrary power or a prorogation of the Council, which last
would be equivalent to a great victory of the minority.
There was no want of attempts to get up an agitation
for an adjournment. It seemed a happy escape from
grave embarrassments to those secular and untheological
counsellors of the Pope, who have given up the notion
of infallibility, and on the contrary are convinced that
the definition involves the separation of Church and
State, the fall of the temporal power and the loss of
the accustomed resources of the Papacy. These men
do not expect an isle of Delos to rise out of the sea for

the Pope when the States of the Church are swallowed up, but they are excluded from any influence on the Council. The more full the Pope is of the one grand subject of his infallibility, the less will he listen to Antonelli, to whom the mysteries in which he is not initiated are a nuisance, and who hates the line taken by Manning and the French zealots and apostolic Janissaries, and would like nothing better than an ambiguous formula leaving things just where they are.

But as soon as the majority became aware that some of the more colourless Bishops of the middle party were working for the prorogation of the Council, they resolved to be beforehand with them. Their *postulatum* for closing the debate with its 150 signatures was got ready on Thursday the 2d, but was not meant to be presented till the Saturday. But the great excitement at the close of Maret's speech gave them the opportunity for striking the blow on Friday, when the close of the general debate was carried by a large majority. The order of business undoubtedly gave the Presidents the right of putting it to the vote, and moreover they have more than the letter of the law on their side. They might have urged that, as the general and special debates were not kept separate, most of what was now omitted might be supplied afterwards, and the Fathers who had missed their turn would have five other opportunities of speaking. They might have also alleged, in excuse of hurrying the proceedings, the constantly growing impatience and disgust generally manifested in the assembly, and the uselessness of all minute discussion of details. It is enough to mention as indicative of the prevalent feeling of the majority, that they received the Bishop of Pittsburg with derisive laughter when he ascended the tribune, and that they muttered at every affectionate or respectful allusion to the Pope by an Opposition speaker, "Et osculatus est Illum." [1] Under these circumstances Conolly omitted nearly half his manuscript. The majority might have urged the further excuse that far more of their own speakers than of their opponents were excluded by the close of the debate. Some 27 of the latter had as yet spoken against 36 infallibilists, which however, considering that the minority are only a fourth of the Council, tells in their favour.

But if we examine the matter more closely, the Opposition has lost all it had left by the close of the general debate, viz., freedom of speech. It has been sacrificed

[1] Matt. xxvi. 49.

to the caprice of the majority, for the subsequent debates may be closed in the same way : that on the primacy because it is no new subject, and that on infallibility because the general debate turned wholly upon it.   So the Opposition had nothing left them but to protest, unless they would summon courage for a decisive act.   But their protest is as feeble as the last ; it is simply directed against the abuse of an order of business they had already protested against, and then themselves accepted by continuing to take part in the Council.   A party intoxicated with success cannot be restrained or conquered by these paper demonstrations, nor even the sympathy of the Catholic world be gained ; a definite and firm principle is requisite for that.   After all their experiences it may be called a harmless amusement for the minority to present protest after protest, with the certainty that they will be laid by unnoticed and unanswered.

The French Bishops of the minority held a meeting on the 3d, from which they came away troubled and undecided.   The Germans take the matter less seriously. Their past presses heavily upon them.   They had an opportunity, when the second *regolamento* was issued at the end of February, and again at the Solemn Session at the end of April, of either getting their views accepted or bringing the Council to an end. But they were not then strong enough for that. Now at the eleventh hour a last though less favourable opportunity is offered them. But at the international meeting at Cardinal Rauscher's last Saturday, their views were again set aside, for the assemblage of the whole body of Opposition Bishops brought to light the unpleasant fact of a gulf between the intellectual leaders and the mass of the minority, which makes any real leadership impossible. And this is the more lamentable, because the men who since the opening of the Council have risen to so important a position were almost unanimous; for Hefele and Rivet, Bishop of Dijon, were almost the only ones among them, except Ketteler, who rejected the energetic measure of holding aloof from the debates for the future and protesting by silence. It seems that Hefele wanted to recognise the Council as still having some claim. The other leaders succumbed, unwillingly and predicting evils, to the will of the majority, who were satisfied with the protest drawn up by Rauscher.

But all is not yet lost, and the tactics actually adopted may perhaps in skilful hands be made as effective as the rejected policy. Between Pentecost and the feast

of the Apostles from 80 to 90 speakers might make
their voices heard.   If we consider that more than 100
speakers had enrolled their names for the first and
tolerably irregular debate, and that 49 speeches were
suppressed, it is clear that the great question of the
primacy and infallibility of the Pope would require a
much longer time for uninterrupted and complete discussion, and thus the adjournment would remain as
probable and as inevitable as before.   The Court and
the majority would perhaps shrink from depriving the
proceedings of all dignity, weight and completeness by
a fresh *coup d'église*, as such an attempt might appear
even to them too bold and dangerous in the special
debate on the principles of the Church.   And if such
an attempt was made, it would perhaps exhaust at last
even the patience of the patient Germans, and lead
them to muster all their forces for the last contest.
One must admit that if orthodox Catholicism is only
to be saved by an adjournment of the Council this is
not much to the credit of the Church.   But the reason
why so many prefer a prorogation to a decisive conflict
is because they fear that many present opponents of the
doctrine might at last vote for its definition and betray
their consciences through fear of men, and that many

who vote against it and insist on the necessity of unanimity would ultimately accept and teach a dogma false in itself and carried by illegitimate means.

I will merely mention, in illustration of this, that it was lately thought very necessary to distribute a *Disquisitio Moralis de Officio Episcoporum*, discussing whether a Bishop does not greatly violate his conscience by voting for a decree to define the personal and independent infallibility of the Pope, without having any previous conviction of its being a revealed doctrine always held and handed down in the Church as such. The treatise is well written, but no such bitter irony against the Episcopate is contained in the pasquinades, and it is obvious that the author has not underrated their weakness from the fact that many Bishops would vote differently if the voting was secret. There are some among them too who doubt if papal absolutism and a power which kills out all intellectual movement is not better than truth and purity of doctrine, and if the responsibility of individual Bishops is not superseded by a decree of the Pope, at least when issued " sacro approbante Concilio."

To judge from to-day's debate on the preamble, one would imagine the Opposition neither knew how to speak nor how to keep silence.   None but the French, who have put down their names to speak, appear to have much desire to take any further part in the discussion.   Perhaps they think it ludicrous to take any serious part in a debate which may be suddenly broken off, and speak, as it were, with a halter round their necks.   And those who had thought the right plan was to keep silence henceforth were the best speakers of the Opposition ; they do not therefore fall readily into a policy they disapproved.   Their view is that, as the majority has done its worst and the minority has not the spirit to follow the counsel of its leaders, it is no longer worth while to fight against a result which cannot be permanent.

This weak and vacillating attitude may possibly only be a momentary consequence of the sudden commencement of a discussion which seemed distant and for which they were unprepared.   On the other hand the confidence of the majority increases, and they announce the close of the debate on Corpus Christi.   If the minority remain as undecided as they were at the Conference at Cardinal Rauscher's, an unfavourable issue must be feared, and this will be their own fault, for sacrificing their cause at the very moment they have for six months been preparing for, through some of them not choosing to be silent and the others not choosing to speak.

The main argument urged against taking further part in the discussion is that the historical and traditional evidences against infallibility had been prepared by men who lost their turn through the closing of the general debate, and cannot be brought forward in the special debate which is only about changes in the text of the decree. The majority have thereby testified their refusal to listen, not to certain speakers, but to a certain portion of the theological argument, and thus they prevent the investigation of tradition which is so unwelcome to them. Only secondary matters can be discussed now, while the main point is left untouched. To many, and especially the Hungarians, this seemed a betraying of the cause. The Hungarians absolutely refuse to take any further part in the debates, for in their eyes the Council has already condemned itself, and they cannot too soon publish their opinion to the world by recording their *non placet*. They are therefore dissatisfied with the Germans, who prevented stronger measures being adopted, and some of them—like Simor, who would not go on attending the sittings

—have even refused to sign the Protest to the Pope, because it involves too much deference to the Council. There are accordingly only 81 signatures, for the Archbishop of Cologne has also refused to sign, but on grounds precisely opposite to those of the Archbishop of Gran.

Meanwhile the Vicar-General here is organizing all sorts of demonstrations for the happy result of the Council in the sense of the Court party. There were to be three processions this week, and no pains were spared to induce persons of rank, including ladies, to take part in them. In many cases the attempt failed, for it is idle to deny that a large portion of the Roman citizens of all ranks turn away with indifference and contempt from St. Peter's, and of course from all religion too.

The *Unità Cattolica* predicts with triumphant confidence that God will yield to their pious importunities (*Iddio obbedirà*), the Holy Ghost will fill the Council Hall, descend upon each of the Fathers and work the miracle of making them all boldly confess the infallibilist doctrine. As in the year 33 the people, who surrounded the house where the Pentecostal miracle was wrought, asked, in amazement at the new tongues of the Apostles, "Are these who speak Galileans?" so in 1870 they will hear the Bishops and Cardinals proclaim papal infallibility and will ask themselves, "Are not these the men who wrote as zealous Gallicans?" The Spirit of God will work this "noisy miracle" (*strepitoso miracolo*).

A remarkable Petition has for some time been hawked about, begging the Pope to promote St. Joseph to be General Protector of the Catholic Church. Many have objected that it is unfair to disturb the "riposo di San Giuseppe," but the notion finds much favour in the Vatican.

It is impossible to foresee at this moment how the great decision will turn out. The majority are evidently consolidating their plans, and the argument may be heard among them that, if papal infallibility were an error, the devil would not have stirred up the war which is being carried on against it. But one may still always assume that 120 Bishops will say *Non placet*, unless some miserable formula of compromise is hit upon. But the real decision will be when the Pope determines to ignore these 120 opponents and proceed to the order of the day.

FIFTY-FIFTH LETTER.

Rome, June 10, 1870.—If we look at the many minor subdivisions of the two great parties and consider the individual differences even within that narrower circle, it is impossible to form any approximately sure conjecture about the immediate issue of the contest. All are agreed that the definition must be attempted or the Council prorogued within the next few weeks, and many Bishops are already preparing for departure. The majority, with Manning at its head, insists on the dogma being defined, however numerous and strong the minority may prove, as being the very way to exhibit most clearly the power and right of the Pope to make a new article of faith with only a fraction of the Council; and there can be no doubt that the Pope inclines decidedly to this view himself. He is so completely in the hands of the Jesuits that he will not listen to counsellors like, *e.g.*, Antonelli, who makes no secret in his confidential intercourse of the fact that he has lost all influence in the matter and has no opinion to give. The Pope's feeling towards the Opposition, and especially towards its leaders, grows more bitter every day. Strossmayer he regards as the mere head of a sect (*caposetta*), and he termed another German Cardinal and Archbishop the other day " quell' asino." The Jesuits make capital out of this disposition of Pius IX. for effecting the ruin of all the men of the old school who yet remain to him from his earlier and more liberal days, while he leaves no stone unturned to win over wavering Bishops to the infallibilist side. He tried to work on the Portuguese lately by a visit, on which a French prelate observed, " On n'a plus de scrupules, ce qu'on fait pour gagner les voix, c'est un horreur. Il n'y a jamais rien eu de pareil dans l'Église." The most urgent next to Manning is Deschamps. He has proposed canons anathematizing all those Bishops who claim a share for the Episcopate in the sovereign rights of the Church—a measure expressly aimed at the Opposition and the views professed by Maret both in his book and in the Council.

Meanwhile some differences have arisen among the majority, branching off at last into what may be called a middle party. Even Pie of Poitiers is no longer altogether in accord with Manning and Deschamps, and Fessler said lately that a definition could not be carried against 80 dissentient votes. This party disapproves Bilio's treatment of Maret, which is disowned by Cardinal de Luca, who in other respects often speaks openly against Manning. Others, including Cardinals, say plainly in reference to the minority Bishops that the Papacy is threatened with destruction. The definition must, if possible, be prevented by proroguing the Council, and, failing that, the difficulties must be evaded by an ambiguous formula. The prelates who speak thus are too sober-minded not to perceive the political dangers the new dogma would bring with it. They not only think the price too high, but they dread being themselves reduced by the definition under the intolerable dominion of the Jesuit party. They frequently confer with members of the Opposition with the view of devising a compromise.

The French Opposition Bishops have lately had another meeting and resolved to continue to take part in the debates. The little misunderstanding between them and the Hungarians has quite disappeared, and several of the latter—*e.g.*, Simor—are said to be again disposed to speak. And it is thought that many speeches, suppressed by the violent closing of the general discussion, will be delivered at the supreme moment in the debate on the fourth chapter of the *Schema*, which deals with infallibility.

The debate on the separate chapters has reached as far as the third section " on the meaning and nature of the Roman primacy." As twenty-six speakers are inscribed the discussion may last to the middle of next month, and then will immediately follow the debate on the fourth and most important chapter, which a great number are likely to take part in, and there will be no want of amendments. Conolly will propose the formula that the Pope is infallible " as head of the Church teaching with him " (*tanquam caput Ecclesiæ secum docentis*), while others, as Dupanloup and Rauscher, will reproduce the formula of St. Antoninus of Florence, declaring the Pope infallible when he follows the judgment of the Universal Church, " utens consilio," or " accipiens consilium Universalis Ecclesiæ." This amendment is said to have been seriously discussed in the sitting of the Deputation on Faith on June 8, though it amounts to pure Gallicanism, for Antoninus says plainly (about 1450), " In concernentibus fidem Concilium est supra Papam." It is certain that the Deputation will labour to make some changes in the *Schema* in view of the Opposition. Lastly, men like Strossmayer press for an unambiguous denial of the personal infallibility of the Pope.

The more recklessly the Court party are resolved to advance, and the less they care for the destruction of the Church which must result from a decree irregularly enacted, the more are the Opposition disturbed at this prospect, and often made irresolute, but these are only passing moments of temptation. " Conscience before everything," said a German Bishop to me the other day, who was weighed down by his gloomy views of the future of the Church. Even men who are infalli- bilists at heart speak of the terrible crisis in the Church, and think only God can save her. The most decided I meet are the Hungarians.

In the present debates from four to five speeches are delivered at each sitting. The most remarkable were those of Landriot and Dupanloup. The Presidents are very ready to interrupt, as Bilio did when Verot, Bishop of Savannah, was speaking on the preamble. Verot,

who is a man of high character but very singular,
submitted and left the tribune, saying, "Humiliter me
subjicio." This conduct might suggest to the Presidents that the definition would be hastened by a second
grand interruption.

FIFTY-SIXTH LETTER.

Rome, June 11, 1870.—If the new article of faith is accepted and proclaimed throughout the Catholic world, what will be its retrospective force? On what decisions and doctrines of previous Popes will it set the seal of infallibility? What amplifications and corrections of Catholic theology will it involve? These questions are naturally raised here, not indeed by the Bishops of the majority but by many of the Opposition; only no one is in a position to give even an approximately accurate answer from want of the necessary books, and the Court party reckoned on this "penuria librorum," which Cardinal Rauscher has already complained of. A German theologian who had previously examined and studied the subject, undertook to answer the anxious question of the Bishops, and I send you his collection, which makes no claim to completeness, as a not unimportant contribution to the history of the Council.

The Jesuit Schrader, who is the most considerable theologian of his Order since Passaglia's retirement, and who has been employed both before and during the Council for drawing up the *Schemata*, on account of the special confidence reposed in him by the Pope, has shown, in his great work on *Roman Unity*,[1] that, as soon as papal infallibility resting on divine guidance and inspiration is made into an article of faith, it must by logical necessity include all public ordinances, decrees and decisions of the Popes. For every one of these is indissolubly connected with their teaching office, and contains, whatever be its particular subject, a *doctrina veritatis* either moral or religious. Papal infallibility is not a robe of office which can be put on for certain occasions and then laid aside again. The Pope is infallible, because he is, in the fullest sense of the word, the representative of Christ on earth, and like Christ he teaches and proclaims the truth by his acts as well as his words ; in short no public act or direction of his can be conceived of as not having a doctrinal significance. And thus Catholic theology and morality

[1] *Von der Römischen Einheit*, Wien. 1866, vol. ii. pp. 444 *seq.*

will be enriched by the new dogma with not a few fresh articles of faith, which will then possess the same authority and dignity as those already universally received as such.

There are indeed former papal decisions which, in becoming themselves infallible through the proclamation of infallibility, will in turn cover and guarantee the infallible character of the collective Constitutions of all Popes.   The first of these decisions is the statement of Leo X. in his Bull of 1520 against Luther, " It is clear as the noonday sun that the Popes, my predecessors, have never erred in their canons or constitutions."   The second is the declaration of Pius IX. in his Syllabus, " The Popes have never exceeded the limits of their power."   This assertion too will become an infallible dogma, and history must succumb and adapt itself to the dogma.   Let us however specify some of the new articles of faith thus declared to be infallible.

1. According to the teaching of the Church, the validity of the sacraments, and especially of ordination, depends on the use of the right form and matter.   The whole Church for a thousand years regarded the imposition of the Bishop's hands as the divinely ordained matter of priestly ordination.   But Eugenius IV., in his

dogmatic decree, decided that the delivery of the Eucharistic vessels is the matter of the sacrament of Orders, and the words used in their delivery the form.[1] If the doctrine of this decree, solemnly issued by the Pope *ex cathedrâ* and in the name of the Council of Florence—which however was no longer in existence— was to be accepted as true and infallible, it would follow that the Western Church for a thousand years, and the Greek Church up to this day, had no validly ordained priests. Nay more, there would at this moment be no validly ordained priest or Bishop in the Church at all, for there would be no succession. And Eugenius gave an equally false definition of the form of the sacraments of Penance and Confirmation.

2. According to the teaching of Innocent III., in the decretal *Novit*, and other Popes after him, the Pope is able and is bound, whenever he believes a question of sin to be involved, to interfere, first with admonition and then with punishments. He can on this ground reverse any judicial sentence, bring any cause before his own tribunal, summon any sovereign before him, simply to answer for a grave sin or what he considers

[1] See the decree of Eugenius in Porter's *Systema Decretorum*, p. 535, and in Raynaldus.

such, annul his ordinances, and eventually excommunicate and depose him.[1]

3. God has given to the Pope supreme jurisdiction over all kings and princes, not only of Christendom but of the whole earth.   The Pope has plenary jurisdiction over the nations and kingdoms, he judges all and can be judged by none in the world, according to Paul IV. in the Bull *Cum ex Apostolatus Officio,* and Sixtus V. in the Bull *Inscrutabilis.*   It is also a doctrine of faith, to be received on pain of eternal damnation, that the whole world is subject to the Pope even in temporal and political matters, according to the Bull of Boniface VIII., *Unam Sanctam.*   Boniface adds that the Pope holds all rights " in scrinio pectoris sui."

4. According to papal teaching, it is the will of God that the Popes should rule and " govern," not only the Church, but all secular matters and literally the whole world.   Thus Innocent III. says : " Dominus Petro non solum universam Ecclesiam sed etiam sæculum reliquit gubernandum."

5. According to papal teaching, as proclaimed by

---

[1] " Ad officium nostrum spectat de *quocumque* mortali peccato corripere quemlibet Christianum ; et, si correptionem contempserit, per districtionem ecclesiasticam coercere."—*Decretal. Novit,* c. 13, De Judic. [Cf. *Janus,* p. 158.]

Gregory VII. at the Roman Council of 1080, the Popes with the Fathers assembled in Council under their presidency are not only able, by virtue of their power of binding and loosing, to take away and bestow empires, kingdoms and princedoms, but can take any man's property from him or adjudge it to any one.[1]

6. According to papal teaching the Pope alone can remit all sins of all men. Thus Innocent III. says in his letter to the Patriarch of Constantinople.[2]

7. According to papal teaching the Pope is ruler by divine right of Germany and Italy during the vacancy of the Imperial throne, because he has received from God both powers, the spiritual and the temporal, in their fulness (*jura terreni simul et cœlestis imperii*). So John XXII. has declared in his Bull of 1317.[3] On account of this doctrine millions of German and Italian Christians, from 1318 to 1348, were placed under ban and interdict and deprived of the sacraments by the Popes.

8. The Pope by divine right can give whole nations into slavery on account of some measure of their sovereign. Thus Clement V. and Julius II. dealt with the

[1] *Concil.* ed. Labbé, x. 384.
[2] Innoc. *Epist.* ii. 209, p. 473, ed. Paris.
[3] Raynald. *Annal.* xv. 156.

2 T

Venetians on account of territorial quarrels, Gregory XI. with the Florentines,[1] and Paul III. with the English on account of Henry VIII.'s revolting from him.

9. The Pope can also give full authority to make slaves of a foreign nation merely because they are not Catholics. Thus Nicolas V. in 1454 authorized King Alfonso of Portugal to appropriate the property of all Mahometans and heathens of Western Africa, and to reduce them to perpetual slavery.[2] Alexander VI. in 1493 gave similar rights to the Kings of Spain over all inhabitants of America, when bestowing on them that quarter of the world with all its peoples.[3]

10. According to papal teaching it is just and in consonance with the Gospel to rob innocent populations, cities, regions, or countries *en masse*, with the sole exception of the infants and the dying, of divine service and sacraments, by an interdict, merely because the Sovereign or Government of the country has violated a papal command or some right of the Church. Innocent III., Innocent IV., Martin IV., Clement V., John XXIV., Clement VI., and others have done so.

[1] Raynald. *Annal.* an. 1376, 1.

[2] See Bull *Romanus Pontifex* confirmed by Callixtus III. in 1456 and Sixtus IV. in 1481.—Morelli, *Fasti Novi Orbis*, p. 58.

[3] See Bull *Inter Cæteræ* in Raynald. *Annal.*

11. The Popes as God's vicars on earth can make a present of whole countries inhabited by non-Christian peoples, and hand over all rights of sovereignty and property in them to any Christian prince they please. Alexander v. did this in his Bull addressed to Ferdinand the Catholic and Isabella, as he declares, "auctoritate omnipotentis Dei nobis in B. Petro concessâ ac Vicariatûs Jesu Christi, quâ fungimur in terris."[1] Historically it may be said with perfect truth, that the peoples of the southern and middle regions of America have been made the victims of the theory of papal infallibility. The Spanish Church and nation, as well as the sovereigns, have willingly received and maintained this doctrine, because their claim both to Navarre and America rested solely upon it, primarily on the Bulls of Alexander vi. and Julius ii. With the Gallican doctrine both claims would fall through. Alexander had empowered the Spaniards to make the Indians slaves. All Spanish theologians appeal with Las Casas to "el divino poder del Papa," as he calls it, as the basis of the Spanish dominion in America, and no one dared to call in question the divine right of the infallible vicar of God, by virtue whereof he had given over

[1] Raynald. *Annal.* an. 1493, 19.

millions of Indians to slavery, and thereby to extermination; within eighty years whole countries were
depopulated.

12. It is just and consonant with the Gospel to burn
to death as heretics those who appeal from the sentence
of the Pope to a General Council. So Leo X. declares
in his Bull of 1517, *Pastor Æternus* (issued in the fifth
Lateran Synod).

13. Leo X. declared in another Bull, *Supernæ Dispo-
sitionis,* also published in the Lateran Synod, that all
clerics are wholly exempt by divine right from all civil
jurisdiction, and therefore not bound in conscience by
the civil law.[1]

14. According to the teaching of the Church, every
Christian is bound before God to do penance for his
sins by ascetic exercises of abstinence, self-denial and
almsgiving. On Church principles no one can dispense
from this obligation, because it rests on divine ordinance. But the Popes teach that it may be relaxed or
superseded by means of plenary or particular indulgences
granted by themselves. They teach that to take part
in a war against enemies of the Holy See and in the
extermination of heretics is an effectual means for

[1] Harduin. *Concil* ix. 1756.

gaining pardon of sins, and a complete substitute for all works of penance. Thus did Paschal II. instruct Count Robert of Flanders in 1102, that for him and his warriors the surest means of obtaining forgiveness of sins and heaven was to make war upon the clergy of Liége and all adherents of the German Emperor, Henry IV.[1] Innocent III. charged King Philip Augustus of France with the conquest of England, after he had deposed King John, as a means for obtaining remission of sin.[2] Martin IV. again impelled the French in 1283 to make war on the Aragonese by the promise of plenary remission of their sins.[3] And whenever there was a war to be undertaken in the territorial interests of the Holy See, or for the extermination of heretics, the Popes urged men to take part in it as the surest and most effectual means for cleansing them from all their sins and attaining eternal happiness.

15. The Inquisition, both Spanish and Italian, is so pure a product of papal teaching on faith and morals, that there never was an Inquisitor who did not exercise his office by virtue of Papal authority and in the Pope's name, or whose power the Pope could not at any moment

---

[1] Baron. *Annal. Eccl.* an. 1102, sect. 18.
[2] Rog. Wendover, *Hist.* iii. 251.
[3] Raynald. *Annal.* an. 1283-4.

he chose have wholly or partially withdrawn. All essential laws and regulations of the Inquisition—the accused being deprived of any advocate to defend him, the admission of infamous and perjured witnesses, the frequent application of the torture, the obliging the civil magistrates to carry out capital sentences of the Inquisitors, the prohibition to spare the life of any lapsed heretic even on his conversion—all this emanates from the direct and personal legislation of the Popes, and has always been confirmed by their successors.

16. Gregory IX., Innocent IV., and Alexander IV. teach that it is in accordance with the principles of morality and the Gospel to condemn a heretic seized by the Inquisition, who has recanted, to lifelong imprisonment.[1]

17. Alexander IV. teaches that it is lawful for the Pope to have the goods of those condemned for heresy sold by his inquisitors, and to take the proceeds for himself.[2]

18. Innocent III., Alexander IV., and Boniface VIII. teach that it is just and consonant with the Gospel to deprive the sons and daughters of heretics, though

---

[1] *Litera Apost. Summorum Pontif. pro offic. S. Inquis.*, Venet. 1607, p. 3.　　[2] *Ib.* p. 39.

themselves Catholics, of their hereditary property. But if the sons themselves accuse their parents and get them burnt, then their inherited property, according to papal doctrine, is exempt from confiscation.

19. According to papal teaching torture is an institution thoroughly in harmony with morality and the spirit of the Gospel, and should be employed particularly against those accused of heresy. Thus Innocent IV. and many later Popes have directed, and Paul IV. ordered the rack to be very extensively used.

20. It is especially just and Christian, according to the teaching and regulation of Pius V. in 1569, to torture persons who have confessed or been convicted of heresy, in order to make them give up their accomplices.[1]

21. This same canonized Pope has ordered in a Bull that even the sons of a man who has once offended an inquisitor should be punished with infamy and confiscation of their goods.

22. There is a whole string of papal decrees declaring it a duty of conscience for every Christian to denounce even his nearest relations to the Inquisition, and give them up to prison, torture and death, if he perceives

[1] Del Bene, *Decreta et Constitt. Pontif.* in his *De Offic. Inquis.* ii. 647.

any trace of heretical opinions or of anything forbidden by the Church in them.[1]

23. The same Popes have declared it to be just and evangelical, and have ordered, that a relapsed heretic, even if he recants, should be put to death.[2]   They have further declared it to be moral and Christian-like that in trials for heresy witnesses should be admitted to accuse or give evidence against the accused, whose testimony would not be admitted in any other court on account of their former crimes or their infamy.[3]

24. According to papal teaching it is just and Christian forcibly to deprive heretics of their children, in order to bring them up Catholics.   Thus Innocent XII., by a sentence of the Holy Office at Rome, pronounced null and void the edict of Duke Victor Amadeus of Savoy in 1694 ordering their children, who had been forcibly taken from them, to be restored to the unfortunate and cruelly persecuted Waldenses under his government.[4]

---

[1] [That this is no mere abstract theory, even in quite recent days, may be seen from Blanco White's account of his mother's agony of mind when she began to suspect his opinions and feared it might become her duty to denounce him to the Inquisition.—TR.]

[2] *Decr.* v. 7, 9, and Lucius III. and Alexander IV. in Lib. vi. 5. 2. 4.

[3] *Ib.* 5, 2, 5.

[4] Carsetti, *Storia del Regno di Vittorio Amadeo di Savoia,* Torino, 1856, p. 178.   The Pope said it was "cosa da non potersi dir senza lagrime."

25. The Popes teach that a sentence once pronounced for heresy can never be mitigated, nor pardon ever granted to any one sentenced to death or perpetual imprisonment for heresy. Thus Innocent IV. rules in his Bull *Ad Exstirpanda.*[1]

26. Up to 1555 it was the teaching of the Popes that only those should be burnt who persisted obstinately in maintaining a doctrine condemned by the Church, and those who had relapsed after recanting into the same or some other heresy. But in that year Paul IV. established the new principle that certain doctrines, if only just put forward and at once retracted, should be punished with death. Thus whoever rejected any ecclesiastical definition on the Trinity, or denied the perpetual virginity of Mary and maintained that the scriptural language about "brothers of Jesus" was to be taken literally of children of Mary, was to be classed with the "relapsed" and to be executed, even though he recanted.

27. Up to 1751, theologians, especially Italians, who defended trials for witchcraft and the reality of an express compact with Satan, together with the various preternatural crimes wrought thereby and the carnal

[1] Guerra, *Pontif. Constit.* i. 177.

intercourse of men and demons (*incubi et succubi*), used to appeal to the infallible authority of the Popes, the Bulls of Innocent VIII., Sixtus V., Gregory XV. and several more besides, in which these things are affirmed and assumed and the due penalties prescribed for them.[1]

28. If an oath that has been taken is prejudicial to the interests of the Church (*e.g.*, in money matters), it must be broken. So teaches Innocent III.[2]

29. The Popes can dispense at their pleasure oaths of allegiance taken by a people to their King, as Gregory VII., Alexander III., Innocent III., and many others have done.

30. They can also absolve a sovereign from the treaties he has sworn to observe or from his oath to the Constitution of his country, or give full power to his confessor to absolve him from any oath he finds it inconvenient to keep. Such a plenary power Clement VI. gave to King John of France and his successors.[3] Thus

---

[1] See, *e.g.*, Tartarotti, *Apologia del Congresso*, etc., p. 176.

[2] *Decr.* ii. 24, 27.

[3] D'Achery, *Spicileg.* iii. 714. ["Vobis et successoribus vestris Regibus et Reginis Franciæ in perpetuum indulgemus, ut confessor religiosus vel sæcularis quem vestrûm vel eorum quilibet duxerit eligendum, vota per vos forsitan jam emissa, *ac per vos et successores vestros in posterum emittenda* . . . necnon juramenta per vos præstita, *et per vos et eos præstanda in posterum,* quæ vos et illi *servare commode non possitis,* vobis et eis commutare valeat in alia opera pietatis." Two cases are reserved, viz., vows of chastity and *vows taken to the Pope.*—TR.]

Clement VII. absolved the Emperor Charles V. from his oath restricting his absolutism over popular rights in Belgium, and again from his oath not to banish the Moriscos from their home. And Paul IV. announced to the Emperors Charles and Ferdinand that he dispensed their oath to observe the Augsburg religious peace.[1]

31. In 1648 a prospect of toleration was held out to the sorely oppressed Catholics of England and Ireland, if they would sign a renunciation of the following principles, (*a*) The Pope can dispense any one from obedience to the existing Government; (*β*) The Pope can absolve from an oath taken to a heretic; (*γ*) Those who have been condemned as heretics by the Pope may at his command, or with his dispensation, be put to death or otherwise injured. This renunciation was signed by fifty-nine English noblemen and several ecclesiastics, but Pope Innocent X. declared that all who had signed it had incurred the penalties denounced against those who deny papal authority, *i.e.*, excommunication, etc. And so the penal laws against Catholics remained in force for another century. Paul V. had previously condemned the oath of allegiance prescribed

[1] Bzov. *Annal. Eccl.* an. 1555, p. 306, ed. Colon.

by James I. for the English Catholics, and the execu-
tion of a considerable number of them was the
result.[1]

32. The Popes teach that they can absolve men from
any vow made to God or empower others to do so, and
can even give them powers prospectively for dispens-
ing vows to be made hereafter. And thus they have
empowered royal confessors to absolve kings from any
future vow they may find reason to repent of.[2]

33. The Popes have declared, by granting indulgences,
that their jurisdiction extends over Purgatory also, and
that it depends on them to deliver the dead who are
there and transfer them into heaven. Thus Julius II.
bestowed on the Order of Knights of St. George, restored by the Emperor Maximilian, the privilege that,
on assuming the habit of the Order, the Knights "con-
fessi et contriti, a pœnâ et a culpâ et a carcere Purgatorii
et pœnis ejusdem mox et penitus absoluti et quittandi
esse debeant, planè et liberè Paradisum et regnum in-
traturi."[3]   Then or shortly before (1500) the doctrine
was first propounded in Rome, that the Popes could

---

[1] Dodd, *Church History of England*, iii. 288 ; *Tractat. Dogmat. et Schol-
ast. de Ecclesiâ*, Romæ, 1782, ii. 245.

[2] D'Acheray, *Spicileg.* iii. 721.

[3] *Acta Sanct. Bolland.* Ap. 23, p. 157.

attach to certain altars by special privileges the power of delivering one or more souls from Purgatory.

34. The Pope can dissolve a marriage by placing one of the parties under the greater excommunication, and thus declaring him a heathen and infidel. Urban v. did this in 1363, when he excommunicated Bernabó Visconti, Duke of Milan, depriving him and all his children of all their rights and property and absolving his subjects from their allegiance to him, and at the same time pronouncing his wife free to marry again: " Uxorem ejus uti Christianam a vinculo matrimonii cum hære-tico et infideli liberavit."[1]

35. Innocent III. had paved the way for this by establishing the doctrine that the bond between a Bishop and his diocese is stronger than the marriage bond between man and wife, and therefore as indissoluble by man as the latter, and that God alone could dissolve it, and the Pope as God's vicegerent.[2] It followed that the Pope, and he alone, could also dissolve a validly contracted marriage.

36. According to papal teaching it is praiseworthy and Christian for a man, who has promised a woman

---

[1] Spondani, *Annal. Eccl. Contin.* ii. 595.
[2] *Decr. de Transl.* c. ii. 3, 4. [Cf. *Janus,* pp. 55, 56.]

with an oath to marry her, to deceive her by a sham marriage, and then break the bond and retire into a monastery. This recommendation (to commit an act of treachery at once and of sacrilege) was given by Alexander III. in 1172, and it has been incorporated in the code of canon law drawn up by command of the Popes.[1]

37. The Popes teach that any one attending a service celebrated by a married priest commits sacrilege, because the blessing he gives turns to a curse. So Gregory VII. teaches, in direct contradiction to the doctrine of the ancient Church, and even to modern theology.[2] The notion has long since been exploded.[3]

38. The Popes teach that they have the power of rewarding services done to themselves with a higher degree of eternal beatitude. Thus Nicolas V. promised all who should take up arms against Amadeus of Savoy (the antipope Felix) and his adherents, not only remission of all their sins, but an increase of heavenly happiness, and gave his lands and property at the same time to the King of France.[4]

---

[1] *Decr.* iv. 1, 16.
[2] *Dist.* 81, c. 15.
[3] *Concil. Gangrens.* can. 4.
[4] *Concil.* ed. Labbé, t. xiii. pp. 1322, 3.

39. The Popes teach that it is false and damnable to maintain that a Christian ought not to abstain from doing his duty from fear of an unjust excommunication. Clement XI. declares the contrary to be true in his Bull *Unigenitus,* prop. 91.

40. Those who die wearing the Carmelite scapular have papal assurance, resting on a revelation granted to John XXII., that they will be delivered on the next Saturday after their death by the Virgin Mary from Purgatory and conveyed straight to heaven. So says the Bull *Sabbathina,* confirmed by Alexander V., Clement VII., Pius V., Gregory XIII., and Paul V., by the last after long and careful examination, and with indulgences attached to it.[1]

41. According to papal decisions it is an excess of extravagance and folly, and a detestable innovation, to translate the Roman missal into the vernacular. It is to violate and trample under foot the majesty of the ritual composed in Latin words, to expose the dignity of the holy mysteries to the gaze of the rabble, to produce disobedience, audacity, insolence, sedition and many other evils. The authors of such translations are

[1] See Amort, *De Indulg.* i. 146.

" sons of perdition." Alexander III. says this *totidem verbis* in his Brief of Jan. 12, 1661.[1] Nevertheless the translated missal is in general circulation in France, England and Germany, and is daily used by all the most pious persons.

42. To receive interest on invested money is a grievous sin according to papal teaching, and any one who has done so is bound to make restitution. Papal legislation makes it, under the name of usury, an ecclesiastical offence to be judged by the spiritual tribunals. The principle established by the Popes was, that it is unlawful and sinful to ask for any compensation for the use of capital lent out. And under the head of usury, which was strictly forbidden, was included anything whatever received by the lender in compensation for his capital, every kind of interest, commercial business and the like. Thus Clement V. pronounced it heresy to defend taking interest, and liable to the penalties of the papal law against heresy.[2] His successors, Pius V., Sixtus V., and especially Benedict XIV., adhered to this condemnation of all taking of interest. The results

[1] D'Argentré, *Collectio Judiciorum*, Paris, 1728, iii. 297.
[2] *Clementin.* i. 5, De Usuris, tit. 5.

were that real usury was greatly advanced thereby,
that all sorts of evasions and illusory contracts came
into actual use, that the wealth of whole countries was
damaged, and commercial greatness, banished from
Catholic countries, became the monopoly of Protestant
countries.[1]

[1] [On this subject, as also on persecution, the reader may profitably consult *Papal Infallibility and Persecution ; Papal Infallibility and Usury.*
By an English Catholic. Macmillan, 1870.—TR.]

FIFTY-SEVENTH LETTER.

Rome, June 18, 1870.—The great merits of Cardoni are at length to receive their fitting reward. He has hitherto been only Archbishop of Nisibis, a city that has long ceased to exist; he has now become keeper of the archives of the Roman Church. He was the principal person intrusted last year with the grand mystery of the fabrication of the new dogma, which required for its success the strictest secrecy; the Bishops, with the exception of course of the initiated, were to be drawn to Rome unprepared and innocent of the design and then to be taken by surprise. Had the real object of the Council become known in the spring of 1869, it might easily have proved a complete failure. It was therefore intrusted to Cardoni's experienced hands, who managed matters so well in the Commission that the Bishops were kept in the dark, and his lucubrations on infallibility were first printed in April,

—it is said after being considerably altered by the Jesuits. The reward of Cardoni is a punishment for Theiner, who has to suffer for his Life of Clement XIV. and for communicating to some of the Bishops a paper on the order of business at Trent. The archives are now closed to him, and he has had to surrender the keys to Cardoni, though he nominally retains his office. Every German scholar knows that Theiner, after coming to Rome, became extremely reserved in his communications and very cautious in his own publications, always suppressing whatever might excite displeasure there, and throw a slur on the Roman authorities. It was much easier under his predecessor Marini—as German and French scholars, such as Pertz, Raumer and Cherrier, and the British Museum can testify—to get a sight of documents or even transcripts, of course for a good remuneration. Theiner, who was inaccessible to bribery, knew that he had an abundance of enemies and jealous rivals watching him, and carefully guarded against giving them any handle against him. But the original sin of his German origin clung to him; he was not a Reisach and could not Italianize himself. There is great joy in the Gesù, the German College, and the offices of the *Civiltà* !

Theiner's great offence is his letting certain Bishops, viz., Hefele and Strossmayer, see the account of the order of business at the Council of Trent, showing the striking difference between that and the present regulations and the greater freedom of the Tridentine synod. But Hefele had seen the Tridentine Acts in the spring of 1869, and knew about it without Theiner's help.

Meanwhile there is no abatement of the bitter exasperation in the highest circles. The three chief organs of the Court—the *Civiltà*, the *Unità* and the *Univers*—have evidently received orders to vie with each other in their descriptions of the " Liberal Catholics " as the most abandoned and dangerous of men. For the moment nobody is more abominated than a Catholic who is opposed to infallibility and unwilling to see the teaching of the Church brought into contradiction with the laws of his country, which is what they mean by a Liberal Catholic ; such persons are worse than Freemasons. The *Civiltà* says they are more dangerous to " the cause of God " than atheists, and have already proved so. We know how his confessors, La Chaise and Le Tellier, explained to Louis XIV. that a Jansenist is worse and more dangerous than an atheist.

In convents and girls' schools the new article of
faith is already strong enough to work miracles. The
Univers relates " a miraculous cure wrought through an
act of faith in the infallibility of the Vicar of Christ,"
at Vienna on May 24. But that is little in comparison with the greater and more difficult miracles which
the dogma will have to accomplish. If the English
proverb is true, there is nothing more stubborn than
facts ; to remove them from history or change their
nature will be harder than to move mountains. Here
in Rome we are daily assured that the dogma has conquered history, but these anticipated conquests will
have to be fought out, at least everywhere north of the
Alps, and cannot be won without great miracles. But
the Jesuits have never of course been without their
thaumaturgists, and they have been able to accomplish
the impossible even in the historical domain.

The Pope seems peculiarly annoyed at some of the
English Bishops opposing infallibility, probably because
Manning had told him that the English above all
others reverenced him as the organ of the Holy Ghost.
He lately broke out into most bitter reproaches against
Bishop Clifford of Clifton, before an assemblage of
Frenchmen, most of whom did not even know him by

name, and accused him of low ambition, saying that he knew " ex certâ scientiâ " the only reason why Clifford would not believe in his infallibility was because he had not made him Archbishop of Westminster. Yet there is perhaps no member of the Council whom every one credits with so entire an absence of any ambitious thought. The spectacle of such conduct on the part of the man, who for twenty-four years has held the highest earthly dignity, produces a painful feeling in some, and contempt in others.

It is indeed disgusting to see the Court party compelling men, most of them aged, to remain here to the great injury of their health at a season when all who are able to do so leave Rome, although many of them are accustomed to a different climate and feel sick and exhausted. They are treated like prisoners, and not even allowed a holiday without special leave. No such egotistic and unscrupulous absolutism, as what now prevails here, has been seen in the Christian world since the days of the first Napoleon. If there were any persons here besides courtiers who could advise the Pope, as friends, they would have to tell him that his credit before the world demanded that an end should be put to this state of torture, and the Bishops be allowed to depart, many of whom are already dead. But, as was observed before, even Antonelli does not conceal his impotence as regards the Council, and as to others, it may suffice to acquaint Transalpine readers with one detail of Roman Court etiquette. If the Pope sneezes, the attendant prelate must immediately fall on his knees, and cry " Evviva !" in that position. Every man is at last what his *entourage* has made him, and Pius has for twenty-four years had every one kneeling before him, and has been daily overwhelmed with adorations and acts of homage, the effect of which may be read in Suetonius' biographies of the Emperors.

The affair of the Prince Bishop of Breslau, who was not allowed to leave Rome, has been arranged, by Cardinal Antonelli ordering an apology to be made.. The regulations about refusing visas were only meant for the Orientals, who are certainly detained in Rome against their will, but in extending the same treatment to German prelates the police had exceeded their instructions and must be severely punished. Förster answered that he did not wish this, and that Cardinal de Angelis in his note had fully approved their conduct. Meanwhile the same thing has been repeated : the visa was refused to the suffragan Bishop of Erlau in Hungary, who wanted to go to Naples, because he had received no permission from the Secretary, Bishop Fessler.

The Franciscan, Hötzl, has made an explanation satisfactory to the authorities, and is now again received into favour, but he is to stay here for the festival of June 29, on which day, as Pius was at least convinced a week ago, the proclamation of the new dogma with all imaginable pomp will take place. We live in very humane times, and so the good Father from Munich has suffered no worse martyrdom than the heat. He has been instructed, the *genius loci* has done its work, his Spanish General has simply reminded him of certain rules of the Order—and so his conversion has been very quickly, easily and happily accomplished. He was not even threatened, I believe, with the Inquisition, and even there he would not have fared as ill as Galileo in 1633.

You must allow me, before relating the events of the last few days in the Council Hall, to recur to the occurrences of June 3, which I am now better acquainted with, and which have proved to be sufficiently important and eventful to deserve more detailed mention.

On the motion of Cardinal Bonnechose, who belongs to the middle party, Cardinal de Angelis had asked the

Pope, directly after the session of June 2, whether he would not permit the prorogation of the Council, in view of the intolerable heat and the too long absence already of so many Bishops from their dioceses. The reply was a decided negative; there should be no adjournment till the infallibilist *Schema* was disposed of. That was a hint to the majority, which they used next day, as the wish to cut short the debates had been loudly expressed for some days previously.

On the same day the Bishop of Pittsburg in North America spoke against infallibility and defended the Catholics of his country, who had hitherto known nothing of this doctrine, but were yet genuine Catholics in life and practice and not in name only, like the Italians. Capalti immediately attacked him and imposed silence. Bishop Dinkel of Augsburg followed. Senestrey, Bishop of Ratisbon, in the previous sitting had assured the prelates, who listened eagerly, that all Germany, so far as it was Catholic, thought as he did, and that every one was deeply penetrated with reverence for the infallible Pope, while it was a mere invention of certain evil-minded persons that there were those in Germany who doubted this divine prerogative of the Vicar of God. The astonishment was great; they had heard so often that the aversion to the new dogma was most deeply rooted and most widely spread in Germany. Dinkel pointedly contradicted his colleague, and warned them against being misled by such tricks. He won great commendation, and his Biblical comments were also found to be well grounded and to the purpose.

Bishop Maret of Sura next ascended the tribune. He like others has made advances since being in the Roman school. If he had to write his work on the Pope and Council now, he would take a far more decided and bolder line. It was not without reason that he pointedly distinguished the two things, papal infallibility based and dependent on episcopal consent, and the personal infallibility of the Pope deciding alone, as the real subject of the controversy; for during the last few days there have been Bishops who excused their adhesion to the majority on the pretext that they only found the former kind of infallibility in the *Schema*. Maret then showed in what a labyrinth the majority was on the point of involving the Council. Either the Council was to give the Pope an infallibility he did not yet possess, in which case the donor was higher than the receiver by divine and therefore inalienable rights; or the Pope was to give himself an infallibility he had not hitherto possessed, in which case he could change the divine constitution of the Church by his own plenary power; and if so why summon a Council and ask its vote? There Bilio angrily interrupted him, exclaiming to one of the most learned and respected men of the French clergy, the president of the Paris Theological Faculty, "Tu non nôsti prima rudimenta fidei." And then he gave the explanation I mentioned before, that it did not belong to the Council to bear witness, to judge and to decide, but only to acknowledge the truth and give its vote, and then to leave the Pope to define what he chose by the inspiration of the Holy Ghost. There could be no talk here of majority or minority, but only of the Council. The majority applauded. Maret remained quiet, and asked without changing countenance, after this effusion of Bilio's was at an end, "Licitumne est ac liberum continuare sermonem." Then all was silence, and he was able to finish his speech without further interruption.

Hereupon followed the violent closing of the discussion by a decree of the majority. The euphemistic language in which the *Giornale di Roma* announced it next day was remarkable :—" Fù *terminata* la discussione generale intorno alla materia di fede, che cominciata con la Congregazione del 14 Maggio, era stata proseguita per tutte le adunanze tenute nel suddetto spazio di tempo, nelle quali ebbero parlato in proposito 65 padri," etc.—such an obituary announcement as those which used to be put into the Russian newspapers on the death of a Czar, and which led Talleyrand to say, " Il serait enfin temps que les Empereurs de Russie changeassent de maladie."

At the international meeting at Cardinal Rauscher's on the 4th, when about 100 Bishops were present, some of the bolder and more vigorous of them thought they ought to show by observing complete silence that there was no freedom at the Council. This view, as was said before, did not prevail; and the alternative of a protest was again adopted. On June 6, when the special debate began, Bishop Verot of Savannah in Georgia was the speaker who incurred the peculiar displeasure of the Court party, and was maltreated by Bilio. He objected to the words of the preamble " juxta communem et universalem doctrinam," as not being true, because the doctrine referred to was not universal or everywhere received, but was only the doctrine of the so-called ultramontane school. At this murmurs arose, and Verot remarked that a previous speaker-- Valerga—had been quietly listened to while he talked for an hour and a half about the Gallican school, and compared them with the Monothelite heretics ; it was only fair therefore to let him call the other school by its name. Hereupon Bilio, who has assumed the rôle of *ex officio* blusterer and terrorist, interposed in his manner of a brawling monk, saying this topic had nothing to do with the preamble, and could be introduced afterwards in the discussion on the four chapters.

Bishop Pie of Poitiers had proposed to his colleagues on the Commission *de Fide* to put the article on infallibility, which was too crudely worded, into a shape which all could accept ; to which Manning and Dechamps replied that it could not be improved upon, and they would allow not the slightest change. And as they had a majority in the Commission, Pie's wish was strangled before its birth.

There is no want of restless activity and agitation in favour of infallibility. The processions to obtain the gift of infallibility from the Holy Virgin and the numerous Saints, whose bones and relics fill the Roman

Churches, march with sonorous devotion through the streets; the lazy and lukewarm are urged not to remain idle at so important a time, and there is no lack of intimations of the real profits which the dogma must yield to the city. The Bishops of the minority must have had marble hearts if they had continued proof against so many fervent prayers for their conversion, and wished still to defend their Gallican citadel in spite of the general assault upon it. The Roman parish priests have already presented an address in favour of the dogma, but not—as I hear—till after the opposition among them had been put down by the highest authority. And now an urgent admonition has been addressed to the University Professors either to signify their desire for the definition or resign their offices. All who receive salaries here have long been accustomed to the soft pressure put upon them from above, and are hastening, with a correct appreciation of the importance of the wish of the authorities, to follow lead. In the last few days we have had an address from 40 Chamberlains of the Fathers of the Council who "prostrate at the Pope's most sacred feet earnestly desire to have the opportunity of sharing the wholesome fruits (*saluberrimi frutti*) of infallibility and

the exultation felt by all true believers at the decree."
The text of the address is given in the *Unita Cattolica.*

Meanwhile the chief Pontiff himself speaks in
most emphatic terms. The *Tedeschi,* notwithstanding
Senestrey's assurances, are in bad odour here. A letter
of the Papal Secretary in the *Univers* of June 2
describes the Opposition Bishops as *amateurs de nouve-
autés dangereuses,* and I understand that in a letter to
Chigi, the nuncio at Paris, the Pope speaks of his infallibility as " that pious doctrine, which for so many centuries nobody questioned." This expression is peculiarly
suggestive. That the Pope uses it in good faith is certain, and that he has not gained his conviction by any
study of his own is equally certain. He has been
deluded by this monstrous lie, which no single even
half-educated infallibilist will make himself responsible
for, and thus has been driven into his perilous course.
No one, who has but glanced at the official Roman
historians, such as Baronius or Orsi or Saccarelli, can
possibly maintain seriously that there has been no
doubt for centuries about papal infallibility. This saying
lifts the veil and affords us a glance into the workshop,
where the Pandora's basket was fabricated which has
now been opened before our eyes. Future theologians

will know how to appreciate that weighty saying, " no one for many centuries," and I for my part would say, like Gratiano to Shylock, " I thank thee for teaching me that word."

Cardinal Schwarzenberg, who spoke on the 7th against the second chapter, was not, I think, interrupted, as was however the Bishop of Biella, Losanna, on the pretext that he did not keep to the subject. The old man is a doubly unpleasant phenomenon to the Court party, both from his boldness and clearness of view, and as being a living proof that even an Italian may be a decided opponent of infallibilism. At the international meeting at Cardinal Rauscher's on the 8th it was determined that the third chapter was to be especially attacked in the speeches.

This third chapter deals with matters of very pregnant import. It binds the Bishops to the acknowledgment that all men are immediately and directly under the Pope, which means that the so-called papal system is to be made exclusively dominant in the Church, in place of the old episcopal system, or in other words is to displace the latter, as it existed in the ancient Church, altogether. Bishops remain only as Papal Commissaries, possessed of so much power as the Pope finds good to leave them, and exercising such authority only as he does not directly exercise himself; there is no longer any episcopate, and thus one grade of the hierarchy is abolished. The persons bearing the name of Bishops are wholly different from the old and real Bishops; they have nothing more to do with the higher teaching office (*magisterium*), and have no authority or sphere of their own, but only delegated functions and powers, which the Pope or any one appointed by him can encroach upon at pleasure. Even this is not enough for Archbishop Dechamps of Mechlin, who has now proposed four canons anathematizing all defenders of the episcopal system; this has roused the suspicions even of several Bishops of the majority. These four canons are so significant an illustration of the aims of the party that they deserve to be put on record here:—

(1.) " Si quis dixerit Romanum Pontificem habere qui-dem in Ecclesia primatum jurisdictionis, non vero etiam supremam potestatem docendi, regendi et gubernandi Ecclesiam, perinde ac si primatus jurisdictionis ab illâ supremâ potestate distingui posset—anathema sit.

(2.) " Si quis dixerit talem potestatem Romani Pon-tificis non esse plenam, sed divisam inter S. Pontifi-cem et episcopos, quasi episcopi a Spiritu S. positi ad

2 x

Ecclesiam Dei docendam et regendam sub unico summo pastore etiam divinitus vocati fuerint, ut in supremâ potestate totius Ecclesiæ capitis participent—anathema sit.

(3.) " Si quis dixerit supremam in Ecclesia potestatem non residere in universæ Ecclesiæ capite, sed in episcoporum pluralitate—anathema sit.

(4.) " Si quis dixerit Romano Pontifici datam quidem esse plenam potestatem regendi et gubernandi, non autem etiam plenam potestatem docendi universalem Ecclesiam, fideles et pastores—anathema sit."

FIFTY-EIGHTH LETTER.

Rome, June 21, 1870.—What I have to communicate in this letter is so important, that I find it desirable to take it out of the historical order of events and let it precede the detailed account of what occurred between June 8 and 17.

A circumstance occurred on Saturday, which has kept all who are interested about the Council in breathless suspense ever since. Nothing in fact could be more unexpected than that, at the moment when the Opposition, though still maintaining the contest from a sense of conscientious duty, almost despairs of success, a fresh ally should join its ranks in the person of a Roman Cardinal, whose accession is the more valuable because he does not only speak in his own name, but has concerted his speech with the fifteen Bishops of his Order. In fact I hear his speech spoken of in many quarters as the most important and unexpected event in the Council. It must not of course be supposed that Guidi's spirited speech represents adequately the tendencies of the Opposition, but still it must be affirmed that it involves a complete, and as we believe irreconcilable, breach with the majority. In order to enable people to appreciate the full weight of the speech it is of some importance to premise a brief account of the speaker.

Cardinal Guidi has belonged, almost ever since his entering the Dominican Order, to the convent of the Minerva. For a long time he belonged to the theological professoriate connected with the convent, and enjoyed, as such, the well-earned reputation of great learning and strict orthodoxy. When eleven years ago Pius IX. wished to send thoroughly trustworthy and learned Roman theologians to the University of Vienna, to inculcate genuine Roman science and views on the young clergy, his eye fell on Father Guidi. After working there for some years he returned to Rome, having been meanwhile appointed Cardinal, and was soon afterwards made Archbishop of Bologna; and as the Italian Government promised to place no impediment in the way of his residing there, he actually betook himself to his See. But he soon found that it was not the place for him. The Dominican Order had seriously compromised itself in the notorious Mortara affair, and accordingly the Bolognese rabble broke out repeatedly into the most deplorable demonstrations against the new Archbishop as a member of the hated Order. He therefore returned to Rome, and administered his diocese from hence. And here he was one of the Pope's favourites, only during the last year he has lost favour through his freedom of speech. Since then he has been prosecuting his theological studies in retirement, and it was pretty well known what he thought about the personal infallibility of the Pope. Several months ago he had assembled the Dominican Bishops at the Minerva about this affair. His view prevailed, and when Father Jandel, the General imposed on the Order by the Pope and reluctantly accepted, tried to put a pressure on them, they replied that they were Bishops, and were bound, as such, to consult their consciences when called to act as judges of faith. Then began a notable agitation in the Order, which was already divided into two camps. One arbitrary act followed another. A so-called academy of St. Thomas was opened, and hardly had the President taken his seat, when he made a long speech, expounding the doctrine of St. Thomas and the Order on papal infallibility in the most tactless and violent manner to his episcopal audience. A Dominican Bishop delighted the Pope by getting up an infallibilist address among his episcopal colleagues. Then followed a series of writings defending St. Thomas against *Janus*. A member of the Order was forbidden by the General, Jandel, "to speak either publicly or privately about infallibility," and the *Civiltà Cattolica* of June 18 praised the General for prefixing to the infallibilist writing of a Dominican the approbation that in the Dominican Order papal infallibility has always been held as a Catholic truth.

Under these circumstances people were the less prepared to find Cardinal Guidi, in contrast with his numerous sympathizers in the College of Cardinals, venturing boldly on a step which must embitter his whole existence at Rome. The very first sentence of his momentous speech must have concentrated the anger of the majority on a Cardinal, as they thought, so confused and oblivious of his duty. Guidi began by affirming that the separate and personal infallibility of the Pope, as stated in the amended chapter of the *Schema*, was wholly unknown in the Church up to the fourteenth century inclusive. Proofs for it are vainly sought in Scripture and Tradition. The whole question, he added, reduces itself to the point whether the Pope has defined even one dogma alone and without the co-operation of the Church. No man could claim divine inspiration (*doctrina infusa*). An act might be infallible, a person never. But every infallible act had always proceeded from the Church herself only, either "per consilium Ecclesiæ sparsæ," or "per Concilium." To know "quid ubique credatur, si omnes Ecclesiæ cum Romanâ Ecclesiâ concordent," information is indispensably required. After this examination the Pope sanctions doctrine "finaliter," as St. Thomas says, and only so can it be rightly said "Omnes per Papam docent." He then showed from the works of the Jesuits Bellarmine and Perrone, " in definendis dogmatibus Papas nunquam ex se solis egisse, nunquam hæresim per se solos condemnâsse." As Guidi uttered these words the majority began to make a tumult under the lead of the Italian Spaccapietra, Bishop of Smyrna. The Cardinal saw he could not continue his speech. One bishop cried " birbante " (scoundrel) and another " brigantino." But Guidi did not let himself be put out of countenance ; he answered with astonishing firmness and calmness that he had a right to be heard, and that no one had given to the Bishops the right of the Presidents. "However, the time will come yet for saying your *Placet* or your *Non placet,* and then every one will be free to vote according to his conscience." Here for the first time his speech was interrupted by loud applause, and the words " Optime, optime " resounded from every side among the Opposition Bishops. Manning was asked by one of them, who stood near him, " Etes-vous d'accord, Monsigneur ?" He replied, " Le Cardinal est une tête confuse." On this a high-spirited Bishop could not refrain from observing to the powerful Archbishop of Westminster, " C'est bien votre tête, Monseigneur, qui est confuse et plus qu'à moitié Protestante."

After this pretty long interruption Guidi went on to require a change in the chapter on infallibility " ut clare appareat Papam agere consentientibus episcopis et illis occasione errorum qui sparguntur petentibus, factâ inquisitione in aliis Ecclesiis, præmisso maturo examine et judicio et consiliis fratrum aut collecto Concilio." This was the true doctrine of St. Thomas ; " finaliter " implied something to precede, and the words " supremus magister et judex" pre-suppose other "magistri" and "tribunalia." He concluded by proposing these canons :—

(1.) " Si quis dixerit decreta seu constitutiones a Petri

successore editas, continentes quandam fidei vel morum veritatem Ecclesiæ universæ ab ipso pro supremâ suâ et apostolicâ auctoritate propositas non esse extemplo omnimodo venerandas et toto corde credendas vel posse reformari—anathema sit.

(2.) " Si quis dixerit Pontificem, cum talia edit decreta, posse agere arbitrio et ex se solo non autem ex consilio episcoporum traditionem Ecclesiarum exhibentium— anathema sit."

On sitting down he gave his manuscript to the Secretary, and was soon surrounded by the leaders of the Opposition, some of whom complimented him on his speech, while others expressed their admiration of his courage in resisting the attempts to interrupt him. When a learned Italian Bishop asked Valerga, Patriarch of Jerusalem, what he thought of this speech, he replied audibly with the pun, " Si e squidato," and on his inter-rogator rejoining that anyhow the speech contained nothing but the truth, Valerga let slip an expression very characteristic of himself and his party, " Si, ma non convien sempre dir la verità."

After this speech a large number of Bishops left the Council Hall, and excited groups of prelates might be seen standing about in all directions. Cardinals Bonnechose and Cullen addressed their very pointless speeches to empty benches. Both pleaded for the pro-clamation of the fourth chapter, as it stood. Bonne-chose, from whom Ginoulhiac and others had expected a very moderate speech, proved that he had completely gone over into Manning's camp, which cannot surprise any one in the case of a man who himself made no secret of his having no clear views on the question. Cullen destroyed by his last speech the impression made by the first, which had been admired, not for its contents but for its strictly parliamentary form.

Cardinal Guidi's courageous speech was destined soon to bear its fruits. The Pope—the dearest object of whose heart is the perfect freedom of the Council, as the official journal stated the other day—sent for him at once, and next day boasted to several Cardinals of having energetically rebuked their undutiful colleague for his heresy and ingratitude, and threatened him with being called on to renew his profession of faith. But the Cardinal may consider himself indemnified for these hard words of the Pope by the homage he re-ceived the day after his speech from almost the whole body of the Opposition Bishops who came to visit him. And he knows that the best of them were even worse treated by his Holiness than himself, where it was possible.

FIFTY-NINTH LETTER.

Rome, June 22, 1870.—On the 13th the votes were taken on the changes proposed in the preamble, and taken by rising and sitting down.[1] Instead of "Vis et salus Ecclesiæ ab eo (Papâ) dependet" was proposed "Vis et soliditas in eo (Papâ) consistit." The majority seem to have thought that stronger. The debate began with the speech of the Irish Archbishop of Cashel, a member of the Commission. It is precisely in our days, he said, that it is so necessary for the Pope to have absolute and irresponsible authority, for therein lies the one safeguard, first, against the encroachments of Liberalism; secondly, against the Radical and anti-Church policy of the Governments; thirdly, against the poisonous and unbridled influence of journalism; and fourthly, the absolute Pope can alone meet the ecclesiastical and national enterprises of Russia or subdue

[1] [This had been protested against by the minority. Cf. *supr.* pp. 327-8.]

the political sects and ward off the Revolution which is impending everywhere. In short, human society requires a deliverer, and this deliverer must be omnipotent and infallible. So it is said in the Commission, and the Irish prelate, who was specially alarmed by Fenianism, spoke in its name. As soon as the Pope with the assent of the Council—or indeed without it—has ruled his own omnipotence and infallibility, the deliverance of mankind is accomplished.

The French Benedictine, Cardinal Pitra, undertook to lift the assembly out of this cloudy region back to the firm ground of facts, viz., the facts disclosed by himself. He expatiated on the collection of canons in the Greek Church, saying that those relating to the Roman See had been falsified, and the Russian Church was above all implicated in this system of forgery, which had brought things to such a pass that there was no authentic collection of canons in the Oriental Church. This was probably intended to serve as a diversion, for the enormous fabrications in favour of papal omnipotence, which were carried on for centuries and are incorporated in the codes of canon law, had been frequently before referred to in a very suspicious manner in the Council. Even the Bishop of Saluzzo, who is almost a thorough-going Roman absolutist, had called the collection of canons (Gratian's, etc.) an Augean stable. Pitra went on to indulge in an uncommonly fervid philippic against the Machiavellian and persecuting Russia. But he forgot to say one thing, viz., that in no country would the impending decrees be received with such satisfaction as in Russia, nowhere would they give greater pleasure than in that great Northern State which considers itself the happy heir of Rome in the East. So much must be known even in Rome, that on the day the dogma is promulgated all the bells in Mohilew, Wilna, Minsk, etc., will resound to ring the knell of Rome. Pitra was followed by Ramirez y Vasquez, Bishop of Badajoz. He maintained in the style and tone of Don Gerundio de Canpazes, the doctrine that the Pope is Christ in the Church, the continuation of the Incarnation of the Son of God, whence to him belongs the same extent of power as to Christ Himself when visibly on earth. Maret had announced his intention of speaking, with the view of combating the four anathemas of Dechamps, which were so manifestly directed against his book. But Dechamps, on learning this, told the Bishop of Sura that, if he would keep silence, he would withdraw his anathemas, and excused himself by alleging his zeal for the new dogma, assuring Maret that he had a good heart and meant no harm. So Maret renounced his design of speaking.

On the 14th, Haynald, in spite of his bodily suffering, delivered a long polemical speech against the majority, and maintained his reputation of being the best Latin speaker after Strossmayer. Jussuf, the Melchite Patriarch of Antioch, came next with an apology for the Oriental Churches and their liberties. He pointed out in earnest words the danger of their defection, if the present design of taking away their ancient rights was carried out. He produced letters from his home telling him that he had better not return at all than bring back from Rome decrees curtailing their eccle-siastical liberties. And if the Pope chose to send back another Patriarch instead of him, they might be very sure he would not be received. Bishop Krementz of Ermeland observed that Holy Scripture made, not Peter, or as is here understood the Pope, the foundation of the Church, but Christ, and then as secondary foundation the Apostles and Prophets. Only after these and in dependence on them could this designation be applied to the See of Rome.

It had indeed been already observed among the

minority how monstrous it was to make the Pope "the principle of unity in the Church," as the *Schema* puts it, and that the ancient Fathers speak indeed of an "exordium unitatis" established in the person of Peter, but had never called him, and still less the Bishop of Rome, the principle of ecclesiastical unity, which would be logically inconceivable. In the voting, which was again taken by rising and sitting down, the little band of dissentients disappeared before the consentient mass, and the expression "principium unitatis," opposed as it is both to logic and tradition, was accepted. Before the voting Bishop Gallo of Avellino had uttered in the name of the Commission some Neapolitan mysticism about Adam and Eve and the mysteries already revealed in Adam and Eve of the Church resting on the Pope.

Cardinal Mathieu was the first speaker on the fourth chapter on infallibility. His long and powerful speech was mainly directed against Valerga, who had outraged the French by his attack on the "Gallican errors." It was a well-delivered panegyric on the French nation, which had shed the blood of her sons to restore Rome to the Pope, and without whose troops at Civita Vecchia the Council could not remain in Rome. The only doubt is whether this Valerga is worth as much notice

as the French have accorded to him.   After Mathieu
Cardinal Rauscher spoke.   His speech was very inaudible owing to the nature of the Council Hall, but
was clear and well grounded, and showed how the
acceptance of a personal infallibility, by virtue of which
every utterance of a Pope must be believed by all
Christians under pain of eternal damnation, is equally at
issue with facts and with the former tradition of the
Church, and must have a fatal effect in the future.   He
referred to Vigilius, Honorius, the reordinations of Sergius and Stephen, and the contradiction between
Nicolas III. and John XXII., and commended the formula
of Antoninus requiring the consent of the Church as a
condition.   He could never assent to the *Schema* without
mortal sin.   " We knew all that from your pamphlet,"
said Dechamps while he was speaking.   " But you have
never refuted it," replied Rauscher.

Cardinal Pitra was to have followed, but he was
unwell, and the sitting was broken off.   The Presidents
had issued an instruction that no one should speak out
of his turn, and if prevented on the regular day should
lose his right altogether.   The rule in this case affected
the zealous infallibilist Pitra, and accordingly the
Bishops were dismissed before the usual hour.

The two next days, the 17th and 18th, were festivals, and there was no sitting held. As there are already 75 speakers enrolled for the fourth chapter, the promulgation obviously cannot take place on June 29, and the Council will last on into July. There is indeed a simple means of gratifying the desire of the Pope and curtailing the pains of the Bishops, who are now absolutely tortured by the heat : the majority can any day cut short the special debate, as they have already cut short the general discussion. It may of course be objected that this procedure, of depriving the Bishops of their right of speaking and violently imposing silence upon them, overthrows the nature of a Church Council, where every Bishop is meant to bear witness not only to his own belief, but to the tradition of his country and the faith of his diocese. If the Bishops are deprived of this right—and that too where so momentous a question is at issue and there is such diversity of opinion—the freedom essential to a Council is wanting.

The Pope becomes more lavish of his admonitions and instructions every day. In the last Papal *Capella* Patrizzi assured him the faithful were impatiently awaiting the proclamation of infallibility, whereon Pius, in presence of several Bishops of the minority, replied that

2 Y

there were three classes of opponents of the dogma, *first*, the gross ignoramuses, who did not know what it meant; *secondly*, the slaves of princes, he said " of Cæsar," referring both to Vienna and Paris ; *thirdly*, the cowards, who feared the judgment of this evil world. But he prayed for their enlightenment and conversion.[1] This was of course applied here universally to the Bishops of the Opposition. Moreover the Pope had just before had a letter written to certain canons of Besançon, saying that all the objections raised now had been triumphantly refuted a hundred times over, and that as to appealing to the results of historical criticism and the examination of texts, viz., to the huge mass of deliberate falsifications and forgeries, these were " des anciens sophismes ou mensonges contraires aux prérogatives du St. Siége." The remark touches Rauscher, Schwarzenberg, Dupanloup, Hefele, Maret, Kenrick, Ketteler (in the pamphlet he circulated), and some thirty more. There is much dispute here as to the paternity of those views which Pius emits both orally and in writing. Has he got them from the *Civiltà*, or are the Jesuit writers of that journal only the

---

[1] The text of the speech, as it is now printed in the journals, has been subsequently corrected and toned down.

pupils of the Pope, who has received this information "by infused science" from the Virgin Mary? On that point opinions differ. The majority, who are quite aware that every one would think it a joke to call Giovanni Maria Mastai a learned theologian, hold to the latter view, and to the well-known picture painted by the Pope's own order, where the "actus infusionis" is represented to the eye. Their favourite watchword is that every one who does not accept the decree is, or in a few days will be, a heretic and enemy of the Church; his *non placet* consummates his separation from her, and hence Manning has already proposed that each of these Bishops should have his excommunication handed him with his railway-ticket when he leaves Rome. Livy says, "Hæc natura multitudinis est, aut servit humiliter aut superbe dominatur;" the "multitude" in the Hall combines both characteristics.

On June 18 the Pope observed a German priest among those admitted to an audience, and asked who he was, when he replied that he was secretary to a Bishop, who is well known for his learning and his fallibilist views. Pius turned away with an exclamation of disgust. Of another very eminent dignitary of similar views he is wont to say in the bitterest terms, that his opinions are prompted solely by personal enmity to himself.

The majority are said to be very impatient, so that many anticipate the violent closing of the debate on Saturday, the 25th.   And the greater number of the intending speakers on the fourth chapter, now increased to a hundred, belong to the Court party, who might say that they are only willingly renouncing the pleasure of hearing their own ideas put forward.   But then the speeches of Darboy, Place (of Marseilles), Maret, Clifford, Schwarzenberg, Simor, Dupanloup, and Haynald would also be suppressed.   Hefele was the first to put down his name, as he was not allowed at the time to answer the fierce attack of Cullen.   On his inquiring after some days when his turn would come, he was told that he was the fifty-first in order, as all who came before him in age and rank must speak before he could be permitted to open his mouth.   A little later he was told he came seventy-first, so that his hope of being able to vindicate himself in the Council is almost at an end.   Meanwhile he has had a brief reply to the attack of a Frenchman, de la Margerie, printed at Naples.

The minority have resolved to send a deputation to

the Pope to petition for the adjournment of the Council, since it is horrible to detain so many aged men, many of whom are sick, by violence in this unhealthy city. They will of course meet with a positive refusal, for the Jesuits and the holy Virgin, who is always appealed to, are for carrying out the compulsory system to the last. But you may judge how the heat and the moral and physical miasmas are working on the Bishops from the fact that there are now only five or six on a bench where thirty Bishops used to sit, though most of the others are in Rome or the neighbourhood. Indeed they are kept prisoners here, and Antonelli said recently to a diplomatist, " Si quelque Evêque veut faire une partie de campagne (like Förster) la police n'a rien à y voir, mais s'il voulait quitter le Concile, alors ce serait différent," so that every foreign Bishop lives here under the inspection of the police, who are to take care that he does not escape. This statement seemed to the diplomat to whom it was made so seriously to affect the sovereign rights of his Government, that he at once reported it.

The Roman logic, as may be seen from the *Civiltà*, is simply this : the Council is what it is through the Pope alone ; without him it can do nothing and is an empty shadow.   Freedom of the Council therefore means freedom of the Pope : if he is free, it is free.   You may infer what reception will be accorded in the Vatican to the petition just resolved upon for a secret voting on the Papal *Schema*.   There could be no more eloquent testimony to the real state of things and the estimate formed of the freedom of the Council, for it is dictated by the knowledge that a secret ballot would give a very considerable number of negative votes, at least 200, if the private expressions of opinion of the Bishops may be relied upon, while no one here ventures to hope for more than 110 or 115 *non placets* in a public voting. There are certainly some hundred, even of the Papal boarders, who would say *Non placet*, if their votes were sheltered by secrecy.   Neither the Catholic nor the non-Catholic public has any idea of the extent to which a Bishop in the present day is dependent on Rome, and how difficult or impossible the administration of his office would be made for him by the disfavour of Rome.   The worst off of all are the Bishops under Propaganda, who have simply no rights.   For them to speak of freedom, after the Pope has announced his wish, would be ludicrous, and to this category belong not only all the Oriental and Missionary Bishops, but the American and English also. And even for the Bishops of the older Sees, who are under the *Congregatio Episcoporum et Regularium,* and are protected by the common law or by Concordats, the practice of the *Curia* is a field full of man-traps, a belt studded with nails, which only needs to be drawn in by curialistic hands to make the nails pierce the body of the obnoxious Bishop. As things now are here, and after Pius has gone further than any Pope for centuries in glaring partisan-ship and open threats of enmity against all dissentients, secret voting must appear the only possible means of securing even a shadow of freedom for the decrees of the Council. If the voting is public, the word free-dom, as used of the Council, could only be regarded as a mockery. And it is very well known here that the Pope's *entourage* do everything in their power to main-tain him in his belief that the Opposition will melt away at last like snow before the sun, and hardly four negative votes will remain.

Last year the theologians summoned for the prelimi-nary work were sent home at the beginning of June, and scarcely one or two even of the directing Commission of Cardinals stayed longer in Rome. Now the 15th or 20th of July is spoken of as the day for the promulga-

tion, and if it should be a little earlier there will still
be many of the prelates who will return from Rome ill
and with their constitutions permanently shattered.
The ancients found the word "amor" reversed in the
name of the eternal city (*Roma*), and the Bishops are daily
reminded of it.   Meanwhile the brilliant recompense
of Cardoni's services has rekindled the hopes of the
majority; there are fifteen or sixteen vacant Hats, which
will be given to those who have deserved best of the
new dogma.   The merits of the Italians are not conspicuous ; they have most of them done moles' work,
chiefly as spies, for that business is conducted here to
an extent almost unheard of in Europe.   Valerga is of
course an exception, who has excelled all the Italians
as a speaker.   After him, Mgr. Nardi has so greatly
distinguished himself by his active zeal that a red Hat
would seem a fitting ornament of his head, but then
there are very suspicious circumstances, only too
notorious in Rome.   The men who have done and will
do the most important services, who are indeed the
modern Atlases to carry the main weight of the new
dogma on their lusty shoulders, are of course the
Jesuits.   Pius is penetrated with the feeling that their
services are above all praise and recompense.   A

Jesuit cannot be rewarded with titles and colours and dresses, but he can receive a Cardinal's Hat. The names of Toletus, Bellarmine, Pallavicini, de Lugo, recall grand memories. Not long before its dissolution in 1736, three of the Order were in the Sacred College together—Tolomei, Eienfuegos and Salerno. That might happen again, and the College would gain in capacity and working power. As Kleutgen cannot be thought of, on account of his trial before the Inquisition, and Perrone is too old, the next candidates would be Curci, Schrader and Franzelin. Father Piccirillo, from his intimate relations to the highest personage, would possess the first reversionary claim, and his services have been rewarded in a manner greatly desired and long aimed at by his Order, for he has received the permission, unprecedented in the history of Rome, to go alone into the secret archives and there work. Such an event would at other times have been regarded at Rome as a downfall of the heavens or a sign of the last judgment, and even now it has produced perplexity and amazement in genuine Roman circles. For every one who passes the threshold of the chamber of archives incurs *ipso facto* excommunication. So the Order is firmly seated in this unapproachable sanctuary. There is no fear of indiscreet publications. Piccirillo, far from publishing anything, will excel in mere negative activity.

Among foreign candidates for the Cardinalate Manning stands out as a star of the first rank in the Roman firmament. He may claim some paternity of the great idea of at last treating the apotheosis of the Papacy seriously, and he long ago suggested to Darboy how nice it would be for the two chief capitals of Europe, London and Paris, each to have its Cardinal, which could be best brought about by furthering the infallibilist definition. But Darboy would hear nothing of it. Next to Manning comes Dechamps of Mechlin; but as the Pope has named him primate, which is indeed a mere title, he is thought here to have had his reward. Spalding, who has deserved so well of Rome, would of course create a great sensation in the United States by the red hat, which has never yet been seen there. Among the French, Dreux-Brézé of Moulins and Pie of Poitiers come first in order. There is great difficulty about Simor, the ill-advised and ungrateful son who had the Cardinalate, so to speak, in his pocket, and is now causing such distress to the lofty giver. How fortunate, say the Court party, that d'Andrea is no longer alive. Rauscher, Schwarzenburg, Guidi, d'Andrea, Simor—that would be too much. But now for the Germans! There it is difficult to select; all the faithful ones must be rewarded, who have literally sweated and are sweating daily in the interest of the good cause —Fessler, Martin, Senestrey, and then Stahl, Leonrod, Rudigier and the Tyrolese Gasser and Riccabona. The Tyrol has had no Cardinal since Nicolas of Cusa (Bishop of Brixen) and Madrucci (Bishop of Trent), and there most especially would the return of a countryman with a red hat be kept as a national festival.

Margotti has had a denial inserted in the *Univers* of the fact that a Sicilian Bishop related the story of St. Peter and the Virgin Mary in the Council Hall. On this I have merely to remark that it was told me the same evening by three Bishops, none of whom heard it from one of the others, and the speaker was Natoli, Archbishop of Messina. We know what Margotti's assertions and denials are worth.

SIXTIETH LETTER.

Rome, June 23, 1870.—On reading the last document emanating from the Council, composed by the
most distinguished of the American Bishops, an inex-
pressible feeling of astonishment comes over me, as
often before, at the new and unprecedented spectacle
so boldly offered to the startled world, and I again
recognise the necessity of accounting to myself for the
condition of the Catholic Church which has made this
possible, and remembering that the position of the
Papacy in the modern Church for some time past has
been hardly less novel and strange than this present
infallibilist Council.

The two great events of modern history, the Reformation and the Revolution, have made the Papacy what
it is,—the Reformation by forcibly driving the Catholic
half of Christendom into centralization, the Revolution
by removing the last remaining independent powers

within the Church, viz., the Gallican Church with the Sorbonne and Parliament. So it came to pass that with the Restoration the Church was surrendered to the discretion of the Papacy, just as at the same time the Roman States, by the withdrawal of all provincial and corporate independence, became a uniform and absolute monarchy. The very spirit of the nineteenth century, without much help from Rome, contributed to the consolidation and strengthening of this new system. The re-awakening and growth of distinct Church feeling in powerful classes of the educated nations, the legitimist ideas of the ruling classes of Europe, and later on the combined Catholic and Liberal interest of the struggle against hostile bureaucracies and the antipathy of parliamentary majorities—principles of reaction and principles of freedom all alike in turn subserved the cause of the Church, *i.e.*, the Papacy. For although Papacy and Church were still not wholly identified in fact, to say nothing of right, the times did not suggest the need for distinguishing between them.

There was opportunity given, one might suppose, for a great display of activity. A fresh creative spirit passed here and there through the new world of the nineteenth century, and not least through the Catholic portion of it, which produced in individuals many fair flowers of art and science, and also of practical piety. It was enough to catch the inspiration, in the sense of the age and of the eternal needs of mankind, and as the wilderness blossoms under the hand of a gardener, there grew out of the ruins of the Revolution a new era of rich Christian life. But the destiny of Catholicism was to be the reverse. There was indeed then, and is now, urgent need of an immense deal to be done in the Church; to carry on the daily ecclesiastical administration by no means satisfied the requirements of the age, but the Church herself needed and needs reform— reform everywhere from the outer rind to the marrow. But reform, whether in Church or State, generally results from the struggle of rival forces. And the only power surviving in the Church possessed neither the capacity nor the inclination for acts of world-wide import; it seemed to have no sense but for the maintenance and extension of its own dominion. Such Catholic works as the nineteenth century has produced did not emanate from Rome, and were little if at all helped on by her. On the contrary, Rome put a restraint on everything which did not serve directly as an instrument of her power. Every germ of relative independence seemed to be viewed with distrust. Here and there the intellectual labour of a lifetime of Catholic study was simply extinguished. The youth of talent turned from a path which led only to unfruitful conflicts. The once promising seed-plot of original Catholic production became dry, and even the noblest creation of the century, the female orders for nursing the sick, are said by those best informed to show symptoms of decay. There was stillness. From Rome one only heard a monologue. The Bishops' Pastorals were its echo, or were so long-winded and verbose that the simple and noble language of the pronunciamento issued by the newly elected Bishop of Rottenburg was quite a phenomenon. Men boasted of the Catholic unity, which had never been so palpable and so undisturbed as in these latter days, but it was a unity of sleep over the grave of intellectual and all higher ecclesiastical life.

Who will bring us deliverance? asked every one who looked at things independently of the mere force of habit with a clear eye. The answer was that there was no longer any independent power anywhere but in the centre, and therefore deliverance could only come from thence; the lever could only be applied in

Rome, and nobody but a future Pope was in a position to do this.

How peculiarly are things disposed! In Rome they had all they could desire. There has never been a time when Catholic Christendom lay so submissively at the Pope's feet. In fact he possessed practically the prerogative of infallibility, for no one contradicted whatever he might say. The Bishops were disused to learning; there was hardly among them a theologian of note, and therefore they had no spirit for theological convictions of their own. It seemed to be the office of their lives to re-echo the Roman oracles. The daring project of defining the Immaculate Conception met with hardly any serious opposition, though many Bishops could not conceal from themselves that the faith of antiquity and the belief of their own dioceses knew nothing of the new dogma. And then in the Encyclical and Syllabus came a perfect flood of irrational and unchristian propositions. What did the Bishops of Christendom, the judges of faith, do? Some put a more rational interpretation on it, the others took it all for granted as it stood; everywhere the new articles of faith and morality were received as though all were in the most regular order. That was in fact a situation without any precedent, and there was nothing left to wish for but its continuance for ever. The talisman to secure this continuance was discovered in the tenet of papal infallibility, and to make this into a dogma and foundation-principle of the Church has been the grand object to which the thoughts and measures of the last ten years have been directed.

Even this last point might perhaps have been attained by adhering to the practice which has prevailed hitherto of quietly collecting the votes of the *Ecclesia dispersa,* and passing over the isolated opponents still left to the order of the day. Why was the perilous plan of a General Council adopted instead of this? Perhaps with the view of extruding and getting rid of for the future all the doubt still attaching to the assent of the Church dispersed; certainly in the full confidence, after all that had occurred previously, that there was absolutely no demand the Bishops would dare to refuse. The authorities felt in the position, ecclesiastically speaking, of being able to challenge the Holy Ghost Himself to say if He would refuse to set His seal to the deformation of the Church.

All the world knows how the Vatican Council has been managed. It was as if they wished to keep the

Holy Ghost a prisoner, with eyes and ears bandaged. But things did not go as they wished. On the contrary this extreme step of the *Curia* roused a reaction, which seems likely to lead to a revolution that will take its place in history and introduce a complete change in the future. Certainly the deliverance is coming from the centre, but not as was thought and desired, not in peace but in storm, not as a gift of the highest human wisdom but as a nemesis. For it is an old law, equally prevalent throughout the Christian and Heathen world, that pride will always bring its punishment.

We are already in the third stage of this movement. First came, quite unexpectedly, protests against infallibility from the lay world, instead of the accustomed clouds of incense, and then still more unexpectedly the military obedience of the clergy was broken through by the most decided intimations of conscientious sincerity and scientific conviction; and now even the princes of the Church are putting themselves at the head of the Opposition. There is still some difference between the Church dispersed and a great assembly, many as are the restrictions imposed here by fraud and violence on the free expression of opinion. The man of knowledge and character, who would there remain alone and isolated, gains tenfold power and energy here. Consciences are aroused. Many a Bishop who left home with his head wholly or half involved in the haze of Jesuit doctrine, receives the impulse here to unprejudiced study and is irresistibly driven to the side of right and truth. Besides, it is no small thing to have seen the state of things at Rome for six months with one's own eyes.

We shall do well not to raise our expectations too high. The spirit of slavery, which has become ingrained in one generation after another, cannot be scared away in weeks and months from men's minds and the conduct of affairs. So much the more noteworthy is every increase of outward or inward strength in the struggling minority at the Council. And so I return to the work already mentioned, to remark that its contents justify us in reckoning the author, the venerable Archbishop Kenrick of St. Louis, with Strossmayer, Hefele, Dupanloup, Darboy, Schwarzenberg, and Rauscher among the heads of the Opposition.

It is only matter of course that much which has often been said before should be repeated here, which we may pass over, without however omitting to notice the impression which the plain and practical nature of the treatise is calculated to produce. What concerns us more nearly is the distinctness and firmness with which the present claims of the *Curia* are repudiated, as, *e.g.*, in pointing out the injury to episcopal rights involved in the desired definition. "The Bishops," says the author, " have always been held judges of faith. But assuming that the Pope alone is infallible, the Bishops may indeed assent to his judgments, but cannot exercise any real judicial office, and thus lose a right inherent in the episcopal office. But this right they are in no position to resign, however much they might wish it, for its connection with the episcopal office rests on the institution of the Saviour." In another passage he says, " Appeal is made to the number of theologians, who in the course of ages have defended infallibility. But that does not make it an article of faith. Divine Providence does not permit such opinions, when they have no true ground or do not agree with the records of revelation, to become articles of faith. It has been a view held for centuries that Christ gave Peter and his successors supreme authority in secular affairs also. But there is no one in our own day who does not reject and deplore it and seek for an excuse for it in the circumstances of the age, except the Roman clergy, in whose *Proprium Officium S.*

Zachariæ we read the other day, that the Pope by his apostolic authority transferred the sovereignty over the Franks from Childeric to Pepin. And yet the Popes have ventured to make this usurped authority, so far as in them lay, into an article of faith." Then follows a reference to the Bull *Unam Sanctam,* and the similar statements of Bellarmine and Suarez. " On the other hand," Kenrick proceeds, " we find at this Council some Bishops, of whom the present writer is one, who have published and solemnly sworn to a declaration that the Pope, at least in England, possesses no such power. This example might teach those who are pressing for the definition of papal infallibility, that even the most solemn papal decree, and though issued like that of Boniface VIII. at a Synod, is null and void if it be not grounded on God's word in Scripture and Tradition. ' Commenta delet dies, judicia naturæ confirmat.' "

We may recognise in the tone of these remarks, with all their moderation, an advance on the part of the Opposition to greater freedom and distinctness of speech. And this impression is still more confirmed by Kenrick's judgment on the well-known proceedings in and out of Council. " There is yet another argument used," he says, " which I can only refer to with reluctance. It is urged that papal infallibility is so vehemently attacked by its opponents that, if it is not now declared to be an article of faith, it is virtually admitted to have no foundation, and surrendered to the daily increasing violence of its assailants without protection. Those who so argue forget that they are themselves responsible for having occasioned this deplorable controversy, by announcing to the astonished world that at the Vatican Council two new dogmas would be proposed to the faithful, papal infallibility and the Assumption of the Blessed Virgin, and in a similar spirit publishing works in England and the United States on the Pope's authority, with a view of preparing men's minds for the acceptance of these dogmas.   In view of this temerity, which has not only not been rebuked but has even been defended in Bishops' Pastorals, and with a clear perception of the unhappy consequences that must follow from it, men, who deserve eternal remembrance and will obtain praise of God, have lifted up their voice to remind the faithful that in matters of faith no innovation is allowed, that papal infallibility as distinct from the infallibility of the Church has no evidence of Scripture and Tradition, and that the office of Councils is to investigate and not to carry decrees by acclamation.

And just because they speak the truth openly, these men are reproached with stirring up the people by the very persons who would eventually have interpreted their silence as assent and have used it as ground for carrying out their own designs. Then again it is urged upon good people that something must be done under the circumstances for maintaining the honour of the Papacy, forgetting that Bishops should have not circumstances but the truth before their eyes, and that it is as little competent to the successors of the Apostles as to the Apostles themselves to do anything against the truth, but only for the truth."

In another passage, after dwelling on the preponderance of the Italian prelates he proceeds, " If they wish to give the decrees of the Council the character of the testimony of the whole of Christendom, without altering the inequality of numbers of the representatives of different nations, there is the precedent of the plan adopted at the Council of Constance with the happiest results, viz., taking the votes by nations or languages and not by heads. And this method would secure the speedier and better settlement of the matters under discussion, for the Bishops of the same tongue or nation know the needs of their Churches better and would understand how to meet them; moreover they could express their views more readily in their mother tongue than is possible in the General Congregation where Latin is obliged to be spoken, which they have perhaps lost their familiarity with through the long course of an active life, so that they have either to keep silent or to speak under difficulties. And by this means a discussion and searching examination would become practicable, which must necessarily take place at a Council, but which is wanting at the Vatican Council. There is indeed abundant opportunity for making speeches, but the great number of Fathers and the order of business imposed on the Council cuts off all opportunity for submitting any point to a close examination by regular debate with one speaker answering another. Five months have already passed since the opening of the Council, with what result need not be said here. Meanwhile the question of the new definition has roused a great excitement throughout the Christian world, which is still on the increase; some desire the definition, others emphatically repudiate it. Bishops have entered the lists against Bishops, priests have written against their own and against other chief pastors, and won commendation from the supreme authority for doing so. The journals of both parties, with their not always true reports or at least crooked reasonings, keep the whole world in a state of agitated suspense as to what is coming. May one say to what all this will lead and what will be the end of this violent tempest which has so suddenly risen in a clear sky and seems likely to produce much mischief? They are certainly deceived who fancy that the promulgation of the new dogma will at once lay the waves ; the contrary is far likelier. Those who would obey the decrees of the Council will find themselves in a most difficult position. The civil Governments will treat them, not without some plausible grounds, as less trustworthy subjects. The enemies of the Church will throw in their teeth the errors said to have been taught by the Popes or sanctioned by their conduct, and will laugh to scorn the only possible answer—that they did not promulgate these errors as Popes but as individual Bishops of Rome. And then the scandals Church history records of certain Popes will be urged as so many proofs of the internal discrepancy of Catholic belief, for men do not distinguish between infallibility and impeccability, which appear to them inseparably connected."

What Kenrick thinks the Opposition ought to do is not expressly stated, but may be gathered from his language. He says indeed that "whoever does not submit to the decisions of an Œcumenical Council does not deserve the name of Catholic," but he adds, " if the indispensable conditions have been observed in holding the Council." And he makes moral unanimity one of these conditions. He does not allow the crude conception which seems to prevail among the majority, that a Council has simply to vote and then the world must reverence the result as the dictate of the Holy Ghost. The infallibility of Councils is to him no miraculous work of inspiration, but a simple result of the constitution the Church received from her Founder, whose assistance will never fail her, if she remains true to Scripture and Tradition and the agreement of the various particular Churches.

Kenrick and all the Bishops who hold firmly with him may meet the impending decision in quietness and confidence, for the defeat of their opponents is certain, whether they persist and define and promulgate the new dogma, or retreat at the last moment. In the former case deliverance will come through a catastrophe whose consequences defy all calculation. And yet even

in Rome there do not lack pious minds which, undisturbed by these terrible dangers, desire to see the
insolent enterprise carried through, in the belief that
the prevalent corruption can only be overcome by a life
and death struggle. " Quod medicina non sanat, ferrum
sanat."

SIXTY-FIRST LETTER.

Rome, June 24, 1870.—Rome is just now like an episcopal lazar-house, so great is the number of the prelates who are sick and suffering and confined to their bed or their chamber. And still greater is the number of those who feel worn out and impatiently long to be gone. But there are persons here who calculate thus—that the Italians, Spaniards and South Americans are accustomed to the heat, and bear it very well, and as to the Germans, French and North Americans—"vile damnum si interierint."

Guidi's speech still occupies men's minds, and forms the topic of conversation in conciliar circles. Men are astonished at the courage of a Cardinal in daring so directly to contradict the Pope. While Pius has word written to Paris that "for many centuries no one doubted the Pope's infallibility," Guidi declares it to be an invention of the fifteenth century.

The following account of the dialogue between the Pope and the Cardinal is current at Rome, and it seems to rest on the authority of Pius himself, who is notoriously fond of telling every one he meets how he has lectured this or that dignitary :—

Guidi, on being summoned by the Pope directly after his speech, was greeted with the words, "You are my enemy, you are the coryphæus of my opponents, ungrateful towards my person; you have propounded heretical doctrine." *Guidi.*—"My speech is in the hands of the Presidents, if your Holiness will read it, and detect what is supposed to be heretical in it. I gave it at once to the under-secretary (*sottosecretario*) that people might not be able to say anything had been interpolated into it." *The Pope.*—"You have given great offence to the majority of the Council; all five Presidents are against you and are displeased." *Guidi.* —"Some material error may have escaped me, but certainly not a formal one : I have simply stated the doctrine of tradition and of St. Thomas. *The Pope.*— "*La tradizione son' io—vi farò far nuovamente la professione di fede.*" *Guidi.*—"I am and remain subject to the authority of the Holy See, but I ventured to discuss a question not yet made an article of faith; if your Holiness decides it to be such in a Constitution, I shall certainly not dare to oppose it." *The Pope.*— "The value of your speech may be measured by those whom it has pleased. Who has been eager to testify to you his joy? That Bishop Strossmayer who is my personal enemy has embraced you; you are in collusion with him." *Guidi.*—"I don't know him, and have never before spoken to him." *The Pope.*—"It is clear you have spoken so as to please the world, the Liberals, the Revolution, and the Government of Florence." *Guidi.*—"Holy Father, have the goodness to have my speech given you."

The same afternoon a Spanish Bishop belonging to the extremest Infallibilists said, "Absque dubio facies Concilii est immutata. Oportet huic sermoni serio studere." When Guidi asked how the Cardinals had taken his speech, Mathieu replied, "Cum seriâ silentiosâ approbatione," on which Guidi observed, "Sunt quidam qui idem mecum sentiunt, sed deest illis animi fortitudo."

"La tradizione son' io"—it would be impossible to give a briefer, more pregnant or more epigrammatic description of the whole system which is now to be made dominant than is contained in those few words. All

the members of the *Civiltà*, the thick volumes of Schrader, Weninger and the Jesuits of Laach are outdone by
this clear and simple utterance. Pius will take rank in
history with the men who have known how by a happy
inspiration to throw a great thought into the most
adequate form of words, which impresses it for ever in-
delibly on the memory. The formula is worthy to be
classed with the equally pregnant saying of Boniface VIII.,
" The Pope holds all rights locked up in his breast."
It is bruited about here from mouth to mouth, and the
analogy of Louis XIV., which inevitably occurs to everybody, reaches even further. Every day since I have
witnessed the drama being enacted here, has the saying suggested itself to me, " L'Église, c'est moi." Any
one who would form a judgment of the state of things
here should be recommended above all to read a work
like, *e.g.*, Lemontey's *Essai sur l'établissement monar-
chique de Louis* XIV., or the instructions of the King for
the Dauphin. One sees there how absolute sovereignty,
the intoxicating sense of irresponsible power—and
spiritual absolutism is far more overpowering than
political—leads almost of necessity to the notion of
infallibility and divine enlightenment. Louis XIV. says
seriously and drily to his son, " As God's representa-

tive we have part in the divine knowledge as well as the divine authority."[1] And he warns him that all his own errors had arisen from his too great modesty in giving ear to extraneous advisers.   For eight hundred years the question has been disputed, why the Popes are so short-lived, and the phenomenon has been ascribed to a special divine dispensation which removes them betimes, that they may not be morally poisoned by too long enjoy-ment of their dignity—" ne malitia mutaret intellec-tum."

The minority perceive, on a calmer consideration, that the two canons proposed by Guidi would not provide sufficient security for the episcopate taking part in the teaching office of the Church according to the integrity of her constitution.   The second indeed, like a well-aimed arrow, hits the mark.   It calls the thing by its right name, and anathematizes the purely personal infallibility of the Pope, independent of the consent of the Church and resting on direct divine inspiration, as a heresy, which it unquestionably is in the eyes of every theologian who knows anything of the Church and her tradition ; but then, after the Pope has so

[1] " Il est sans doute de certaines fonctions où, tenant, pour ainsi dire, la place de Dieu, nous semblons être participants de sa connaissance, aussi bien que de son autorité," etc.—Lemontey, p. 151 (éd. de Bruxelles).

openly and expressly committed himself to precisely this view of the Church, it is thought impossible here in Rome, and close to the Vatican, to throw an anathema in his face. And besides the expression in the first canon, that the consentient " consilium Ecclesiæ " is requisite for an infallible papal utterance, is open to the same charge of vagueness as the notorious and much-abused *ex cathedrâ*, and could as easily be explained away into the mere arbitrary caprice of the Pope. It would always rest with him in the last resort to maintain " ex certâ scientiâ " that the " consilium Ecclesiæ " agreed with his own judgment.

A remodelling of the fourth canon has been undertaken, but the new formula is not known. It is however much talked of among the Bishops, and the general view is that it remains substantially unchanged, and still contains the personal infallibility of the Pope independently of the Church. Manning had said that the utmost regard that was possible should be paid to the views of the Opposition in the alteration of the chapter. And so those Bishops still hope for the accomplishment of their desires who, like Ketteler and Melchers, entreat that only one, however sterile, verbal concession may be made, so as to give them a bridge on which to pass over the gulf safely into the camp of the majority.

I lately heard a Roman layman say that what most surprised him among the many wonderful things he had seen here was the contempt for the Catholic Church which prevails here. For that contempt could not be more emphatically expressed than by the Pope appropriating to himself what according to the ancient doctrine belongs to her, and declaring himself the sole and exclusive organ of the Holy Ghost. It is the same here universally; when one talks with a Roman, the *Curia*, the Pope, is everything, and the Church nothing but the "contribuens plebs." My informant thought it was easy enough to understand the view of born Romans, but difficult to give any rational account of the attitude of the episcopal majority, for it must be clear to every one of them that the promulgation of the new dogma would destroy irrevocably all episcopal independence of Rome, and strip the nimbus from the brow of the Bishop who is a successor of the Apostles. I observed to him that in Romance countries this primitive idea of the episcopate had long since vanished, as he might easily convince himself by asking the next Italian peasant or shopkeeper he met what was his notion of a Bishop. And five-sixths of the majority belong to these countries.

In the Congregation of June 20 the Deputation put up one of its members, Bishop d'Avanzo of Calvi and Teano, to speak. For there was urgent need of promptly meeting the great scandal given by Guidi, and deterring any Cardinal who might be so disposed from following his example. The speaker allowed that in dogmatic decrees the tradition of the Church must be consulted and the Holy Ghost invoked, but how this was to be done was left to the judgment of the Pope. By his second canon Guidi passed over " ad aliena non Catholica castra," exceeded all Gallicans and wanted—he, an Italian, a Dominican and a Cardinal—to canonize Gallicanism. A shudder ran through the ranks of all the Italians who live between Ferrara and Malta, but they remembered for their comfort that the unworthy son of the peninsula had been for some years professor at Vienna, and it was obvious that the German malaria he had caught there was the cause of this matricidal heresy.

Guidi had said that the admonition to Peter to confirm his brethren pre-supposed something to be confirmed, *i.e.*, that the Pope only confirmed the doctrine already maintained by the Bishops. To this d'Avanzo answered that it was utterly uncatholic, and one must rather begin from above and not from below, and ascribe the authorship and initiation of doctrine to the Pope, who was immediately inspired by the Holy Ghost; "causa princeps infallibilitatis est assistentia Spiritûs Sancti." And here followed a statement that must be given word for word : "Supervacaneum est omne additamentum, nulla emendatio in decreto et canone schematis acceptatur ; nulla conditio, nulla limitatio admittetur per deputationem ; inutilis est igitur omnis labor ? 'Animalis homo non percipit quod de cœlo est.'"[1]   To say the definition was inopportune was merely pandering to the corrupt portion of society, and especially to the tribe of Government officials. The speaker added emphatically : "Satis fit servis Satanæ, qui sunt gubernantes, negantes ordinem supernaturalem—ergo Decretum est opportunum. In Pontifice Spiritus Domini vivit et agit, Pontifex ergo hôc Spiritu agente errare non potest." It became known at once in the Council that this declaration, which annihilated so many hopes, had been made in the name and by special command of the Pope, and that "the animal man" meant the Opposition.

[1] 1 Cor. ii. 14.

The two next speakers were the titular Patriarchs Ballerini and Valerga. The first said with notable frankness, " Were we to let personal infallibility drop, we should destroy the obedience due to the Pope and exalt ourselves against God Himself." In other words, the Vice-God orders us to declare him infallible, and of course we obey implicitly.

Valerga's appearance was the beginning of a comedy, which was repeated in subsequent sittings. He wanted to prove papal infallibility by inferences from the Florentine decree, which was received by all; but he was twice interrupted by the Presidents for not keeping to the question. He thereupon left the tribune, not without remarks being made by Opposition Bishops that they saw this treatment was not reserved for them only. The same thing happened on June 22 to Bishop Apuzzo of Sorrento and Archbishop Spaccapietra. On the 20th, towards the end of the debate, Archbishop MacHale of Tuam in Ireland spoke with great severity against the decree, the fatal consequences of which he seems to appreciate better than most of his Irish colleagues. Bishop Apuzzo reminded the Hungarians that they once had a primate (Szelepcsenyi, a pupil of the Jesuits) who had summoned a synod to condemn the

Gallican Articles of 1682, and that quite recently a Provincial Synod at Colocza had used language of very infallibilist sound. Haynald took part in that Synod, and he, as well as Rauscher, to whom the same reproach was addressed, had already observed that it would not do to put a strictly logical interpretation on mere complimentary phrases. In the course of his speech Apuzzo became still more abusive. "Those are the sons of Satan," he exclaimed at last, "who say the Bishops are judges in the Church. No! we are but poor sinners." At the same time he proposed a supplement still more peremptory than the chapter. Spaccapietra came to grief in Church history, which is more grossly mishandled at Rome and in the Council Hall, when it is appealed to at all, than anywhere else. This time St. Polycarp's yielding to the Pope about the observance of Easter—he notoriously did just the reverse—was to serve as an example to the Opposition. When the speaker went on to utter fierce invectives against Cardinal Guidi, he was interrupted. He declared he had only something to say against the schismatics, but the President closed his mouth in theatrical fashion saying, " Cedat verbum tintinnabulo." So he left the rostrum.

Men breathed more freely when, after these hollow declamations, two British Bishops brought the clear practical sense of their race and country to bear on the question and the previous discussion of it. The first of them, Archbishop Errington, who was formerly Cardinal Wiseman's coadjutor but soon got out of favour at Rome, pointedly characterized the vicious nature of the whole transaction; there were speeches on both sides, one affirming, another denying, and no one could feel that he had refuted anything or advanced his cause the least by his words. The Deputation alone had the privilege of referring to the speeches and examining them, and it belonged to the majority, not to the Council; "how it was formed, we know." As a tribunal the Council was bound to institute a calm and searching investigation of facts, tradition and testimonies, and for this only one means was available, which was employed at the former great Councils including the Tridentine, to form deputations from both parties for earnest conference, where scientific examination might take the place of rhetorical harangues—from both parties, for it was idle with Bilio to bid them ignore the existence of two parties. " Modo in hôc Concilio fit aliter et illud ineptissime," he concluded, and he proposed the formula, " Magisterium universalis Ecclesiæ est infallibile."

The next speech, of Vitelleschi, who is Archbishop of Osimo but has never been in his diocese, though it is so near, left no impression ; it was an exhortation to vote infallibility unanimously.   And then followed Archbishop Conolly of Halifax with a speech such as has seldom been heard here.   " Thrice," he said, " have I asked for proof from Scripture according to its authentic interpretation, from Tradition and from Councils, that the Bishops of the Catholic Church ought to be excluded from the definition of dogmas ; but my request has not been complied with, and now I adjure you, like the blind man on the way to Jericho, to give us sight that we may believe.   Hitherto we have recognised the strongest motive for the credibility of Catholic doctrine in the general consent of the Church notified through the collective episcopate ; this has been our shield against all external assailants, and by this powerful magnet we have drawn hundreds of thousands into the Church.   Is this our invincible weapon of attack and defence now to be broken and trampled under foot, and the thousand-headed episcopate with the millions of faithful at its back to shrink into the voice and witness of a single man? Let the Deputation prove to us that it has really been always the belief of the Church that the Pope is everything and the Bishops nothing. The Council of Jerusalem did not adopt the formula of Peter but of John, who spoke before him, and in the Apostles' Creed we do not say ' Credo in Petrum et successores ejus,' but ' Credo in unam Ecclesiam Catholicam.' We Bishops have no right to renounce for ourselves and our successors the hereditary and original rights of the episcopate, to renounce the promise of Christ, ' I am with you to the end of the world.' But now they want to reduce us to nullities, to tear the noblest jewel from our pontifical breastplate, to deprive us of the highest prerogative of our office, and to transform the whole Church and the Bishops with it into a rabble of blind men, among whom is one alone who sees, so that they must shut their eyes and believe whatever he tells them."

Was it confidence of victory that moved the Legates to allow the bold and free-minded American, who spoke with the full weight of a deep and laboriously attained conviction, to bring these earnest words to a close without interruption, after they had recently reduced three of their own speakers in succession to silence? I know not. It was the unenviable lot of the Archbishop of Granada, Monzon y Martins Benvenuto, to follow Conolly. No one expects at this Council ideas or facts from a Spaniard, but merely bombast and abject protestations of homage. Since they no longer have Queen Isabella and the throne has been vacant, these prelates have transferred their undivided devotion to the Pope, and among the reptiles here they are the most cringing after the Neapolitans. Monzon said he thirsted for new dogmas, and the infallibility of the Pope did not satisfy him; he earnestly desired a second dogma, viz., the divine and inviolable nature of the States of the Church.

It was reported two days ago that Cardinal Morichini, who formerly as nuncio breathed some German air, intends to speak in Guidi's sense, but since the scene between the Pope and Guidi has become known, it is generally thought that no Cardinal will be so foolhardy as to express any other opinion in Council than that of the inspired Pope. Meanwhile there are new speakers enrolled, among whom are Haynald, Strossmayer, the Bishops of Dijon, Constantine, Tarentaise, etc. The number considerably exceeds a hundred, but Errington has only too much reason for saying the debates are like a boy riding a rocking-horse—movement without advance.

You may imagine what capital the Jesuits make out of the speech of the Dominican Guidi. They are the supreme and thoroughly devoted body-guard of the Roman See, and can alone be implicitly trusted. And in fact nobody thinks it possible that a Jesuit should speak in Council like Guidi, as neither does any one here credit a Jesuit with sincere conviction of what he says ; it is always known beforehand what he will say on any question, viz., what the Order considers for its interest and imposes as a corporate doctrine on its individual members. The sons of Ignatius remember now that the Dominicans have never been trustworthy. As early as 1303 the French appeal from Pope Boniface VIII. to a General Council was supported by 130 Dominicans at Paris, and at the Councils of Constance and Basle they took the most active part in the measures against papal omnipotence and in framing the mischievous canons of the fourth and fifth sessions of Constance ; they joined Savonarola in opposing Alexander VI. and preferred being burned to submitting. And again they gave powerful aid in France to the establishment of the Gallican doctrine. And what, say the

Jesuits, is the great Church history of the Dominican Natalis Alexander but an arsenal from which to this day the opponents of infallibility get their weapons?

Preparations are already being made for the festivities which are to accompany the promulgation of the new dogma. The Romans—the native population—cannot understand why a part of the Bishops resist it so stoutly, and no less mysterious to them is the fiery zeal of foreigners, especially Frenchmen, in its favour. Their view is that infallibility, as being likely to bring large sums of money into Rome, is certainly a profitable and praiseworthy affair, and they are accordingly ready for noisy demonstrations of joy. Plenty of sky-rockets will go up, there will be illuminations, the pillars of the churches will be clothed in red damask according to the local usage, and numberless wax-candles will be burnt. Some enthusiasts think the fountain of Trevi will that day flow with wine instead of water, and it is hoped that at nightfall a transparency of the famous picture painted by the Pope's command to represent his infallibility will be shown to the faithful people. And next time the French Veuillotists choose to cry in the streets " Long live the infallible Pope !" some Romans will join the cry.

The festivities will absorb large sums of money, and the financiers are not without anxiety ; for however lucrative the new dogma may prove by and bye, for the moment it is an unproductive capital, and the annual deficit of thirty million franks cannot be covered by promises of future prosperity. It has now been determined, since the huge bankruptcy of Langrand-Dumonceaux, who had been named a Roman Count, has created some alarm, to take in the Rhenish and Westphalian nobility with the ecclesiastical unions there as sureties, and thus to negotiate a loan of twenty million franks " al pari." The noble presidents of the unions are said to have already signified their willingness.

The rewards of those for whom there are no Cardinal's hats are already under consideration. It is said that about a hundred Bishops will be named "assistants at the Pontifical Throne" in recognition of their services. Others will be made "protonotarii apostolici;" most of them only "protonotarii sopranumerarii non participanti." Several priests especially zealous for the good cause will be made titular Bishops, and others " prelati domestici" and "monsignori," or " camerieri segreti," etc. Then there are the distinctions by means of colours, and soon we shall be able to measure a man's zeal for the new dogma at the first glance by seeing whether he wears the "abito paonazzo" or violet or scarlet. And there are exceptional decorations for use in church kept in reserve, like what the Archbishop of Algiers had given him.

The attitude of Ketteler creates astonishment and is studied as a riddle to which no solution can be found. The Pope said to-day, " Io non capisco, cosa vuole quel Ketteler, che un giorno distribuisce delle brochure contro di me e contro della mia infallibilità, e che il giorno dopo scrive nei giornali che sia pieno di devozione per me, e che crede alla mia infallibilità, pare che sia proprio mezzo," and thereupon he made a gesture indicating that the Bishop of Mayence was not quite right in his head.

In fact Ketteler is the only man here who perplexes a reporter or historian. He has a work printed and distributed, in which infallibility is declared to be an unscriptural and unecclesiastical doctrine, and he says in his attack on me that according to his view Scripture and Tradition (*i.e.*, the two only sources for the Church's faith) do not justify its dogmatic definition. Yet he affirms that he was always an infallibilist believer and will soon be more so than ever. It is difficult to report on the performances of a theological gymnast who seems rather to balance himself in mid air than to have firm ground under his feet. Here it is thought that he follows the counsel of his powerful patrons in the German College and the Gesù, who have made him understand that the new dogma will certainly be proclaimed, and that he would do well to change as speedily as he can from an inopportunist to a zealous advocate and executor of the decree. He has lately been reproached by an influential theologian (Gass) with making his own Church worse than it is by his doctrine that the Catholic Church knows of no duty of obedience against conscience. It will certainly never occur to me, now or at any future time, to have recourse to the conscience of Bishop Ketteler; that would indeed be the last refuge one would fly to!

SIXTY-SECOND LETTER.

Rome, June 30, 1870.—In the middle ages ecclesiastical controversies were decided by the ordeal of the cross. The representatives of both parties placed themselves before a large cross, with their arms stretched out in the form of a cross, and he whose arms first sank, or who fell exhausted to the ground, was conquered. The heat and the Roman fever have replaced this ordeal at the Council. The process which is to test the result has been going on for six weeks, and the majority will evidently come out of it with flying colours. It is composed chiefly of Italians and Spaniards of both hemispheres, who can bear such things much better than northerners, and as it is four times as numerous as the minority, gaps made in its ranks by sickness and death are soon filled up, and the phalanx remains firmly closed, while the Opposition receives the news of the sickness or departure of one of its members as heralding its growing discouragement and final defeat. How well the authorities understand the inestimable value of this new ally, the heat and mephitic exhalations, is shown by the laconic but significant words of the papal journalist, Veuillot, in his 125th Letter on the Council, " Et si la définition ne peut mûrir qu'au soleil, eh bien, on grillera." As before, so now again Roman orthodoxy seems to have called fire to its aid, and for Bishops, who do not wish to be roasted according to Veuillot's wish, flight is the only alternative.

Cardinal Guidi has received the most peremptory orders from the Pope to make a formal retractation of his speech in Council. The form and occasion of making it he may arrange with the Legates. He has already had an interview with Bilio. The Pope has forbidden him to receive visits, that he may be free to consider without distraction the greatness of his error. Solitary confinement is adopted in the penal legislation of other countries too as an efficient instrument of reformation. Guidi has told the Presidents that he is ready to give an explanation of his speech in a public sitting, if they will announce beforehand that he does so by the Pope's desire ; but he can make no retractation. Jandel, the Dominican General, intends now to deliver a speech

in refutation of Guidi's theory, which has been composed
for him in the Gesù.   Many think that Guidi will be
deterred from letting things come to extremities by the
terrible example of Cardinal Andrea, who was worried
to death.   A Cardinal, who lives out of the Roman
States, may maintain a certain independence or even
opposition, as the precedent of Cardinal Noailles shows,
but in Rome this is impossible.   As Archbishop of
Bologna Guidi would be under the protection of the
Italian Government, but thither he will never be allowed
to return.

Heat, fever and intrigues—this is a brief description
of the state of Rome, as regards the Council.   The heat
and pestilential miasmas are unendurable for foreigners
from the north ; already six French and four American
Bishops have been obliged to save their lives by departure, and of those who stay in Rome a third are unable
from their bodily ailments to attend the sittings.   A
Petition to the Pope is now in course of signature
praying for a prorogation, on account of the danger
to the lives of many foreign and aged prelates at this
season of the year.   I give you the text, but will
observe that I hear most refuse to sign, some thinking
the case a hopeless one, others of very ill repute in the

Vatican fearing their adherence would only make it more so. The Petition runs thus—

"Beatissime Pater ! Episcopi infrascripti, tam proprio quam aliorum permultorum Patrum nomine a benignitate S. V. reverenter, fiducialiter et enixe expostulant, ut ea, quæ sequuntur, paterne dignetur excipere :

"Ad Patres in Concilio Lateranensi v. sedentes hoc habebat, die XVII. Junii, Leo X. Papa 'Quia jam temporis dispositione . . . concedimus' simulque Concilium Pontifex ad tempus autumnale prorogabat.—Pejor certe inpræsentiarum conditio nostra est. Calor æstivus, jam desinente mense Junio, nimius est, et de die in diem intolerabilior crescit; unde RR. Patrum, inter quos tot seniores sunt, annorum pondere pressi, et laboribus confecti, valetudo graviter periclitatur.—Timentur inprimis febres, quibus magis obnoxii sunt extranei hujusce temperiei regionis non assuefacti.

"Quidquid vero tentaverit et feliciter perfecerit liberalitas S. V., ut non paucis episcopis hospitia bona præberentur, plerique tamen relegati sunt in habitationes nimis angustas, sine aëre, calidissimas omninoque insalubres. Unde jam plures episcopi ob infirmitatem corporis abire coacti sunt; multi etiam Romæ infirmantur et Concilio adesse nequeunt, ut patet ex tot sedibus quæ in aulâ conciliari vacuæ apparent.

"Antequam igitur magis ac magis creverit ægrotorum numerus, quorum plures periculo hic occumbendi exponerentur, instantissime postulamus, B. Pater, ut S. V. aliquam Concilii suspensionem, quæ post festum S. Petri convenienter inciperet, concedere dignetur.

"Etenim, B. Pater, cum centum et viginti episcopi nomen suum dederint, ut in tanti momenti quæstione audiantur, evidens est, discussionem non posse intra paucos dies præcipitari, nisi magno rerum ac pacis religiosæ dispendio. Multo magis congruum esset atque necessarium brevem aliquam, ob ingruentes gravissimos æstatis calores, Concilio suspensionem dari.

"Nova vero Synodi periodus ad primam diem mensis Octobris forsitan indicari posset.

"S. V., si hoc, ut fidenter speramus, concesserit, gratissimos sensus nobis populisque nostris excitabit, utpote quæ gravissimæ omnium necessitati consuluerit.

"Pedes S. V. devote osculantes nosmet dicimus S. V. humillimos et obsequentissimos famulos in Christo filios."

Attempts have already been made by word of mouth to secure some compassion from the Pope for the severe sufferings of the Bishops, but wholly in vain. His comments on the members of the minority, if rightly reported here, are so irritable and bitter that I scruple to mention them. But I must relate what occurred to-day at a farewell audience given to some Maltese Knights, who had come to exercise their privilege of keeping guard at an Œcumenical Council. The Pope first turned to an English member of the Order and wished him success in the scheme for introducing it into England, and then expressed his sympathy for that nation in his confident expectation of the speedy and innumerable conversions promised by Manning, adding the remark that the Italians were somewhat volatile. And the mildness of the expression, compared with former ebullitions of anger, proved that the infallibilist line of the Italian Bishops had covered in his eyes the political sins of the nation. But then he turned to the Germans, who were present in the greatest number, with the words, " I piu cattivi sono i Tedeschi, sono i piu cattivi di tutti, lo spirito Tedesco a guastato tutto." Even that was not enough, but a Bohemian knight who was present had to listen to a stream of invectives against the conduct of Cardinal Schwarzenberg, which made a very unpleasant impression on him.

As a French Bishop said to me to-day, it is a humiliating spectacle to see a man who, at the very moment when he is assimilating his office to the Godhead, recklessly displays the little weaknesses and passions which people are generally ashamed to expose to view.

It was clearly shown in the Congregations of 23d and 25th June that the majority only continue to tolerate the speeches of the Opposition as an almost unendurable nuisance. Loud murmurs alternated with the ringing of the Presidents' bell. When Bishop Losanna of Biella, the senior of the Council, was speaking against burdening the Christian world with the new dogma, the Legate tried to ring him down. He entreated that at least out of regard for his advanced age they would let him finish the little he still had to say. In vain. The Legate went on ringing and the Bishop speaking, so that the assembly for some time was regaled with a duet between a bell and an—of course inaudible—human voice.

In the Congregation of the 23d Bishop Landriot of Rheims made a long speech in the interests of mediation and mutual concessions, which showed careful study, but was received with every sign of displeasure by the majority : he also proposed what Errington had wanted, that a Commission formed from both parties should examine the whole tradition on the subject and report the result to the Council. At this cries of " Oho, oho !" rose from the majority. Discouraged and intimidated the Archbishop concluded with the declaration that, if the Pope pleased to confirm the *Schema,* he submitted by anticipation, at which the faces which had grown black brightened up again and the apology for the French Church which he ended with was condoned.

The most remarkable speeches in the sitting of 25th June were those of the Bishop Legate of Trieste and Ketteler of Mayence. The first had the courage to say plainly that the manipulation of Scripture texts, which were pressed into the service of the new dogma in glaring contradiction to the authentic interpretation of the Church, was a sin. Ketteler's speech created the greatest sensation from its decided tone, and its not betraying the contradiction in which he seems to find himself involved after his public declarations in Germany. I must indeed reckon on my report again displeasing and angering him, for this " mobile ingegno usato ad amar e a disamar in un punto " is wont to take it very ill if his bold transitions do not leave the same impression on others which floats before his own

memory. But I will fulfil my duty as historian of the
Council in spite of this. Ketteler urged that nobody
had alleged any clear evidence for a personal and
separate infallibility of the Pope being really contained
in Scripture, Tradition and the consciousness of all
Churches; it was only the opinion of a certain school—
"placita cujusdam scholæ" he repeated several times
emphatically. The Pope certainly had the right of
proscribing doctrines which contradicted the dogmas
already decided by the Church, but by no means the
totally different right of formulating a new dogma without the consent of the episcopate. It was the greatest
absurdity to believe or say "Pontificem in pectoris sui
scrinio omnem traditionem repositam et infusam habere." At these words murmurs arose in the assembly;
all had shortly before heard and repeated to one another
the Pope's assertion, "La tradizione son' io." Then
Ketteler attacked the theory of Cardinal Cajetan, the
well-known first opponent of Luther, that Peter alone
among the Apostles had a "potestas ordinaria" to
be transmitted to his successors, while the "potestas
specialis" conferred by Christ on the rest expired at
their death, so that the Bishops are not successors of
the Apostles but derive all their authority from the

Pope. This mischievous system had been adopted by a certain school, and the *Schema* before them was drawn up in accordance with it and in contradiction to all Catholic tradition. It placed the Bishops in the same relation to the Pope as priests occupied towards Bishops, which was unheard of. He protested against the whole system, and desired that in every dogmatic decree Holy Scripture and Tradition should be taken full account of: the Pope needed the co-operation of the Bishops as representatives of tradition. It was utterly wrong to believe that the *depositum fidei* was committed to the Pope alone.

If the force and clearness of Ketteler's speech evoked deep and serious reflection, an amusing episode occurred at the close of the sitting. The Irish Bishop Keane of Cloyne ascended the tribune. There is a story told of a German city whose sapient councillors carried the sunlight out of the street in sacks to light their town-hall, which had no windows; and so Keane informed his hearers that St. Peter brought the whole body of tradition with him to Rome well stored up; here and here alone it was still kept, and every Pope took what was required from the stock which he possessed as a whole genuine and entire.

Those who wish to prosecute pyschological and ethical studies should come to Rome. Here they may observe how the three great powers of the world, as St. Augustine calls them, " Errores, amores, terrores," work together in full harmony and activity ; the last especially will aid the victory of the first—for how long He only knows who rules the destiny of man.

SIXTY-THIRD LETTER.

Rome, July 2, 1870.—The Pope's reported answer
to those who spoke to him of the sufferings of the
Bishops and their danger of death, and the consequent
need for proroguing the Council, is passing from mouth
to mouth. I should consider it a sin to publish it.
Were it true, one would have to treat the man who
could so speak as the Orsini treated Boniface VIII. in
his last days. If it is not true, it is very remarkable
that the Romans have no hesitation in circulating it
and really credit their Pope with it. This and the
disdain bordering on simple contempt with which the
Romans look down on the Bishops are among the
indelible impressions they will take back with them
over the Alps.

In the sitting of 28th June Bishop Vitali of Ferentino
in the Roman States first inveighed against the long
speeches of the Bishops, and then broke into a dithy-

rambic panegyric on his master, the Pope, who, like
the Emperor Titus, was the "deliciæ orbis terrarum."
He was somewhat abruptly interrupted by the Legates
in the middle of his rhapsody.   Ginoulhiac, Archbishop
of Lyons, who is the most learned member of the French
episcopate after Maret, next delivered an ably and
carefully composed speech, which was not interrupted.
He appealed to the words and example of former
Popes who had acknowledged—like *e.g.*, Celestine I. in
430—that they were not masters of the faith but only
guardians of the traditional doctrine, and that not singly
but in unison with all Churches and their Bishops, as
was clearly expressed in the decree.   Pius VI., strong
as was the pressure put upon him by France, delayed a
long time the issue of the decree against the civil Constitution of the clergy of 1790, because, as he wrote to
the King, the Pope must first conscientiously ascertain
how the faithful will receive his decision.   But a large
section of Catholics were not at all disposed to receive
this *Schema*, and the decree would evidently evoke the
bitterest hostility to the Church where it did not already
exist, and immensely increase it where it did.   Pius VI.
then said that, if the Roman See, the centre of the
Church, lost its authority through exaggerating its claims,

all was lost. Pius IX. should take care that this doctrine did not become a snare to innumerable Catholics. He concluded by commending the formula of St. Antoninus, which requires the consent of the episcopate.

In the sitting of 30th June a member of the almost extinct third party among the French, Sergent, Bishop of Quimper or Cornouailles, came forward. He proposed adding to the *Schema*, which might then be accepted, words requiring the co-operation for decisions on faith of the "episcopi, sive dispersi sive in Concilio congregati." But he insisted on the superiority of the Pope to a Council according to the decree of Leo. x.,— or, as he said, the fifth Lateran Council, and defended the order of business imposed on this Council by Pius IX. But here he touched on a very sore place ; the Bishops sit here under the continual conviction of having their hands tied in an illegitimate and tyrannical fashion, and knowing that the order of business is in direct contradiction to the independence of the ancient Councils. The Legates must have felt that the Opposition would say, "Hæc excusatio est accusatio," and that it would give the requisite handle for again renewing their written protests by word of mouth now at the decisive moment. Sergent was therefore called to order.

After the Bishop of Aversa, who spoke as an ordinary infallibilist, Bishop Martin of Paderborn came forward and created a sensation. A German infallibilist, like Martin, who was not kneaded and dressed in the Jesuit school, is an interesting and curious phenomenon of itself, and produces somewhat the same impression as an European who voluntarily lives among savages and adopts their language and customs. But Bishop Martin's appearance was remarkable on other grounds also. It was long since any one had been heard in the Council who spoke in so angry a tone and with such noise and visible endeavour to supplement his stammering utterance by the action of hands and feet. It was a difficult labour that Martin achieved, like a singer drowning his own voice, and doubly meritorious in these melting days. And here I may make a remark that should have been made before : the Hall has really gained lately in acoustic qualities, from having an awning stretched over it which acts as a sounding-board.

Martin shouted into the Hall that the personal infallibility of every Pope was inseparable from the primacy, for the Pope was the supreme legislator, and therefore he must of necessity be divinely preserved from all error. The Bishops of the minority were amazed at this statement, for none of them had expected a German Bishop to declare the whole code of the Inquisition, as promulgated by the Popes from Innocent III. to Paul V., infallible and inspired. But there was still better behind. Two German witnesses for infallibility were cited, Dr. Luther, on account of his letter to the Pope in 1518, and Dr. Pichler of 1870. Up to 1763 all Germans were stanch infallibilists, but then Febronianism came in and for a time obscured this light of pure doctrine, which had previously shone so bright in Catholic Germany. But an orthodox reaction had followed, thanks to the excellent catechism of the Jesuit Deharbe, the Provincial Synod of Cologne and several Pastorals. Martin then referred to Döllinger, and reproached him with having in his earlier works—which were not named —taught papal infallibility, whereas he now assailed it. The Bishop, who is a member of the Deputation, then proposed a formula he had devised, "Traditioni inhærentes docemus Pontificem, cum universalem Ecclesiam docet, vi divinæ assistentiæ errare non posse." But that was not enough, without smiting down the opponents of the doctrine by a solemn anathema, as follows, "Si quis dixerit non nisi accedente consensu Episcoporum Romanum Pontificem errare non posse, anathema sit." He moreover agreed with Spalding and Dechamps that parish priests and others having cure of souls should be required by a special admonition addressed to them to impress this doctrine of infallibility on their people often and emphatically from the pulpit.

The speech was delivered in the tone and manner of a confessor dealing with a hardened sinner in his last moments, and the Germans, from whose ranks the speaker had issued,—men like Rauscher, Haynald, Strossmayer, Hefele—sat shamefaced with their eyes on the ground, while the delight of the Italians and Spaniards could be read on their countenances at this humiliation of the nation which prides itself on the superior culture of its clergy.   But they were surprised at Martin's concluding declaration that no doubt in Germany great dangers for the Church would follow from the promulgation of the doctrine.   It was mentioned in the Council Hall that, in a widely circulated school-book which had passed through eleven or twelve editions, Martin had taught the exact reverse of the doctrine he now so noisily and peremptorily maintained; but then it was observed in excuse for him that the heterodoxies of this book, though it bore his name, were no fault of his, as he had simply transcribed it from the papers of the late Professor Diekhoff, which were left in his charge.

SIXTY-FOURTH LETTER.

Rome, July 5, 1870.—Rome is an excellent school for Bishops ; a course of seven months at the Council produces wonderful results. One illusion after another is laid aside and an insight gained into the working of the huge machine and the forces that put it in motion, and the Bishops learn at last, though it be laboriously and not without tears, why they were summoned and what services alone are demanded of them. The historian Pachymeres relates that, when the people of Constantinople demanded a Council in 1282 in order to judge the unionist Patriarch, Bekkus, Bishop Theoktistus of Adrianople said that they treated Bishops like wooden spits on which Bekkus might be roasted, and which might then be thrown into the fire.[1] A very similar feeling has come over many Bishops here ; they know that if they say *Non placet* at last, they will be cast into the fire, after they have helped by their

---

[1] *Pachym.* II. 20, ed. Bonn.

reluctant practical recognition of both the first and second order of business—destructive as both are to all real freedom—to forge the new spiritual yoke. And then they find their schoolroom a very narrow and uncomfortable one, and have at last discovered that it looks very like a prison cell.

It is but a game of moves and counter-moves as on a chessboard, only that no one dares to incur the penalty of high treason by saying " Check to the king," or lifting a finger for such an audacious move. The minority were so confounded and irritated by the abrupt closing of the general debate, because they hoped to prolong it till prorogation became inevitable. For nobody doubted in April and May that this would follow at the end of June, and the notion was sedulously fostered by the official staff of the Council—the Legates and Secretary Fessler—and by the Pope himself. It is not long since Pius said to a French Bishop, " It would be barbarity on my part to want to keep the Bishops here in July." And thus the Opposition, whenever they were shaken and disturbed by some violent act, let matters be hushed up and never gave any practical effect to their protests and complaints. But now the Court party say that it would indeed be tyrannical cruelty to keep us here, under ordinary circumstances, imprisoned in this furnace full of fevers, but it is justified by the abnormal situation. The grand and saving act of the infallibilist definition, which is to quicken the whole Church with new powers of life and introduce the golden age of absolute ecclesiastical dominion, cannot any longer be held in suspense. "You surely will not wish," said Cardinal de Angelis to a Bishop who was urging the necessity of a prorogation, "that the Pope, after spending so many thousand scudi on the Bishops, should now be left alone in the Vatican without any recompense." And Antonelli thinks the Bishops have only themselves to blame for their present suffering condition; why have they wasted so much time in speeches?

Since that shocking saying of the Pope's, which I referred to in my last letter, has became known here, the Bishops have abandoned as hopeless the design of making a direct appeal to him for the prorogation of the Council on the score of the health and lives of its members. And this conviction has been further strengthened by the insolence of the Court theologian, Louis Veuillot. "Let yourselves be roasted, since it is only through this fiery ordeal that the precious wine of infallibility can be matured," he exclaims to them, and they know now that they are inside a door over which the inscription is written

" Lasciate ogni speranza voi ch' intrate."

And now there is a new cause of alarm. It is said —perhaps the report is spread on purpose—that at last no Bishop will be allowed to depart till he has signed a bond laid before him declaring his entire and unconditional submission. We actually hear that, by a recent decision, leave of absence is only to be given to the Bishops in case of serious illness, that is, when they are no longer equal to the journey. Several prelates therefore have already inquired of the ambassadors of their Governments, what means of protection they could afford them in case of such violence being exercised. The ambassadors will be obliged to write home for further instructions, as it seems no such case had been foreseen as possible to occur. But so many astonishing and seemingly impossible things have happened during the last seven months that such an act would no longer excite even any particular surprise.

Guidi still appears in Council and shows himself in his votes an independent thinker and by no means a humiliated or broken man, but in his convent he is guarded like a prisoner and constantly urged by threats and persuasions to recant. When a remark was made to the Pope about his harsh treatment of this man, who still as Cardinal shares the numerous privileges of his order, he is reported to have said, "I summoned him, not as Cardinal, but as brother Guidi, whom I lifted out of the dust." Guidi had drawn great displeasure on himself before by joining Cardinals Corsi and Riario Sforza in making representations to the Pope against the alteration introduced by his order in the sequence of the subjects for discussion, by which means the infallibilist *Schema* was interpolated before its time. He lived in the Minerva with certain Bishops of his Order, Milella, Pastero, Alcazar and Manucillo, and their mutual conferences led to the matured conviction that the personal infallibility of the Pope is a novel doctrine, of late invention and unknown even to the great Thomas and the Thomist school, chiefly introduced in substance by the Jesuits. Guidi appeals to the fact that years ago he has taught this at Vienna, as was or easily might have been known. If he keeps firm, and Cardinal Silvestri, who often votes with the Opposition, joins their side in good earnest—five dissentient Cardinals, including Mathieu, Rauscher and Schwarzenberg ——more Italian Bishops than the Court would like, may say *Non placet.* It is already remarked that they earnestly inquire among themselves whether the German and French minority are likely to remain firm at the decisive moment and not melt away, in which case they would be ready to vote with them. You may imagine how intensely Guidi is hated here. For the moment he might make O'Connell's boast his own when he said he was "the best abused man in the British Empire." What Persius said is equally true of the clerical " turba Remi " now,—" sequitur fortunam ut semper, et odit damnatos." I may mention in illustration of the view prevalent among the majority, that Manning the other day told one of the most illustrious Bishops of the minority he had no further business in the Catholic Church and had better leave it. Even in the Council Hall Bishop Gastaldi of Saluzzo exclaimed to the minority that they were already blotted out of the book of life.

The internal history of the minority since the end of June consists mainly of their endeavours to avert the departure of the timid and home-sick and those attacked by fever. Hitherto leave has been given them readily enough when asked, but it is said this will not be so for the future. The Prince Bishop of Breslau, Förster, was urgently entreated to remain, and he seemed to be persuaded, but now he is gone,[1] and so are Purcell of Cincinnati, Vancsa, Archbishop of Fogaras, Greith of St. Gall, and others—a serious loss under present circumstances. The feeling of self-preservation at last overpowers every other; and what answer can be given to a man who says, when required to stay and help to save the truth, "If I am ill in bed with fever on the critical day, my vote is lost"? Moreover the burning atmosphere peculiar to Rome, impregnated with exhalations from the Pontine marshes, oppresses and enervates mind as well as body and cripples the energy of the will.

So on the 1st July an understanding was arrived at among the Opposition Bishops. It was felt more and more clearly that to go on with the speeches was a sterile and dreary business. For one solid and thoughtful speech from, *e.g.*, Darboy, Strossmayer, Haynald, Guidi, Dupanloup, Ginoulhiac, Ketteler or Maret, one had to listen for long hours to the effusions of Spanish, Sicilian and Calabrian infallibilists, and the speeches of this party sound as if their authors had first studied

---

[1] According to a letter of his which reached Breslau the 12th July, permission to depart has been refused him.

the dedicatory epistles to the Popes which the Jesuits prefix to their works, and strung together the sonorous phrases contained in them.   Moreover the conduct of the Legates had become palpable partisanship.   For several days they offered demonstrative thanks to every speaker who gave up his turn; the bitterest attacks of the majority on their opponents passed unrebuked, and the murmurs and signs of impatience whenever infallibility was called in question grew more and more pronounced.   It became evident that there was nothing really to be gained by prolonging the speeches, when all hope of getting the Council prorogued had to be abandoned.

At the sitting of July 2 the affair was to have been brought to a settlement.   The minority had sketched out a notice in the Council Hall, stating that all speakers on their side withdrew, and handed it to Cardinal Mathieu to communicate to the French, but they declined to accept it, saying every one should be free to decide for himself.   And so, on that day, out of twenty-two Fathers only four spoke, including Meignan of Chalons and Ramadie of Perpignan.

But it soon became irresistibly evident to both parties that it was advisable for them to put an end to the oratorical exercises. The Legates had frequently used the formula of the Index when a speaker gave up his turn, saying, " laudabiliter orationi renunciavit," or " magnas ipsi agimus gratias." The majority had two reasons for wanting the speeches to go on—first the wish of particular individuals to signalize themselves and lay up a stock of merits deserving reward; and secondly, that the Northern Bishops might succumb to the rays of the July sun, as Homer's Achæans sunk under the arrows of Apollo. But they were made to understand that the Pope would account their simple " *Placet*, sans phrase " a sufficient service, and reward it according to their wish.

Moreover they felt secure about the eventual attitude of the minority, or at least a considerable portion of them, for it was known that two German Bishops had said, " We shall resist to the last moment, but then we shall submit, for we don't wish to cause a schism." This gave great joy to the Court party. I heard a monsignore say, " These are our best friends, more so than those who already vote for and with us, for their coming over at the critical moment can only be ascribed to the triumphant and irresistible power of the Holy Ghost poured out through the Pope upon the Council; each of them is a Saul converted into a Paul, who has found his Damascus here at Rome, and becomes a living trophy of the vice-godship of the Pope and the legitimacy and œcumenicity of this Council. We can desire nothing better for our cause than these late and sudden conversions." And thus at last an understanding satisfactory to all parties was come to ; on July 4 all the speakers enrolled withdrew, only reserving their right of presenting their observations in writing to the Deputation.

SIXTY-FIFTH LETTER.

Rome, July 7, 1870.—I must go back a few days and tell you something more of the speeches made since St. Peter's Day. It is for the interest of the contemporary world and of posterity that the Roman system of hushing up and deathlike silence should not be fully carried out, and that it should be known what truths have been uttered and what grounds alleged against the fatal decision of the majority and rejected by them.

Soon after Bishop Martin a man spoke who had gained the highest respect from all quarters, Verot, Bishop of Savannah, a really apostolical character, compared in America with St. Francis of Sales. On a former occasion, on June 15, he had pointedly criticised the conduct of the Court party and the attempt to surrender all that yet remains of the ancient constitution of the Church to a centralized papal absolutism. "If," he said, "the Pope wants to possess and exercise a direct and immediate jurisdiction in my diocese, only let him come over to America himself, and bring with him plenty of the priests who are so abundant here to my country where there are so few; gladly will I attend him as a servant and observe how he, riding about in my huge diocese, judges and arranges everything on the spot." And, as some Bishops of the majority had given out the favourite Roman watchword, that historical facts must yield to the clearness and *a priori* certainty of doctrine, Verot replied briefly, " To me an ounce of historical facts outweighs a thousand pounds of your theories." This time he was not interrupted, as he had always been before,—by most no doubt not understood. Maret too, in the sitting of July 1, attacked the projected absolutism which the Church was now to be saddled with. In the political world, he said, it is done away with and disappears more and more under a common feeling of repugnance, and now it is for the first time to be confirmed in the Church, and Christians, " the children of heavenly freedom," are to be reduced, after the protection afforded by the consent of the episcopate is abolished, to spiritual slavery, and forced into blind subjection to the dictates of a single man. He said this in more courteous language than this brief epitome gives scope for.

Among the most important speeches was that which followed, of Bishop David of Saint Brieuc in Bretagne. It was one of the speeches of a kind I said in an early letter would not be tolerated ; the result has refuted me. The Bishop said that the proposed article of faith was first invented in the fifteenth century, when a new form, different from that ordained by Christ, was given to the Church, at the expense of the inalienable rights both of the Bishops and the faithful. If the hypothesis of papal infallibility really belonged to the deposit of faith, it must have been defined and universally acknowledged in the earliest ages, as it would evidently be a fundamental doctrine indispensable for the whole Church. The parallel drawn beween this and the lately defined and previously undetermined and open doctrine of the Immaculate Conception is quite irrelevant. It is clearly evident, he added, that this new attempt to exalt the Papacy will produce the same disturbance as the earlier one in the sixteenth century. A sign of it is the sudden and rapidly growing alienation of the French clergy from their Bishops, which is instigated from a distance. Passing on to a vindication of the much abused Gallican doctrine, he showed that the former Popes themselves declared it to be allowable and only reprobated the attempt to make it into a special and separate rule of faith for the French Church alone.

The Spanish Bishop of Cuenca, Payà-y-Rico, followed, and began by affirming in the bragging and bombastic style of his country, that in Spain the infallibilist doctrine had always prevailed. This was a glaring false-hood; it would have been enough to cite against him the names of Tostado, Escobar, Victoria, and others, the Spanish Bishops and theologians at Trent, and the fact that the Inquisition first made the doctrine dominant in Spain. But immediate replies are not permitted in the Council Hall, and the majority were so charmed with his disclosures that they loudly applauded him. Encouraged by this he turned round upon the Opposition, observing that a short interval was still allowed them to come over to the majority, and that, unless they made a good use of it, their only choice lay between a subsequent meritorious submission or condemnation for heresy.

The minority, who meet daily either in national or international conferences, were engaged in drawing up a formula requiring the consent of the episcopate as indispensable, but soon gave this up and resolved to abstain from any demonstration, as they could gain nothing by it. Several thought this would compel the majority, if they really wanted to gain the concurrence of the Opposition, to make proposals on their side for some tolerable formula. But at present that is highly improbable.

In the sitting of July 5, where the only business was to vote on the third chapter, in consequence of the general withdrawal of the speakers, an unexpected occurrence intervened. Some days before Bishop Martin of Paderborn had proposed in his own name and that of some of his colleagues that in a Supplement, designated as a *monitum*, the doctrinal authority of the Bishops should be mentioned, but only incidentally and in a sense compatible with the Pope's prerogative of personal infallibility. When the Pope heard of this, he was much displeased, and peremptorily ordered that a canon should be laid before the Council for acceptance enouncing emphatically and under anathema the papal omnipotence over the whole Church. The Deputation had already had the third canon printed and distributed in the following amended form :—" Si quis dixerit, Romani Pontificis Primatum esse tantum officium inspectionis et directionis et supremam ipsius potestatem jurisdictionis in universam Ecclesiam non esse plenam, sed tantum extraordinariam et mediatam—anathema sit." But in order to carry out the Pope's command, the Bishop of Rovigo, as a member of the Deputation, read the canon in a more stringent form, which in fact left the extremest absolutist nothing to desire, but which was not in the printed text and was either not heard or not understood by the greater part of the Bishops, while yet it was to be voted on on the spot —in contradiction to the distinct directions of the order of business.   This more stringent version of the canon runs thus :—

"Si quis dixerit, Romanum Pontificem habere tantummodo officium inspectionis vel directionis, non autem plenam et supremam potestatem jurisdictionis in universam Ecclesiam, tum in rebus, quæ ad fidem et mores, tum quæ ad disciplinam et regimen Ecclesiæ per totum orbem diffusæ pertinent; aut eum habere tantum potiores partes, non vero totam plenitudinem hujus supremæ potestatis; aut hanc ejus potestatem non esse ordinariam et immediatam sive in omnes ac singulas Ecclesias, sive in omnes et singulos pastores et fideles —anathema sit."

A more shameless outwitting of a Council has never been attempted. Archbishop Darboy at once rose and protested against this juggling manœuvre, and the

Legates were obliged, humiliating as it was for them, to let the matter drop for the present; but the addition will be brought forward again in a few days.

A proof has lately forced itself on my attention of the confusion of mind habitual to many of the Bishops of the majority. I asked one of them, who had expressed his surprise that so much fuss was made about this one dogma, whether he had formed any clear conception of its retrospective force and examined all the papal decisions, from Siricius in 385 to the Syllabus of 1864, which would be made by the infallibilist dogma into articles of faith. And it came out that this pastor of above a hundred thousand souls imagined that every Pope would be declared infallible, not for the past but for the future only![1] But he was somewhat perplexed when I mentioned to him on the spur of the moment merely a couple of papal maxims on moral theology, which were now to be stamped with the seal of divinely inspired truths.

On Saturday the 9th the special voting is to take place on the emendation just mentioned of the third chapter of the third canon in the interests of papal

---

1 [The same strange confusion of thought seems still to prevail among some fervid infallibilists of the English and Irish Episcopate, to judge from their pastorals issued since the decree of July 18.—Tr.]

absolutism, and on the same day or Monday the whole of the third chapter and the amendments on the fourth are to be voted on; on Wednesday, the 13th, the votes are to be taken on the whole *Schema* "en bloc." As yet the Opposition can still be reckoned at 97, exclusive of Guidi and the Dominican Bishops, who may not improbably come to its aid at the critical moment.

One of the witticisms circulating here, for which the Council affords matter to genuine Romans, is the following, that in the sitting of July 4 there was a great uproar among the Bishops, they were all set by the ears and the Pope himself ran away, and why all this? " E perchè tutta questa cagniara? perchè il Papa vuole esser *impeccabile,* e i vescovi non lo vogliono."

SIXTY-SIXTH LETTER.

Rome, July 14, 1870.—I must again interrupt my narrative of the occurrences and speeches between June 5 and 10 to communicate the details of the great event of the session of July 13—an event which has falsified all expectations on both sides, and created a sensation and astonishment in Rome which it will take people some time to recover from. Even beyond the Alps, in spite of the all-absorbing question of the war, it will rouse interest and joyful surprise. In the last few days before the critical morning of the 13th there was much discussion among the Bishops of the various nations as to whether they should vote a simple "No" or a conditional "Yes,"—a *Non placet* or a *Placet juxta modum.* It was not merely the fourth chapter that was in question, which deals with infallibility, but the whole *Schema* on the Papacy, which contains also the

much-decried third canon of the third chapter, establishing for the first time the theory of the universal
episcopate of the Pope, the very theory Pope Gregory the
Great characterized as an abomination and a blasphemy.
It was known that the Bishops who are mere dilettantis
in theology—and their number is legion, as is natural
under the present system of episcopal appointments—
would greatly prefer voting *juxta modum, i.e.,* with a conditioned "Yes."   That would always leave them free to
reserve their further decision till the public voting "coram
Sanctissimo" (as the Pope is here called), when only a
direct "Yes" or "No" can be voted.   Each of them
could present in writing the conditions or wishes on
which he desired to make his *Placet* dependent, and
then say "Yes" or "No" according to his pleasure in
the Solemn Session, if his suggestions were disregarded
—"Yes," if he wished to direct the lightning flashes of
the angry Jupiter to other heads than his own ; "No,"
if he could summon manliness and courage enough at
the last moment. The Court party and the majority
had neglected no means of impressing on the recalci-
trants the uselessness of their negative votes and the
personal disadvantages to themselves. Every one was
told, "It is determined irrevocably to take no account

of your ' No,' and to go on to the promulgation of the
dogma. Supported by at least 500 favourable votes,
and throwing the surplus weight of his own vote into
the scale, the Pope, on the 17th or 24th July, will
walk over your heads amid the presumed acclamations
of the whole Catholic world ; and how lamentable and
hopeless a situation will yours be then ! You are then
heretics, who have incurred the terrible penalties of the
canon law ; you have surrendered at discretion, bound
hand and foot, to the mercy of the deeply injured Pope.
Consider, ' Quid sum miser tunc dicturus, quem pat-
ronum rogaturus ?' "

Thus they were worked on individually. And more
drastic methods were employed as well. It was asserted
that two documents had already been drawn up in the
Vatican, which every Bishop would be compelled to sign
before being allowed to leave Rome ; the one a profession
of faith comprising the new article of infallibility, and
the other an attestation of the perfect freedom of the
Council throughout its whole course. Whoever refused
to sign either would thereby at once incur papal censures.
" We shall thus have," they were told, " your *Non placet*
and your ' free ' acknowledgment under your hand of
the article of faith you denied a few days before, and

shall show it to the world. Do you wish then morally to annihilate yourselves in public opinion?"

As the Bishops who are resolved to give a negative vote knew well the more timorous temper of many of their colleagues, who were half-ready to be persuaded and half-ready to succumb, and remembered the Scriptural saying that " a high priest must have compassion on our infirmities," some of them drew up a formula stating the basis on which the timid might vote *Placet juxta modum.* In the preamble of the *Schema* the word " principium " was to be exchanged for " exordium," and instead of " vis et virtus in eo (Papâ) consistit," was to be put " præcipue in eo consistit;" the third canon of the third chapter was to be wholly omitted, and the word " episcopalis" left out of the chapter, and lastly, the formula of St. Antoninus was to be substituted for the fourth chapter. The proposed document ends with " Secus in Solemni Sessione dicturus sum, *Non placet.*"

On July 12 the Bishops of the minority held the most largely attended international conference which has yet taken place ; about 70 were present. Three prelates, two German and one French—Ketteler, Melchers and Archbishop Landriot of Rheims—proposed that all should vote *Placet juxta modum,* but at the same time hand in a precise and decided formulaas the condition of their assent, with a declaration that, if their demands were rejected or inadequately complied with, they should be obliged to vote *Non placet* in the Solemn Session. This would have substantially secured the complete victory of the majority and the *Curia*. Every one would have naturally said, "Your 'Yes,' however conditioned, can only bear the sense that in the main point you agree with the *Schema*, and that main point lies in the two new and great articles of faith, which hang together and must shape the future of the Church, the universal episcopate of the Pope and his infallibility. By saying *Placet* you affirm these two new dogmas, and after that it will matter little what particular collateral wishes or conditions you may choose to add. Whether they are acceded to or not, you must in consistency say 'Yes' on the great day of the public profession, when only a simple affirmative or negative vote can be given."

The three Cardinals, the two primates Simor and Ginoulhiac, Strossmayer and others, spoke out repeatedly and emphatically against this mischievous proposal which would at the last moment have frustrated all their hopes, and annihilated the results of seven months' sufferings and labours.   A decisive impression was produced by the remark of the Archbishop of Milan, that there were many infallibilists who on various grounds would vote conditionally, and this peculiar kind of vote, which was better adapted to courtiers than Bishops, had better be left to them.   "The only befitting course for us," he said, "who are convinced of the falsehood of the doctrine, is to say 'No.'"   This was unanimously accepted.   Tarnoczy, who for some time back has withdrawn from his German and Hungarian colleagues, and votes regularly with the majority, was not present.   Cardinal Schwarzenberg said he should be glad if one of the Cardinals voted *Non placet* before him, but if this did not happen he should be the first, and should count it a distinction to stand at the head of this noble band.

It was remarkable how generally the view prevailed that scarcely ten opposing votes would really be given when the time came.   No means were spared, by rumours and inventions, to spread terror and despair among the ranks of the Opposition.   Thus the report was circulated in foreign journals—where you will have read it—as well as here, that a " sauve qui peut," and " débandade " had become the watchword of the Opposition, and not thirty would be left on the day for voting. We see now that this was all pure invention. Even Förster's departure, which I reported myself, had not taken place ; only Greith had gone. When Darboy had an audience of the Pope the day before the voting, and said that there was a considerable number of Bishops who would join him in saying *Non placet,* the Pope replied, " Perhaps many will vote *juxta modum,* but certainly not above ten *Non placet.*" For some time past Pius has notoriously known everything with absolute certainty, even the temper of distant countries. The formulas put into the Pope's mouth by the Roman Chancery, " proprio motu" and " ex certâ scientiâ," have been transmuted by the habit of twenty-four years into actual flesh and blood with him.

At the beginning of the sitting the news had spread among the majority that the negative votes would be much more numerous than had been supposed on the evening before. On this Dechamps of Mechlin went to the heads of the Opposition and entreated them with humble gestures and whining voice to vote *juxta modum,* saying there was really some disposition with the authorities to insert the " consensus" and " testimonium Ecclesiarum" into the fourth chapter. The trick was too barefaced to succeed, and sharp words were spoken on the other side. One of the Bishops said to the new primate, " C'est une impudence sans exemple," and Darboy called the attention of the three Cardinals to this treacherous attempt at the last moment to divide and perplex the Opposition. Now began the voting " sub secreto," as it was again called, and the sub-secretary Jacobini read the names of the Fathers from the pulpit. And then a wholly unexpected phenomenon came to light : out of 600 Fathers present in Rome—there were 764 in January—only 520 had appeared, and it was at once known that very many of the absentees had stayed away from dislike to the *Schema*, and to avoid the disagreeable consequences of a negative vote.

The line taken by the Orientals in the voting excites surprise here. The Propaganda has spared no means of exercising a strict supervision and control over them, and yet the upshot is that the most influential of them have voted *Non placet*, some *juxta modum*, and others have absented themselves. In fact all the real Eastern Bishops —*i.e.*, those who represent dioceses—have voted against the dogma. Every one acquainted with the state of things in Asia foresees that the promulgation of the dogma,

which will follow in spite of this, will lead to the
definitive separation of the Uniate Churches in the East.
But that makes not the slightest impression on the
Pope and the Jesuits.

When the names of the *juxta modum* voters were
read out, the President said " quorum, quantum possi-
bile erit, habebitur ratio." That sounded like open
mockery : it meant, "We (the Deputation) have already
settled among ourselves what is impossible, viz., making
the co-operation of the episcopate a condition, but still
there are some possible things. If, *e.g.*, any Bishops
wish to have 'inerrantia' substituted for 'infallibilitas,'
perhaps they may be gratified." But even concessions
of that sort are doubtful, for one cannot give the lie
to Bishop Gasser of Brixen, who has distinctly declared that " nec verbum addetur nec verbum demetur
amplius."

Among the conditional voters are Dreux-Brézé, certainly only because the decree is not strong enough for
him. The whole Hungarian Episcopate remained firm
in its opposition. The Austrians know now why
Rudigier and Fessler were given them as Bishops. I
send you with this the authentic list of the Fathers who
did not vote with a simple *Placet*. It shows that it

was just the Bishops of capital cities, as well as North American, Irish, English, and beyond expectation many North Italian prelates, who voted against the dogma. Only one, strictly speaking, was wholly false to his professions, the Bishop of Porto Rico.

The Pope is still sure that at the last critical moment a divine miracle will enlighten the benighted minds of the opponents and suddenly reverse their sentiments. The Holy Ghost will and must do this.   Pius seems to have clear assurances on that point.   He had lately a remarkable conversation about it with a French Bishop, whom he had never seen before.   As he regards every opponent of the dogma as his personal enemy, he received him as such and reproached him with being Cæsar's friend instead of the Pope's; the Bishop replied that his white hairs testified to his having nothing to fear or hope for, but simply to follow his conscience, which constrained him with many of his colleagues to vote against the new dogma.   "No," exclaimed Pius, "you will not vote against it; the Holy Ghost at the decisive hour will irresistibly enlighten you, and you will all say *Placet.*"

When the French Government in 1733 had the cemetery of La Chaise surrounded with soldiers, to stop the miraculous cures at the grave of the Abbé Paris, the inscription was found one morning over the entrance—

> De par le roi défense à Dieu,
> De faire miracle en ce lieu.

On the 17th or 24th July 1870 there might be written over the entrance of the Council Hall—

> De par le Pape ordre au bon Dieu
> De faire miracle en ce lieu.

The echo of the Vatican, Veuillot's *Univers*, has just been accusing the Bishops of the minority of ruining the papal treasury by prolonging the debates on infallibility through their opposition, and thus obliging the Pope to go on supporting his 300 episcopal foster sons, and buy his infallibility late and at a high price, when it ought to have been cast into his lap by spontaneous acclamation at the first. A physician has now been discovered for the treasury which has sickened under the infallibility affair. Rothschild is said to have been here and concluded a loan of forty million franks. As the deficit only amounts to thirty million, there remain ten million for fireworks, illuminations and church-decorations, the journey-money of trusty Bishops, and the like. But now the war is impending, and with it the withdrawal of Peter's pence and perhaps still worse.[1]

The following voted *Non-placet :*—1. *Prague,* Cardinal Prince-Archbishop Schwarzenberg; 2. *Besançon,* Cardinal Archbishop Mathieu; 3. *Vienna,* Cardinal Prince-Archbishop Rauscher; 4. *Antioch,* Patriarch Jussuf, of the Melchite Rite; 5. *Babylon,* Patriarch Audu, of the Chaldean Rite; 6. *Gran,* Archbishop

[1] Meanwhile the *Unita* of July 15 has already begun to indicate the wholesome political fruits which may be looked for from the dogma of infallibility. Gallicanism, which demanded fixed guarantees against papal decisions, has paved the way, according to Margotti, for constitutionalism and parliamentarism ; for after a Pope whose decrees *ex cathedrâ* are not irreformable, comes a king limited by the Constitution, and then the era of parliamentary revolutions and political storms is introduced. But now the bright example set by the Bishops in their submission to the infallible Pope will restore not France only, but the whole of Europe. From them the nations will learn to submit as children to their sovereigns, the kingdom of unrighteousness will pass away, and the kingdom of God succeed. That is plain speaking ; absolutism in the Church will lead to absolutism in the State. Margotti then surrenders himself to the most brilliant hopes, predicts unprecedented miracles, and records those which have been already wrought for infallibility during the Council, or will immediately be wrought. We cannot venture to withhold them from our readers. First, it seemed impossible to attain an agreement of the Bishops on the proclamation of infallibility ; all wanted to speak, and the discussion seemed likely to be endless. But the Holy Ghost unexpectedly interposed ; above sixty Bishops waved their right to speak, and the *Schema* was voted and approved. Secondly, a great opposition of all the governments was feared, who only kept quiet while they watched the quarrels of the Bishops themselves in the Council. But scarcely had the Bishops shown themselves unanimous, when the Hohenzollern question turned up, which absorbs everybody's attention, and leaves the Church in peace. The third miracle is still in the future—the dogma will suddenly dissipate the menaces of war, because the word of God, like the Son of God, only comes into the world in the midst of universal peace.

and Primate of Hungary, Simor ; 7. *Lyons,* Archbishop Ginoulhiac ; 8. *Tuam,* Archbishop MacHale ; 9. *Olmütz,* Prince-Archbishop Fürstenberg ; 10. *Trabezund,* Bishop Ghiureghian, of the Armenian Rite ; 11. *Munich,* Archbishop Scherr ; 12. *Bamberg,* Archbishop Deinlein ; 13. *Seert,* Bishop Bar-Tatar, of the Chaldean Rite; 14. *Halifax,* Archbishop Conolly, of the Capuchin Order; 15. *Lemberg,* Archbishop Wierzcheyski, of the Latin Rite ; 16. *Paris,* Archbishop Darboy ; 17. *Kalocsa,* Archbishop Haynald ; 18. *Milan,* Archbishop Nazari di Calabiana ; 19. *Tyre,* Archbishop Kauam, of the Melchite Rite ; 20. *Biella (Italy),* Bishop Losanna ; 21. *Autun,* Bishop Marguerye ; 22. *Ivrea (Piedmont),* Bishop Moreno ; 23. *Dijon,* Bishop Rivet ; 24. *Metz,* Bishop Dupont des Loges ; 25. *Iglesias (Sardinia),* Bishop Montixi ; 26. *Acquapendente* (formerly in the Roman States), Bishop Pellei ; 27. *Trieste,* Bishop Legat ; 28. *Orleans,* Bishop Dupanloup ; 29. *Vezprim,* Bishop Ranolder ; 30. *Mayence,* Bishop Ketteler ; 31. *Bosnia* and *Syrmia,* Bishop Strossmayer ; 32. *Budweis,* Bishop Jirsik ; 33. *Breslau,* Prince-Bishop Förster ; 34. *Kerry,* Bishop Moriarty ; 35. *Leontopolis, in partibus,* Bishop Forwerk, Apostolic Vicar of Saxony ; 36. *Plymouth,* Bishop Vaughan ; 37. *Clifton,* Bishop Clifford ;

38. *Nice,* Bishop Sola; 39. *Parenzo* and *Pola,* Bishop Dobrilla; 40. *Kreutz (in Croatia),* Bishop Smiciklas, of the Ruthenian Rite; 41. *Augsburgh,* Bishop Dinkel; 42. *Gurk,* Bishop Wiery; 43. *Caltanisetta (Sicily),* Bishop Guttadauro di Reburdone; 44. *Vacz (in Hungary),* Bishop Peitler; 45. *Marianne (Syria),* — ? of the Melchite Rite; 46. *Chatham,* Bishop Rogers; 47. *Csanad* and *Temesvar,* Bishop Bonnaz; 48. *Pittsburg,* Bishop Domenec; 49. *Luzonia,* Bishop Colet; 50. *Sura, in partibus,* Bishop Maret; 51. *St. Brieuc,* Bishop David; 52. *Trèves,* Bishop Eberhard; 53. *Coutance,* Bishop Bravard; 54. *Lavant,* Bishop Stepischnigg; 55. *Soissons,* Bishop Dours; 56. *Akra,* Bishop Mellus, of the Chaldean Rite; 57. *Siebenbürgen,* Bishop Fogarasz; 58. *Châlons,* Bishop Meignan; 59. *Valence,* Bishop Gueullette; 60. *Perpignan,* Bishop Ramadié; 61. *Paleopolis, in partibus,* Bishop Mariassy (Hungary); 62. *Petricola* or *Little Rock (United States),* Bishop Fitzgerald; 63. *Marseilles,* Bishop Place; 64. *Cahors,* Bishop Grimardias; 65. *Osnaburgh,* Bishop Beckmann; 66. *Szathmar (Hungary),* Bishop Virò de Keydi Polany; 67. *Munkacs,* Bishop Pankovics, of the Ruthenian Rite; 68. *Bayeux,* Bishop Hugonin; 69. *Raab,* Bishop — ?; 70. *La Rochelle,* Bishop Benedetto; 71. *Nancy,* Bishop Foullon; 72.

Constantine (*Algiers*), Bishop de las Cases; 73. *Oran*
(*Algiers*), Bishop Callot; 74. *Gap,* Bishop Guilbert; 75.
Ermeland, Bishop Crementz; 76. *Rochester,* Bishop
MacQuaid; 77. *Louisville,* Bishop Kenrick; 78. *Cassovia,*
Bishop Perger (Hungary); 79. *Agathopolis,* Bishop
Namszanowski, Provost of the Prussian Army in Berlin;
80. *Montreal* (*Canada*), Bishop Bourget; 81. *Grosswar-
dein,* Bishop Lipovniczky; 82. *Fünfkirchen,* Bishop
Kovacs; 83. *Steinamanger,* Bishop Szenczy; 84. *Rot-
tenburg,* Bishop Hefele; 85. *Ajaccio,* Bishop Sante
Casanelli d'Istria, and three more whose names were
omitted in the official catalogue.

There voted *Placet juxta modum :*—1. De Silvestri,
Cardinal-Priest; 2. Trevisanato, Cardinal Patriarch of
Venice; 3. Guidi, Cardinal Archbishop of Bologna;
4. *Salsburg,* Archbishop and Primate Tarnoczy; 5.
Oregon City, Archbishop Blanchet; 6. *Nisibis, in parti-
bus,* Archbishop Tizzani; 7. *Tyre and Sidon,* Archbishop
Bostani, Maronite; 8. *Manila,* Archbishop Melithon-
Martinez; 9. *Granada,* Archbishop Monzon y Martins;
10. *Avignon,* Archbishop Dubrevil; 11. *New York,*
Archbishop MacCloskey; 12. *Cologne,* Archbishop
Melchers; 13. *Melitene, in partibus,* Archbishop Mérode;
14. *Rheims,* Archbishop Landriot; 15. *Sens,* Arch-

bishop Bernardou; 16. *Burgos*, Archbishop Yusto; 17. *Ventimiglia (Italy)*, Bishop Biale; 18. *Columbica, in partibus*, Bishop Verolles, Apostolic Vicar in Leao-Tung (China); 19. *Canopo, in partibus*, Bishop Besi; 20. *Sira*, Bishop Alberti, Apostolic Delegate in Greece; 21. *Zenopolis, in partibus*, Bishop Moccagatta, Apostolic Vicar in Xan-Tung; 22. *Lipari*, Bishop Ideo; 23. *Birmingham*, Bishop Ullathorne; 24. *Vancouver*, Bishop Demers; 25. *Mileto*, Bishop Mincione; 26. *Moulins*, Bishop Dreux-Brézé; 27. *Gezira*, Bishop Hindi, of the Chaldean Rite; 28. *Hadrianopolis, in partibus*, Bishop De la Place, Apostolic Vicar in Tsche-Kiang; 29. *Tarnovia*, Bishop Pukalski (Galicia); 30. *Chartres*, Bishop Regnault; 31. *Urgel*, Bishop Caixal y Estrade; 32. *Monterey*, Bishop Amat; 33. *Tanes, in partibus*, Bishop Salzano, Dominican; 34. *Newcastle*, Bishop Chadwick; 35. *Lacedonia*, Bishop Majorsini; 36. *Todi*, Bishop Rosati; 37. *Avellino*, Bishop Gallo; 38. *Amelia*, Bishop Pace; 39. *Nola*, Bishop Formisano; 40. *Imola*, Bishop Moretti; 41. *Zamora*, Bishop Condé y Corral; 42. *Avila*, Bishop Blanco, Dominican; 43. *Savannah*, Bishop Verot; 44. *Cuenca*, Bishop Payà y Rico; 45. *Cajazzo*, Bishop Riccio; 46. *Teramo*, Bishop Milella, Dominican; 47. *Nocera*, Bishop Pettinari; 48. *St. Christophori*, Bishop

De Urguinaona; 49. *Clariopolis, in partibus,* Bsciai, Apostolic Vicar in Egypt, of the Coptic Rite ; 50. *Erzeroum,* Bishop Melchisedechian, of the Armenian Rite; 51. *Monte Fiascone,* Bishop Bovieri; 52. *Savona,* Bishop Cerruti; 53. *Agathonica, in partibus,* Bishop Pagnucci ; 54. *Ascalon, in partibus,* Bishop Meurin, Society of Jesus; 55. *Dionysia, in partibus,* Bishop Gentili ; 56. *Cattaro,* Bishop Marchich ; 57. *Serena,* Bishop Orrego ; 58. Mardin, Bishop of the Chaldean Rite ; 59. *Tiberias, in partibus,* Bishop Valeschi; 60. Guardi, General of the Ministers of the Sick; 61. The Abbot of the Camaldolese in Etruria.

The following abstained from voting, though in Rome at the time:—*Cardinals:* 1. Mattei, 2. Orfei, 3. Quaglia, 4. Hohenlohe, 5. Berardi, 6. Antonelli, 7. Grassellini ; 8. The Patriarch Harcus of Antioch, of the Syrian Rite ; 9. The Archbishop and Primate Salomone of Salerno ; 10. The Maronite Archbishop Aun of Beirout ; 11, 12. Two other Archbishops; 13. *Aleppo,* Archbishop Matar, of the Maronite Rite ; 14. *Venezuela,* Archbishop Guevara ; 15. *Utrecht,* Archbishop Zwysen; 16. *Tours,* Archbishop Guibert ; 17. *Rodi, in partibus,* Archbishop Pace-Forno, Bishop of Malta ; 18. *Mardin,* Archbishop Nasarian, of the Armenian Rite ; 19. *Alby,* Archbishop Lyonnet ; 20. Iconium, *in partibus,* Archbishop Pue-

cher Passavalli ; 21. *Guadalaxara,* Archbishop Loya ;
22. *Amida,* Archbishop Bahtiarian, of the Armenian
Rite ; 23. *Tournay,* Bishop Labis ; 24. *Terni,* Bishop
Severa ; 25. *Veglia,* Bishop Vitezich ; 26. *Almira, in
partibus,* Bishop Carli, Capuchin ; 27. *Montauban,*
Bishop Doney ; 28. *Cava,* Bishop Fertilla ; 29. *Curia,
in partibus,* Bishop Grioglio ; 30. *Segni* (Papal State),
Bishop Ricci ; 31. *Paphos, in partibus,* Bishop Alcazar,
Dominican Vicar Apostolic; 32. *Vicenza,* Bishop Varina;
33. *Salford,* Bishop Turner ; 34. *Catanzaro,* Bishop de
Franco; 35. *Bergamo,* Bishop Speranza; 36. *Savannah,*
—(?); 37. *St. Angelo in Lombardy,* Bishop Fanelli; 38.
Dromore, Bishop Leahy, Dominican; 39. *Glarus,* — (?);
40. *Birta, in partibus,* Bishop Pinsoneault ; 41. *Fernes,*
Bishop Furlong ; 42. *Anagni,* Bishop Pagliari ; 43.
Siguenza, Bishop Benavides ; 44. *Ceramo, in partibus,*
Bishop Jeancard, Suffragan of Marseilles ; 45. *Pole-
monia, in partibus,* Bishop Pinchon ; 46. *Lipari,*
Bishop Athanasio ; 47. *Apamea,* Archbishop Ata, of the
Melchite Rite ; 48. *Mindus, in partibus,* Bishop Papardo
del Parco ; 49. *Bursa,* Bishop Tilkian, of the Armenian
Rite; 50.*Astorga,* Bishop Arguelles y Miranda; 51. *Com-
acchio,* Bishop Spoglia ; 52. *Charlottetown,* Bishop Mac-
Intyre ; 53. *Vallis Pratensis,* — (?) ; 54. *Lamego,*

Bishop de Vasconcellos Periera de Mello; 55. *Mont-pellier*, Bishop Curtier; 56. *Barcelona*, Bishop Mon-serrat y Navarro; 57. *Amatunto, in partibus*, Bishop Galezki, Apostolic Vicar in Cracow; 58. *Kilmore*, Bishop Conaty; 59. *Priene, in partibus*, Bishop Cosi; 60. *Tuy*, Bishop Garcia y Anton; 61. *Puno*, Bishop Huerta; 62. *Adelaide*, Bishop Shiel; 63. *Albany (America)*, Bishop Conroy; 64. *Concordia*, Bishop Frangipani; 65. *St. Hyacinth*, Bishop Laroque; 66. *Dubuque*, Bishop Hennessy; 67. *Vannes*, Bishop Becel; 68. *Goulburn*, Bishop Lannigan; 69. *St. Germani bei Monte Cassino*, — (?); 70. *Verdun*, Bishop Hacquard; 71. *Egéa, in partibus*, Bishop Reynaud; 72. *St. Giov. di Cuyo*, Bishop Achaval; 73. *Cirene, in partibus*, Bishop Canzi; 74. *Rodiopolis, in partibus,* Bishop Tosi; 75. *Buffalo*, Bishop Ryan; 76. *Adramyttium, in parti-bus*, Bishop Gibbons; 77. *Coria*, Bishop Nuñez; 78. *Heliopolis*, Bishop Nasser, of the Melchite Rite; 79. *Tito-polis, in partibus,* — (?); 80. 81. Abbates nullius; 82. 83. Burchall, President of the Benedictine Congregation in England; 84. The Abbot of Janow, Apostolic Admini-strator in Russia; 85. Montis Coronæ; 86-91. These names could not be announced on account of the great confusion.

SIXTY-SEVENTH LETTER.

Rome, July 16, 1870.—As I had to report in my last letter, the attempt of the Legates and the Deputation to outwit and catch the minority by a violation of their own order of business had all but succeeded. Darboy and Strossmayer frustrated this plot, on which it is literally true that the fate of the Church was staked. For the third canon of the third chapter had been brought forward in so enlarged and altered a form, that it involved in substance the abolition of the entire episcopate, as an integral constituent of the Christian Church, and substituted for it the papal "totality," as the theologians of the seventeenth century called it; *i.e.,* the theory that in the whole Church there is one sole individual who is in exclusive possession of all plenary powers and all ecclesiastical rights. The weight and importance of the doctrine thereby designed to be

786

for the first time imposed on the Church cannot even be made intelligible in a few words. Most readers are naturally unaware of the sense attached in canon law and the language of the *Curia* to the words, "potestas immediata et ordinaria." Well! they mean that all Christians, whether laymen or clerics, are personally subjects, body and soul, of their lord and master, the Pope, who can impose on them without restriction whatever commands seem good to him. There are, besides the Pope, who exercises immediate authority by virtue of his universal episcopate, papal commis- saries in the separate dioceses, who call themselves Bishops, and are so named by the Roman Chancery. They exercise the powers delegated to them by the one true and universal Bishop, and carry out the particular orders they receive from Rome. According to this view the whole Church has, properly speaking, no other right or law or order but the pleasure of the reigning Pope. This is the most perfect form of absolutism ever yet excogitated in any man's brains.

The order of business prohibits any alteration in the text of the decrees being voted upon without previous discussion in Council. That however was now at- tempted, and the violation of the order of business by the Legates themselves was so flagrant, the design of fraud so palpable, that the incident continued to be the subject of general conversation up to the 12th July. When the plot had miscarried, it was alleged in excuse that the previous discussion had been forgotten!—forgotten precisely in the case of the most important article yet brought forward, and of a change of such immeasurable weight that one may truly say no discussion of equal weight and influence has been passed in any Council during 1800 years. The affair of course made a great sensation. The words "deceit" and "lying" were used more than once in the national meetings of the Opposition Bishops, and it was urged that the whole Deputation *de Fide* were accomplices of the Legates in this unworthy trick, and that the Bishops were being compelled in a truly revolting manner to vote on alterations of the most comprehensive kind, which had only been communicated to them the day before. A short memorandum was issued by the French Bishops, which recommended that this opportunity should be seized for leaving Rome. It runs as follows :—

"(1). L'heure de la Providence a sonné : le moment décisif de sauver l'Église est arrivé. (2.) Par les additions faites au III. canon du 3me chap. la Commission *de Fide* a violé le règlement qui ne permet l'introduction d'aucun amendement sans discussion conciliaire. (3.) L'addition subreptice est d'une importance incalculable ; c'est le changement de la constitution de l'Église, la monarchie pure, absolue, indivisible du Pape, l'abolition de la judicature et de la co-souveraineté des évêques, l'affirmation et la définition anticipée de l'infaillibilité separée et personnelle. (4.) Le devoir et l'honneur ne permettent pas de voter sans discussion ce canon, qui contient une immense révolution. La discussion pourrait et devrait durer six mois, parce qu'il s'agit de la question capitale, la constitution même de la souveraineté dans l'Église. (5.) Cette discussion est impossible à cause des fatigues extrêmes de la saison et des dispositions de la majorité. (6.) Une seule chose, digne et honorable, reste à faire : Demander immédiatement la prorogation du Concile au mois d'Octobre, et présenter une déclaration, où seraient énumérées toutes les protestations déjà faites, et où la dernière violation du règlement, le mépris de la dignité et de la liberté des évêques seraient mis en lumière. Annoncer en même temps un départ, qui ne peut plus être différé. (7.) Par le départ ainsi motivé d'un nombre considérable d'évêques de toutes les nations, l'œcuménicité du Concile cesserait et tous les actes, qu'il pourrait faire ensuite, seraient d'une autorité nulle. (8.) Le courage et le dévouement de la minorité auraient, dans le monde, un retentissement immense. Le Concile se réunirait au mois d'Octobre dans des conditions infiniment meilleures. Toutes les questions, à peine ébauchées, pourraient être reprises, traitées avec dignité et liberté. L'Église et l'ordre moral du monde seraient sauvés."

But the majority of the Opposition did not assent to this ; they resolved to present another Protest, which the Court party might apply, like its predecessors, " ad piper et quidquid chartis amicitur ineptis." It was drawn up by Bishop Dinkel of Augsburgh, and signed, so far as I know, by all of them.

On the evening of the 9th July a proposal of a new formula of infallibility was distributed to the Bishops ; it was apparently designed to split up the Opposition, and was broad, declamatory, full of quotations, and lavish of assurances that the Roman See has always administered its supreme teaching office in the most excellent manner and proclaimed nothing but truth. Now, it was added, since there has been a great deal of contradiction, it is necessary to define that its *ex cathedrâ* decisions are infallible, and its decrees on faith and morals irreformable by virtue of the divine promise given to it. This new production was discussed in the French and German conferences and rejected, although one of the most influential German Bishops, Ketteler, had taken it under his protection. He assured them that the Deputation had unanimously resolved that no change or concession by a hair's-breadth should be allowed in this form of words, for to deny papal infallibility involved a denial of the primacy altogether.

Meanwhile the Jesuit Franzelin had received orders from the highest authority to revise afresh the formula adopted by the Deputation, with which Schrader is said to be very ill satisfied.

In the sitting of July 11, first the Bishop of Trevisa, as a member of the Deputation, defended the notorious decree in the third canon of the third chapter, which is to revolutionize the whole constitution of the Church in the sense of papal absolutism. Then the votes were taken, by rising and sitting down, on the weightiest and most pregnant article that has been laid before any Council for 600 years, and the uncertainty in this method of voting, wholly unprecedented in Church history, was so great that according to the majority only 50 or 60 voted against it, while the minority reckon between 90 and 100 adverse votes.

Then Bishop Gasser of Brixen made a speech three hours long in the name of the Deputation on the infallibility decree, which in its new form—and this he declared to be the *ultimatum*—had been enriched with an anathema against those who " contradicere præsumpserint." Gasser was unwilling to be left behind by Manning, Dechamps, Dreux-Brézé and the Spaniards. He vindicated the doctrines of Cardinal Cajetan against Ketteler.

Meanwhile Cardinal Guidi had been so powerfully belaboured, that it had frightened him, and he now voted for the third chapter with the majority. The process which had been found so effective in France, of raising their diocesan clergy against fallibilist Bishops, had been applied to him too by means of agents sent to Bologna. The apostasy of Archbishop Tarnoczy of Salzburg, who also voted with the majority, excited grief but no surprise. While the occupant of one of the oldest Sees of Germany, the successor of Arno, Pilgrim and Colloredo, flung away his own rights and those of his successors like so many hollow nutshells, even

Cardinal Silvestri voted against the third chapter and the anathema attached to the fourth.

The result of the 13th July has acted like an earth-quake, shaking and confusing for the moment men's heads and plans of operation. Even if half the voters *juxta modum* are abstracted, as belonging to the majority, there remain 31 votes among them in favour of essential changes in the fourth chapter, changes which the Deputation has declared to be absolutely inadmis-sible, and which, if admitted, would offend one section of the majority. This last consequence would not of course matter at all ; a single word from the Pope would set it aside at once, for it is self-evident that no Bishop who is convinced of his unconditional inerrancy could hesitate for a moment to vote for a decree sanctioned by him. Still the perplexity is great. If the decree, as voted by the majority, is brought forward at the public session, some 120 negative votes may be expected. But the Pope is resolved to become infallible " senza conditione," as he says.

It is now often said that on the day of the Solemn Session the Holy Ghost will yet most assuredly work a wonderful miracle and convert the Opposition so sud-denly that, although they had entered the Council Hall

resolved to say "No," they will say "Yes." Some, including Antonelli, vote for conciliatory measures and concessions, which however the Deputation on Faith declares
to be impossible. The other very numerous party says
on the contrary that the unexpected force and extent
of the opposition to so fundamental a dogma makes
an anathema all the more necessary. A new plan of
operations has now been hit upon, which is greatly
favoured by the recent deaths. The grand Session for
proclaiming the dogma had been fixed for the 17th,
and many among the minority were with great difficulty persuaded to remain till that critical day. But
now the 25th is talked of.[1] At the same time the
report is circulated and confirmed by Antonelli, that
there will be no prorogation even at the end of July or
beginning of August, but the Council will continue,
though many Bishops, on requesting leave, will be
permitted to depart. It is urgently necessary, according to Antonelli, to settle the questions about the
Oriental Rite. Yet for centuries the Court of Rome
has not troubled any Council with these affairs, but
settled and regulated them by itself, as is testified by
a whole series of papal decrees. And after infalli-

[1] The impending war led to its being held earlier.

bility is proclaimed, it is utterly superfluous to keep hundreds of foreign Bishops here on that account. But it is known that the new dogma will lead to the separation of the Orientals, and so their Bishops are to be kept here longer as hostages, and the name of the Council is to supply the pretext. And it is hoped that the French and German Bishops will the more certainly ask leave and go home, so that the Opposition may be reduced to a small handful. The Pope himself appears greatly to desire this, as was at once inferred from his remark that the Archbishop of Paris is staying on a long time.

Five Bishops, including Förster of Breslau, actually took their departure on the 14th.

SIXTY-EIGHTH LETTER.

Rome, July 17, 1870.—All the Bishops of the minority have left Rome, after presenting a statement of their attitude towards the decrees on the Papacy. They made a last attempt, immediately before going, to move the Pope at least not to hurry on the affair but to grant some respite by proroguing the Council. At twelve o'clock to-day he received a deputation headed by Darboy and Simor. Darboy, who spoke first, represented to him the great and manifold dangers the definition would unquestionably give rise to for the whole Church. Hitherto Pius had met all suggestions of scruple by appealing to his " I am Tradition "—his already assured infallibility. This time he did not do so. He fell back on the ground of its being " too late." Matters had gone too far, and the whole Christian world was now too much occupied and too powerfully excited about the question. Besides, the Council had already passed a decree by a considerable majority, and he was therefore in no position to put a check on the Council, which was now in full swing and urgently pressing for a final decision on this question. The promulgation of the decree of the majority will accordingly follow to-morrow.

The Orientals have subscribed the declaration of the minority. Two German Bishops only, Melchers and Ketteler, have withheld their signature and presented a separate declaration of their own to the Pope. The manifesto of the minority runs thus :—

"*Beatissime Pater !*

"In Congregatione generali die 13 h. m. habitâ dedimus suffragia nostra super schemate primæ Constitutionis dogmaticæ de Ecclesiâ Christi.

"Notum est Sanctitati Vestræ 88 Patres fuisse, qui, conscientiâ urgente et amore Sanctæ Ecclesiæ permoti, suffragium suum per verba *non placet* emiserunt; 62 alios, qui suffragati sunt per verba *placet juxta modum*, denique 70 circiter qui a congregatione abfuerunt atque a suffragio emittendo abstinuerunt. His accedunt et alii, qui, infirmitatibus aut aliis gravioribus rationibus ducti, ad suas diœceses reversi sunt.

"Hâc ratione Sanctitati Vestræ et toto mundo suffra-

gia nostra nota atque manifesta fuere, patuitque quam
multis episcopis sententia nostra probatur, atque hoc
modo munus officiumque quod nobis incumbit persol-
vimus.

"Ab eo inde tempore nihil prorsus evenit quod
sententiam nostram mutaret, quin imo multa eaque
gravissima acciderunt, quæ nos in proposito nostro
confirmaverunt. Atque ideo nostra jam edita suffragia
nos renovare ac confirmare declaramus.

"Confirmantes itaque per hanc scripturam suffragia
nostra a Sessione publicâ die 18 h. m. habendâ abesse
constituimus. Pietas enim filialis ac reverentia quæ
missos nostros nuperrime ad pedes Sanctitatis Vestræ
adduxere, non sinunt nos in causâ Sanctitatis Vestræ
personam adeo proxime concernente palam et in facie
patris dicere *non placet.*

"Et aliunde suffragia in Solenni Sessione edenda
repeterent dumtaxat suffragia in generali Congregatione
deprompta.

"Redimus itaque sine morâ ad greges nostros, quibus
post tam longam absentiam ob belli timores et præ-
sertim summas eorum spirituales indigentias summo-
pere necessarii sumus; dolentes, quod, ob tristia in
quibus versamur rerum adjuncta etiam conscientiarum

pacem et tranquillitatem turbatam inter fideles nostros reperturi simus.

"Interea Ecclesiam Dei et Sanctitatem Vestram, cui intemeratam fidem et obedientiam profitemur, D. N. J. C. gratiæ et præsidio toto corde commendantes sumus Sanctitatis Vestræ

"devotissimi et obedientissimi filii.

"ROMÆ, 17 *Jul.* 1870."

SIXTY-NINTH LETTER.

Rome, July 19, 1870.—On the evening of the 15th
a deputation of the Bishops of the minority waited
on the Pope, consisting of Simor, Primate of Hungary, Archbishops Ginoulhiac, Darboy and Scherr (of
Munich), Ketteler and Rivet, Bishop of Dijon. After
waiting an hour they were admitted at 9 o'clock in the
evening. What they tried to obtain was in fact much
less than the Opposition had hitherto aimed at : they
only asked for the withdrawal of the addition to the
third chapter, which assigns to the Pope the exclusive
possession of all ecclesiastical powers, and the insertion
in the fourth chapter of a clause limiting his infallibility to those decisions which he pronounces " innixus
testimonio Ecclesiarum." Pius gave an answer which
will sound in Germany like a maliciously invented
fable,—" Je ferai mon possible, mes chers fils, mais je
n'ai pas encore lu le Schéma; je ne sais pas ce qu'il

contient." And he then requested Darboy, who had acted as spokesman, to give him the petition of the minority in writing. He promised to do so, and added, not without irony, that he would take the liberty of sending with it to his Holiness the *Schema*, which the Deputation on Faith and the Legates had with such culpable levity omitted to lay before him, when it wanted only two days to the promulgation of the dogma, thereby exposing him to the peril of having to proclaim a decree he was ignorant of. This Darboy did, and in a second letter to the Deputation severely censured their negligence in not even having communicated the *Schema* to the chief personage, the Pope.

Pius added further, whether ironically or in earnest I know not, that if only the minority would increase their 88 votes to 100, he would see what could be done. He concluded by assuring them it was notorious that the whole Church had always taught the unconditional infallibility of the Pope. Bishop Ketteler then came forward, flung himself on his knees before the Pope, and entreated for several minutes that the Father of the Catholic world would make some concession to restore peace and her lost unity to the Church and the episcopat It was a peculiar spectacle to witness these two men, of kindred and yet widely diverse nature, in such an attitude, the one prostrate on the ground before the other. Pius is "totus teres atque rotundus," firm and immoveable, smooth and hard as marble, infinitely self-satisfied intellectually, mindless and ignorant, without any understanding of the mental conditions and needs of mankind, without any notion of the character of foreign nations, but as credulous as a nun, and above all penetrated through and through with reverence for his own person as the organ of the Holy Ghost, and therefore an absolutist from head to heel, and filled with the thought, "I and none beside me." He knows and believes that the holy Virgin, with whom he is on the most intimate terms, will indemnify him for the loss of land and subjects by means of the infallibility doctrine and the restoration of the papal dominion over states and peoples as well as over Churches. He also believes firmly in the miraculous emanations from the sepulchre of St. Peter. At the feet of this man the German Bishop flung himself, "ipso Papâ papalior," a zealot for the ideal greatness and unapproachable dignity of the Papacy, and at the same time inspired by the aristocratic feeling of a Westphalian nobleman and the hierarchical self-consciousness of a Bishop and successor of the ancient chancellor of the Empire, while yet he is surrounded by the intellectual atmosphere of Germany, and with all his firmness of belief is sickly with the pallor of thought, and inwardly struggling with the terrible misgiving that after all historical facts are right, and that the ship of the *Curia,* though for the moment it proudly rides the waves with its sails swelled by a favourable wind, will be wrecked on that rock at last.

The prostration of the Bishop of Mayence seemed to make some impression on Pius. He dismissed the deputation in a hopeful temper. It was of short duration. For directly the report got about that the Pope was yielding, Manning and Senestrey (*de grands effets par de petites causes*) went to the Pope and assured him that all was now ripe, and the great majority enthusiastically set on the most absolute' and uncompromising form of the infallibilist theory, and at the same time frightened him by the warning that, if he made any concession, he would be disgraced in history as a second Honorius. That was enough to stifle any thought of moderation that might have been awakened in his soul.

The sitting of July 16 was held to consider the pro-posals of those who had voted *juxta modum.* The Legates had promised to pay as much consideration as was possible to their wishes, and they redeemed their pledge by striking out one passage and inserting an-other. The majority decided, on the motion of certain Spaniards, which was adopted by the Deputation on Faith, to strike out the words at the opening of the fourth chapter, saying the Pope will define nothing " nisi quod antiquitus tenet cum cæteris Ecclesiis Apostolica Sedes." This was felt to impose too narrow limits on the Pope's infallibility and arbitrary power of defining. And as the minority had the day before expressed to the Pope their special desire that the consent of the Church should be laid down as a requisite condition of doctrinal definitions, it was now resolved, in direct contradiction to their wishes, again on the motion of Spanish Bishops, not only to leave the words " definitiones Pontificis ex sese seu per sese esse irreformabiles," but to add to them "non autem ex consensu Ecclesiæ." And thus the infallibilist decree, as it is now to be received under anathema by the Catholic world, is an eminently Span-ish production, as is fitting for a doctrine which was born and reared under the shadow of the Inquisition.

In the last sitting of the Congregation three Bishops of the Deputation on Faith spoke, the Neapolitan D'Avanzo, Bishop of Calvi and Teano, Zinelli, Bishop of Rovigo, the author of the notorious addition to the third chapter of the third canon, and Gasser, Bishop of Brixen. D'Avanzo was jocose : " As," said he, " the angel bade the Apostle John swallow a book, telling him it would make his belly bitter but taste sweet as honey in his mouth, so must we Bishops swallow this infallibilist *Schema,* and I have done so already. It will no doubt give many of us a stomach-ache, but we must act as if we had honey in our mouths." Gasser, who as a speaker is " se ipse amans sine rivali," to quote Cicero's saying about Pompey, made a speech of endless length, exhausting the patience of his hearers ; but there was some gold mixed with all this dross. Such was his declaration that Councils had hitherto been useful only for people of unsound faith, who did not chose to believe the Pope's *ipse dixit,* which every good Christian had always believed. But now " quid credendum sit unice ab arbitrio Pontificis in posterum dependebit." On this a well-known Hungarian Bishop could not refrain from observing to his neighbour, " Si etiam in- fallibilitas Pontificis contenta esset in Sacrâ Scripturâ magis compromitti non posset quam hoc levissimo ac ineptissimo sermone, quo auditores ex integro jam lassos ad vomitum movit et martyres reddidit."

An amusing scene occurred at the close of this sitting, the last attended by the Bishops of the minority. A printed address was read out and distributed to the Fathers, in which the Legates complained in the strongest language of certain works describing the course of the Council. Two were named and characterized as " calumnious," both published at Paris. The one, by Gaillard, was *Ce qui se passe au Concile ;* the other was by a man distinguished alike for intellect, eloquence and learning, a member of the Council, who has had almost unique opportunities of seeing through the whole business. It is the work I have before mentioned, *La Dernière Heure du Concile,* in which the personal intervention of the Pope and the pressure brought to bear by him are forcibly depicted in strict accordance with truth. This pamphlet had already created a great sensation, and when the Legates called on the Bishops to join them in condemning it, the Italians and Spaniards, who—being for the most part ignorant of French—had not read it, immediately shouted out " Nos condemnamus." " We do not," cried the Bishops of the minority. Two copies of the address were then handed to each of them, one of which they were ordered to return with their names subscribed. The result was not successful; Haynald told the Legates, in the name of the Hungarian Bishops, that they had better first translate *La Dernière Heure* into Latin, and then he and his colleagues would see whether it was really as bad as the Cardinals maintained.

All the Bishops from South and Central Italy who could be whipped up, or who had previously obtained leave of absence on account of illness or age, were peremptorily recalled for the Solemn Session of July 18. Of the Cardinals, Hohenlohe was absent. The rest appeared, including Antonelli, but only three, Patrizzi, Bonaparte and Pambianco, threw a certain spontaneity and energy of voice and manner into their *Placet* by standing up to deliver it. Guidi was the one most observed; he sat there with an oppressed and abstracted air, and his scarcely audible *Placet* escaped with difficulty from his lips. The two negative voters were Bishops Riccio of Cajazzo and Fitzgerald of Little Rock. When the Monsignore who was repeating the names and votes had credited one of them with a *Placet* out of his own head, the Bishop shouted in a stentorian voice, "No; *Non placet !*"

As all the Bishops of the Opposition but two stayed away, and an *abest* was the answer to every name of the slightest note that was called, the Holy Ghost had no opportunity for working a miracle of conversion, and all went prosaically and smoothly as the wheels of a watch, without any sensation.   Each of the stipendiaries has discharged his obligation, and the Pope and Monsignori find that the Council has cost large sums, but think the money is well spent and will bring in abundant interest.   The most remarkable case of desertion was that of Bishop Landriot of Rheims.   Not one of the Bishops had been so open-mouthed, or had announced his fallibilist opinions with such copious flow of words to everybody he came across.   He now says, like Talleyrand, that he has only deserted before the rest. Clerical Rome, so far as I can yet make out, is not in any very exalted state of enthusiasm ; that is prevented by the political conjunctures, which give Antonelli and Berardi a good deal to think about.   De Banneville has indeed given the most consoling assurances to Antonelli ; the 5000 French troops at Civita Vecchia, who had received orders to hold themselves ready for recall to France, are to be at once replaced by 5000 more— recruits it is believed.   Paris wishes just now to be on the best terms with Rome, who may well prove a useful ally in what the *Monde* has already designated a religious war against Protestantism. Meanwhile they are pleased at the Vatican to have erected their *rocher de bronze* beforehand. The Bishops have—ostensibly of their own free will—abdicated in favour of the monarch, to receive back from him so many rights and commissions as he may think good to delegate to them. The revolution in the Church is accomplished " to enrich *one* among all." Pius himself is more than content; his supreme desire, the crown of his life and work, is attained.

During the voting and promulgation a storm burst over Rome, and made the Council Hall so dark that the Pope could not read the decree of his infallibility without having a candle brought. It was read to an accompaniment of thunder and lightning. Some of the Bishops said that heaven thereby signified its condemnation of Gallicanism, while others thought Pius was receiving a divine attestation, as the new Moses who proclaimed the Law of God, like the old one, amid thunder and lightning. It is remarkable that the days of the opening and closing of this Council were the two darkest and most depressing Rome has

witnessed during the eight months of its session.   It
rained without intermission, so that the promised illumination was partly given up and partly proved a
lamentable failure.   There were few but monks, nuns
and Zouaves, during the session in the very empty-
looking church.   When the Pope at last proclaimed
himself the infallible and absolute ruler of all the
baptized "with the approbation of the holy Council,"
some bravos shouted, several persons clapped, and the
nuns cried in tones of tender rapture, "Papa mio!"
That was the only semblance of a demonstration.   If
any spark of enthusiasm really glimmered in the souls
of the Romans, it was quenched by the downpour of
rain.   The keen-witted Roman, who is accustomed to
speak of this Pope with a certain good-humoured irony,
as a sort of comic personality, thinks there is no harm
in gratifying the wish of the old man who has set his
heart on this infallibility; that will hurt nobody.
All the most important members of the diplomatic
bodies stayed away, in obedience to the instructions of
their governments.   Neither the ambassadors of Austria,
France, Prussia or Bavaria were present.   The Belgian
and Dutch consuls and an agent of some South American Republic attended.   The decrees of July 18, estab-

lishing under anathema the two new dogmas, are the following :—

"(*a.*) Si quis itaque dixerit, Romanum Pontificem habere tantummodo officium inspectionis vel directionis, non autem plenam et supremam potestatem jurisdictionis in universam Ecclesiam, non solum in rebus, quæ ad fidem et mores, sed etiam quæ ad disciplinam et regimen Ecclesiæ per totum orbem diffusæ pertinent; aut eum habere tantum potiores partes, non vero totam plenitudinem hujus supremæ potestatis, aut hanc ejus potestatem non esse ordinariam et immediatam sive in omnes ac singulas Ecclesias sive in omnes et singulos Pastores et fideles—anathema sit.

"(*b.*) Sacro approbante Concilio docemus et divinitus revelatum dogma esse definimus: Romanum Pontificem, cum ex cathedrâ loquitur, id est, cum omnium Christianorum Pastoris et Doctoris munere fungens, pro supremâ suâ apostolicâ auctoritate doctrinam de fide vel moribus ab universâ Ecclesiâ tenendam definit, per assistentiam divinam, ipsi in beato Petro promissam, eâ infallibilitate pollere, quâ divinus Redemptor Ecclesiam suam in definiendâ doctrinâ de fide vel moribus instructam esse voluit; ideoque ejusmodo *Romani Pontificis definitiones esse ex sese, non autem ex consensu Ecclesiæ irreformabiles.* Si quis autem huic Nostræ definitioni contradicere, quod Deus avertat, præsumpserit—anathema sit."

In the work against infallibility circulated here by the Bishop of Mayence occurs the following passage : " Will it not seem to all nations that the authority of all Bishops is suppressed and sentenced to death, only in order to erect on such vast and manifold ruins the unlimited authority of the one Roman Pope ?" When these lines were written, the Bishop and his theologian had no notion, or at least no knowledge, of the third anathema of the third chapter, which was afterwards made still more rigorous. They were only thinking of infallibility, but what would they have said, had they known that the Bishops would be required to subscribe to the abolition of the episcopate and the transference of all conceivable ecclesiastical powers and rights over the 180 million of Catholics in principle and in detail to the Pope alone, as a new article of faith imposed under anathema ? And yet this is what happened on the 13th and 18th July 1870. That the ordinary and immediate jurisdiction of the Bishops still survives, is indeed affirmed in the decree, but the affirmation is contrary to fact. It would be in inevitable collision with the constantly encroaching jurisdiction of the Pope; the earthen vessel dashed against the iron.

The Jewish general and historian, Josephus, relates how he was shut up with forty companions in the valley of Jehoshaphat, and summoned to surrender by the Romans. They resolved to die first. The Bishops are not offered this alternative, but threatened with both at once. They are bidden to submit and then kill themselves, to subscribe the decree of the majority, and thereby sign the sentence which degrades and annihilates them, under pain of incurring anathema. That is the demand. The situation is an unprecedented one. And what of the 532 real or titular Bishops who have made the 13th and 18th July " dies nefasti" for the Church, and renounced so many rights and duties for themselves and their successors, like a cast-off garment? Perhaps it lightens their hearts and is a pleasant feeling to them to be able to say, " Thank God, I need not trouble myself any more about doctrine, tradition, or dogma; henceforth the one infallible oracle in the Vatican will attend to all that, and he again will devolve the burden on the lusty shoulders of the Jesuits, as he has done before. And how sweet and convenient it is to be a mere executor of papal

3 G

decrees, while one's episcopal income remains untouched, and to be able to cover one's-self with the Medusa shield of a papal order in every difficulty, and every conflict with clergy, people or governments !"   I heard a Bishop of this party say the other day, " Now first begin the golden days of the episcopate."

It is reported that on the very day after the promulgation several Bishops experienced a certain reaction of sobriety, a feeling like what German students are wont to attribute to cats, and inquired of the high dogma-fabricating parties, the Legates and some members of the Deputation, whether they were really bound to believe, confess and teach all that is contained in the Syllabus, the Bull *Unam Sanctam,* etc., as *e.g.,* the subjection of the secular powers to the Pope, the Church's power of inflicting bodily punishment with Pius who reigns gloriously, the burning of heretics with Leo x., *et id genus omne.*   They are said to have been answered with a well-known Roman proverb, " Toto devorato bove, turpe est in caudâ deficere "— " You have swallowed the whole ox of papal infallibility, and the last Spanish addition with it, and you need not strain at the tail, *i.e.,* the consequences ; that indeed is the best part of this ox."

The Bishops of the minority agreed before leaving Rome that they would none of them act alone and independently, in such further steps as would have to be taken concerning the decrees of the majority, but would all continue to correspond and act in concert. Meanwhile the Council has not been prorogued, but leave of absence is given to Bishops who can allege urgent reasons up to November 15. Perhaps in the interval the builders of the new Jesuit-Papal Zion, who stay behind, will prepare many a surprise for the Catholic world.

Future historians will begin a new period of Church history with July 18, 1870, as with October 31, 1517.

Are we really at the end of the drama? It appears so. On the same spot where, 1856 years ago, the first monarch of the world, Augustus, bade the attendants on his death-bed clap their hands in token of the rôle being well played out to the end, the Roman courtiers on July 18 have saluted by clapping of hands the first man proclaimed infallible monarch of the world by 532 spiritual satraps. The eight months' campaign has terminated in the preliminary closing act of July 18 ; the absolute Papacy celebrates its financially dear-bought, but otherwise easily obtained, triumph over the Church, which now lies defenceless at the feet of the Italians. It only remains to follow up the anathematized enemy, the Bishops of the minority, into their lurking-places, and compel each man of them to bend under the Caudine yoke amid the scornful laughter of his colleagues of the majority. Anathemas, the "ultima ratio" of Rome, have already been discharged at the fugitives, and every such shot of the Infallible is itself infallible.

Appendix.

APPENDIX I.

THERE seem to me to be three points to be considered in reference to this *Schema :* its origin, its contents and scope, and its practical results.

And first as regards its origin and presentation to the Council at this time, it is enough to mention two facts, from which it may be judged whether the affair has been conducted regularly and in accordance with the dignity and rights of this venerable assembly.

It is certain that the fourth chapter, dealing with the infallibility of the Pope, is the turning-point of the whole *Schema*. For whatever is brought forward in the former chapters about the power and origin of the primacy in Peter and its continuance in the Popes, about which there is no difference among us,—and certainly in the first and second chapters this seems to exceed the right measure—is unmistakeably connected with the infallibility in the fourth chapter. So entirely is this infallibility the grand object of the Vatican Council, that some have indiscreetly asserted it is in a sense the sole object. And with reason, for the

819

fabrication of such a dogma must always remain the weightiest act of an Œcumenical Council; and moreover the other questions to be dealt with are either of far less importance, or have long since been settled and only require revision, as, *e.g.*, questions about the being and attributes of God, the reality and need of revelation, the duty of faith, and the relation of faith to reason. Yet this serious question of infallibility was neither indicated in the Bull convoking the Council nor in the other public announcements referring to it, and with good reason, because on the one hand the Catholic world had no desire for a settlement of this question, nor was there any other ground producible for meddling with what had always hitherto been a subject of free inquiry among theologians, and on the other hand there are many and grave evils, partly endangering the salvation of souls, which the Pope out of his care and affection has thought it more needful to deal with.

It is certain that the first stirring of this question came from without, from religious and secular journalists, and that too in an impertinent manner, against all ecclesiastical and traditional precedent and all rules of hierarchical order and usage, by seeking to put a pressure on the conscience of the Bishops through demagogic agitation, and to intimidate them with the prospect of intrigues in their dioceses which would make the government of them impossible. Nay, matters have come to such a pass that the Fathers of the Council, however piously and courageously they may be simply following their conscience, are accused of having paid an improper deference to party opinion, by promoting the introduction of the infallibility question in consequence of these violent agitations, and all of us appear to have lost something of dignity and freedom through the tumult raised before the doors of the Council-chamber. And such a judgment, which is in the highest degree mischievous and injurious to our honour, can hardly be endured without damage and disgrace to this venerable assembly, an assembly which must act independently and not under pressure from without, which must not only be, but appear to be, free.

It is further certain that the question brought before us to-day has been introduced against the natural and logical order of the subjects in hand, and thereby the cause itself is prejudiced. The rest of the *Schema de Fide* ought first to have been submitted to our consideration, on which we have already debated and have the arguments of both sides so fresh in our memory that the final discussion would have been all the easier. Then again the *Schema de Ecclesiâ* begins quite incorrectly with the primacy. Neither its first compilers nor any theologians before now were of opinion that the treatise on the Church should begin with that. And furthermore, our studies have been directed to the questions intended to come on for consideration according to the order originally announced.

And lastly, it is certain that the precipitate introduction of the question of infallibility by reversing the original order has contributed to the injury rather than the honour of the Holy See. For as, according to the

Bull *Multiplices inter,* motions are to be sent in to a special Congregation, which then reports to the Pope, who either accepts or rejects its decisions, it follows that the authors of this motion have compelled the Holy Father to make a decision in his own case and in reference to a personal prerogative, and have thereby— no doubt unintentionally—failed to show a fitting regard for his high position, if they have not rather directly injured it.

If I am right on all these points—and such appears to be the case—it is impossible to discuss and decide upon the question of infallibility, thus originating and thus introduced, without paving the way for the insults of unbelievers and the reproaches which threaten the moral authority of this Council. And this should the more carefully be avoided, because writings and reports directed against the power and legitimacy of the Council are already current and widely circulated, so that it seems more likely to sow the seeds of contradiction and disunion among Christians than to quiet men's minds and lead to peace. If I may venture to add a practical remark to this portion of my speech, I should say that some have with good reason declared this question to be inopportune, and that there would be equally good reason for abstaining from any decision, even if the discussion of it were opportune.

On the contents and tendency of the *Schema* I shall make only a few observations.

The *Schema* does not deal with the infallibility of the Church, which we all believe, and which has been

proved for twenty centuries, but lays down as an article
of faith that the Pope is, alone and of himself, infallible,
and that he possesses this privilege of inerrancy in all
matters to which the infallibility of the Church herself
extends. It must be well understood that the *Schema*
does not refer to that universally admitted infallibility,
which is the invincible and inviolable strength of dogmatic decrees and decisions binding alike on all the
faithful and all their pastors, and which reposes wholly
and solely on the agreement of the Bishops in union with
the Pope, but that it refers—though this is not expressly
stated—to the personal, absolute and exclusive infallibility of the Pope. On the former kind of infallibility
—that of the Church—complete harmony prevails
among us, and there is therefore no ground for any
discussion, whence it follows that it is the second kind
of infallibility which is in question here. To deny this
would be to disguise and distort the doctrine and spirit
of the *Schema*. And moreover, the Pope's personal infallibility is not maintained there as a mere opinion or
commendable doctrine, but as a dogma of faith. Hitherto
the opportuneness and admissibility of entertaining this
question has been disputed at the Council ; that dispute
is now closed by the Pope's decision that the matter can
no longer be passed over in silence, and we have now to
consider whether it is or is not opportune to declare the
personal infallibility of the Pope a dogma.

To deal rightly with this subject and come to a decision, it is requisite that the formula or definition of
the doctrine should be laid before us, that it should be

proved by sure and unquestionable evidence, and finally, that it should be accepted with moral unanimity.

There is the greatest difficulty in fixing the form or definition of the doctrine, as is shown by the example of those who first composed and then revised the *Schema*, and who seem to have expended much—perhaps fruitless—labour upon it; for they indulge in ambiguous expressions which open the door to endless controversies. What is meant by " exercising the office of the supreme teacher of Christendom " ? What are the external conditions of its exercise ? When is it certain that the Pope has exercised it ? The compilers of the *Schema* think of course that this is as clear as, *e.g.*, the œcumenicity of a Council. But they thereby contradict themselves, for a Council is only then held œcumenical by the body of the faithful scattered over the world when the Bishops are morally unanimous, and therefore infallibility would still depend on the consent of the episcopate if the same principle is to be applied to papal decrees. The authors of the *Schema* either eliminate this consent or they do not. In the former case they are introducing an innovation, and an innovation which is unprecedented and intolerable ; in the latter case they are only expressing an old and universally received view and fighting a man of straw. But in no case can they pass over in silence the necessity or needlessness of the consent of the episcopate, for that would be to infuse doubts into the faithful and throw fresh difficulties in their way in a question of such vast importance and all that at present hinges on it.

The compilers only define the subject-matter of papal infallibility by saying that it is identical with the infallibility of the Church. But that explanation is inadequate until the Council has defined the infallibility of the Church. Hence it is clearly a logical fallacy to prefix the *Schema* on the Primacy to that on the Church. Of the infallibility of the Church we know that it always acts within the proper limits of its subject-matter, both because the common consent of the Bishops is necessary and because the Church is holy and cannot sin, while the compilers of this *Schema* on papal infallibility on the one hand, according to their own statement, exclude the consent of the Bishops, and on the other hand have not undertaken to prove that every Pope is holy and cannot sin.[1]

But if a form of definition was really discovered, it would have to be confirmed by solid and certain proofs. It would have to be shown that this doctrine of personal infallibility is contained in holy Scripture, as it has been always interpreted, and in the tradition of all centuries, that it has the moral assent not merely of some but of all Fathers, Doctors, Bishops and Theologians, and that it is in perfect harmony with all decisions and acts of the General Councils, and therefore with the decrees of the fourth and fifth sessions of the Council of Constance—for even supposing they

[1] [On the essential connection between the infallibility and the impeccability of the Popes, see *Janus*, pp. 113 *sqq.*, and Maret, *Du Concile Général*, vol. ii. ch. 13.—Tr.]

were not œcumenical, which I do not admit, they would show the mind and common opinion of the theologians and Bishops.[1] It would further have to be proved that this doctrine is neither contradicted by historical facts nor by any acts of the Popes themselves, and lastly that it belongs to that class of truths which the Council and Pope in union can decide upon, as having been acknowledged for revealed truth always, everywhere and by all.

All this our *Schema* omits. But when the question is of defining a dogma, the Fathers must have sufficient evidence laid before them and time allowed them for weighing it. As it is, neither the original nor the revised draft of the *Schema* supply such arguments as might illustrate the matter and clear up all doubts, and as little is sufficient time allowed—as is generally notorious—for unravelling this complicated question, solving its difficulties and acquiring the necessary information about it. In such a matter, where a burden is to be laid on the conscience of the faithful, a hasty decision pronounced without absolute certainty is dangerous, while there is no danger in a fuller discussion and in not deciding till it can be done with complete certainty of conscience.

It would finally be necessary that the doctrine of the personal and independent infallibility of the Pope, after being clearly expressed and certainly proved, should be accepted by the Fathers with moral una-

---

[1] [The decree of Constance defines that "every lawfully convoked Œcumenical Council representing the Church derives its authority immediately from Christ, and every one, the Pope included, is subject to it in matters of faith, in the healing of schism, and the reformation of the Church." It was carried in full Council without a dissentient voice.—Tr.]

nimity ; for otherwise we must fear that the definition would be regarded as a papal constitution and not a decree of a Council.[1]   It is a duty to impose a truth of faith on all Christians, but this difficult and sacred right can only be exercised by the Bishops with the greatest caution.   And therefore the Fathers of Trent, as you all know, whatever sophistical objections may be raised, did not pass their decrees on dogmatic questions by numerical majorities, but with moral unanimity. I content myself now with referring to the perplexity of conscience among the faithful, which must arise from passing this dogma over the heads of the minority, and thus giving a handle for questioning the validity and authority of this Council.

Two leading remarks may suffice on the practical consequences of the dogma, for the only object of bringing forward the personal infallibility as an article of faith is to make the unity of the Church more compact and the central authority stronger, and thus to supply an efficient remedy for all abuses.

As regards unity and central authority, I must first make the general observation that they exist and must be preserved, not however in that shape which we may fancy or which approves itself to our reason, but as Jesus Christ our Lord ordained and as our fathers have maintained it.   For it is no business of ours to arrange the Church according to our good pleasure and to alter the foundation of the work of God.   The necessary unity in faith and that of the common central authority

[1] [That in fact is exactly what Antonelli calls it in his circular.—Tr.]

under fatherly guidance exists and has always existed among Catholics, or else one would have to say that there had been some essential defect in the Church of the past, which all will certainly deny.

The unity of doctrine and Church communion and the central authority of the Pope remain then unshaken, as they always flourished and flourish still without any dogmatic definition of infallibility.

Let it not be said that this unity will hereafter be closer when the central authority is stronger, for this inference is fallacious. Mere unity is not enough, but we must have that unity and that measure of it which the nature and scope of the thing, as well as the law and the necessity of life, demand. Else the thing itself might lamentably perish by being forced into too rigid an unity, from its inward vitality being cramped, disturbed and broken through the external pressure. Thus even in civil matters the unity of freemen, who act for themselves under the law, is indeed looser but more honourable than the unity of slaves tormented under an arbitrary tyranny. Permit us to retain that unity which belongs to us by the ordinance of Christ, and that means of unity—viz., the central authority of the Pope—which our forefathers acknowledged and honoured, who neither separated the Bishops from the Pope nor the Pope from the Bishops. Let us loyally hold fast to the ancient rule of faith and the statutes of the Fathers, and the more so since the proposed definition is open to many grave objections.

And again we can hardly doubt that this expedient

would be powerless for healing the evils of our time, and it must be feared would rather tend to the injury of many. The matter must not be regarded only from a theological standpoint, but also in its bearings on civil society. For we in this place are not mere head-sacristans or superiors of a monastery, but men called to share with the Pope his care for the whole Church ; allow us therefore to take the state of the world into our prudent consideration.

Will personal and independent infallibility serve to rouse from their grave those perished Churches on the African coast, or to wake the slumbers of the East, which once bloomed with such flowers of intellect and virtue ? Will it be easier for our brethren, the Vicars-Apostolic, to bring the heathen, Mahometans, and schismatics to the Catholic faith, if they preach the doctrine of the Pope's sole infallibility ? Or will the proposed definition perhaps infuse spirit and strength into Protestants and other heretics to return to the Roman Church and lay aside all prejudices and hatred against it ? And now, first, for Europe ! I say it with pain,—the Church is everywhere under ban. She is excluded from those congresses where nations discuss war and peace, and where once the authority of the Holy See was so powerful, whereas now it is bidden not even to proclaim its views. The Church is shut out in several European countries from the Chambers, and if some prelates or clergymen here and there belong to them, this appears a rare occurrence. The Church is shut out from the school, where grievous errors advance

3 H

unchecked ; from legislation, which manifests a secular and therefore irreligious tendency ; and lastly, from the family, where civil marriage corrupts morals. All those who preside over the public affairs of Europe avoid us or hold us in check.

And what sort of remedy do you offer the world, which is diseased with so many uncertainties about the Church ? On all those who are seeking to shake off from their indocile shoulders even the burdens imposed on them from of old and reverently accepted by their fathers, you would now lay a new, and therefore difficult and odious, burden. All those who are of weak faith are to be crushed by a new and inopportune dogma, a doctrine never hitherto defined, and which, without any amends being made for the injurious manner of its introduction, is to be defined by a Council of which many say that its freedom is insufficiently attested. And yet you hope to remedy everything by this definition of personal and exclusive infallibility, to strengthen the faith and improve the morals of all. Your hopes are vain. The world either remains sick or perishes, not from ignorance of the truth and its teachers, but because it avoids it and will not accept its guidance. But if it now rejects the truth, when proclaimed by the whole teaching body of the Church, the 800 Bishops dispersed over the world and infallible in union with the Pope, how much more will it do so, when the truth is proclaimed by one single infallible teacher, who has only just been declared infallible ? For an authority to be strong and effective, it is not enough for it to be claimed ; it must also be accepted. And thus it is not enough to declare that the Pope is infallible, personally and apart from the Bishops, but he must be acknowledged as such by all, if his office is to be a reality. What is the use, *e.g.*, of an anathema, if the authority which pronounces it is not respected ? The Syllabus circulated through Europe, but what evils could it cure even where it was received as an infallible oracle ? There were only two large countries where religion ruled, not in fact but *de jure*—Austria and Spain. In both of them this Catholic order fell to the ground though commanded by the infallible authority ; perhaps indeed in Austria on that very account.

Let us take things as they are. Not only will the independent infallibility of the Pope not destroy these prejudices and objections which draw away so many from the faith, but it will increase and intensify them. There are many who in heart are not alienated from the Catholic Church, but who yet think of what they term a separation of Church and State. It is certain that several of the leaders of public opinion are on this side, and will take occasion from the proposed definition to effect their object. The example of France will soon be copied more or less all over Europe, and to the greatest injury of the clergy and the Church herself. The compilers of the *Schema*, whether they desire it or not, are introducing a new era of mischief, if the subject-matter of papal infallibility is not accurately defined, or if it can be supposed that under the head of morals the Pope will give decisions on the civil and political acts of sovereigns and nations, laws and rights, to which a public authority will be attributed.[1]   Every one of any political cultivation knows what seeds of discord are contained in our *Schema*, and to what perils it exposes even the temporal power of the Holy See.

To explain this more minutely in detail would take too long and might be indiscreet, for were I to say all, I might easily bring forward things it is more prudent to suppress.   However, I have delivered my conscience, so far as is allowed me, and so let my words be taken in good part.   I know well that everything in the world has its difficulties, and one must not always shrink from action because greater evil may follow.   But I put the matter before the reverend fathers, not that they may instantly conform to my opinion, but in order that they may give a full and ripe consideration to the arguments of all parties.   I know too that we must not childishly quail before public opinion, but neither should we obstinately resist it; it is wiser and more prudent often to reconcile one's-self with it, and in every case to take it into account.   I know, lastly, that the Church needs no arm of flesh, yet she does not reject the approval and aid of civil society, and did not, I think, look back with regret from the time of Constan-

---

[1] This is emphatically asserted in a sermon preached last year at Kensington by Archbishop Manning, where he says, speaking in the Pope's name, " I claim to be the Supreme Judge and director of the consciences of men ; of the peasant that tills the field and the prince that sits on the throne ; of the household that lives in the shade of privacy *and the Legislature that makes laws for kingdoms*—I am the sole last Supreme Judge of what is right and wrong."

tine to the time of Nero. So much for the practical consequences of the *Schema*.

Finally, my desire is (1.) that the *Schema* should be deferred for a later discussion, because it has not been introduced into the Council in a sufficiently worthy manner ; (2.) that it should meanwhile be revised, and the limits of infallibility more accurately marked out, so as to leave no handle for future sophistries and attacks ; (3.) but, best of all, that the question of infallibility should be let drop altogether on account of its manifold inconveniences.

APPENDIX II.

Letters on the Council from French Bishops.[1]

I.

Votre judicieuse dissertation est pleine de sens et de la meilleure critique ; mais c'est bien de cela qu'il s'agit aujourd'hui ! On veut se tromper et tromper ; le reste importe peu. Ce qui importe le plus, ce qui nous sauvera, je l'espère, mieux que toutes discussions avec des gens de mauvaise foi ou de parti pris, c'est d'établir des bases incontestables et de faire que la saine opinion publique soutienne les vrais intérêts de l'Église.

1. Le Gallicanisme n'est pas une doctrine, pas même une opinion, c'est une simple négation de prétentions nées au onzième siècle, et une résistance à ces prétentions, au nom de la tradition ancienne et constante des Églises. L'ultramontanisme, au contraire, est une doctrine, une opinion qui est venue s'entre sur le vieux tronc et qui a poussé des jets de croyances positives. Muselée au Concile de Florence, écartée au Concile de

---

[1] These letters are taken from the *Journal des Débats* of May 6 and 11. The Bishops of Marseilles and Montpellier are said to be the writers.

Trente, cette opinion reparaît furieuse au Concile du Vatican.

2. Le Gallicanisme est improprement nommé. Son *veto* appartient à toutes les nations Catholiques. L'Espagne en soutenait la force antique, Saint François de Sales en vengeait les droits au nom des priviléges de la maison de Savoie, et aujourd'hui, nous autres Français, nous l'avons trouvé faible chez nous, en comparaison de sa vitalité en Allemagne, en Autriche, en Hongrie, en Portugal, en Amérique, et jusqu'au fond de l'Orient.

3. Notre faiblesse, en ce moment, ne vient ni des Écritures, ni de la tradition des Pères, ni des monumens des Conciles Généraux et de l'histoire. Elle vient de notre défaut de liberté, qui est radical. Une minorité imposante qui représente la foi de plus de 100 millions de Catholiques, c'est-à-dire de presque la moitié de l'Église universelle, est écrasée par le joug imposé de règlemens restrictifs et contraires aux traditions conciliaires. Par des députations que nous n'avons pas réellement choisies et qui osent introduire dans le texte discuté des paragraphes non discutés ; par une commission pour les interpellations imposée par l'autorité ; par le défaut absolu de discussion, réplique, objection, interpellation ; par des journaux que l'on encourage pour la traquer, pour soulever contre elle le clergé des diocèses ; par les nonciatures qui viennent à la rescousse, quand les journaux ne suffisent pas pour tout bouleverser, c'est-à-dire pour ériger en témoins de la foi les prêtres contre les évêques, et ne plus laisser à ces juges divins que le rôle de députés du clergé secondaire avec

mandat impératif, et blâme si on ne répond pas au
mandat. La minorité est écrasée surtout par tout le
poids de la suprême autorité qui fait peser sur elle les
éloges et encouragemens qu'elle adresse, *par brefs,* aux
prêtres, et par toutes les manifestations à Dom Guéranger contre M. de Montalembert et autres.

4. La majorité n'est pas libre ; car elle se produit par
un appoint considérable de prélats qui ne sauraient
être témoins de la foi d'Églises naissantes ou mourantes.
Or, cet appoint, qui se compose du chiffre énorme de
tous les vicaires apostoliques, du chiffre relativement
trop fort des évêques Italiens et des États Pontificaux,
cet appoint n'est pas libre. C'est une armée toute faite,
toute acquise, endoctrinée, enrégimentée, disciplinée,
que l'on menace, si elle bronche, de la famine ou de la
disponibilité, et l'on a été jusqu'à donner de l'argent pour
ramener quelques transfuges. Donc, il est évident qu'il
n'y a pas de liberté suffisante.—La conclusion ultérieure
est qu'il n'y a pas *œcuménicité nette et plausible.* Et
ceci n'infirme en rien les vrais principes : l'Église est et
reste infaillible dans les Conciles Généraux ; seulement
il faut que les conciles présentent tous les caractères
d'œcuménicité ; convocation légitime, liberté pleine
pour les jugemens, confirmation par le Pape. Si une
seule de ces conditions manque, tout peut être révoqué
en doute. On a eu le Brigandage d'Ephèse, ce qui n'a
pas empêché d'avoir eu ensuite un vrai Concile de ce
nom. On pourrait avoir *Ludibrium Vaticanum ;* ce qui
n'empêcherait pas de tout réparer dans de nouvelles et
sérieuses assises. . . .

Vous pourrez répandre ces réflexions, je crois que le grand remède aujourd'hui nous doit venir du dehors . . .

II.

Je n'ai point parlé une seule fois, je ne parlerai pas davantage dans la suite. Je n'aime ni les gens qui posent, ni les choses complétement inutiles. *J'agis* depuis quatre mois, et je crois avoir rendu quelques services par ce moyen qui en dépit de toutes les entraves, nous a donné trois représentations, une commission internationale, des commissions de nations et 137 signataires[1] qui succomberont avec honneur et horions, si l'on continue à nous traiter aussi mal.

Je crois inutiles tous efforts pour résister à l'aveuglement de l'orgueil moyen-âge, toutes Notes diplomatiques, toutes menaces qui ne sauraient aboutir, et dont je déplorerais le premier l'exécution, si elle était possible. Le remède n'est pas là ; on se jouera de tout, et on ira triomphalement aux abîmes.

Quand on a affaire à des gens qui ne craignent qu'une chose, il faut se servir de cette chose,—c'est-à-dire de l'opinion publique.

Il faut par ce moyen établir ce qui est vrai—point d'autorité parceque point de liberté. Le défaut de liberté. Le défaut de liberté, gros comme des montagnes, crève les yeux ; il repose sur des faits notoires, appréciables pour tous, et sa constatation publique est la seule planche de salut dans la tourmente inouïe que subit l'Église.

[1] Lire : spartiates.

A notre arrivée, tout était fait sans nous. Toutes les mailles du réseau étaient serrées, et les jésuites qui ont monté le traquenard ne doutaient pas un instant que nous y serions pris. Ils voulaient nous faire poser par enchantement la pierre angulaire de leur fronton, et se seraient chargés ensuite, sans nous, de bâtir le portail de leur édifice en un clin d'œil.

Nous avons donc trouvé un règlement tout fait,— c'est-à-dire des menottes. Pour faire droit à nos plaintes, on a serré de plus belle, et nous jouissons de l'ancien brodequin que Louis XVI. a supprimé. Pour être vrai, il faut dire que les tourmenteurs ont fait la chose avec toute la grâce imaginable. Nous avons trouvé une majorité toute faite, très compacte, plus que suffisante en nombre, parfaitement disciplinée et qui a reçu au besoin instructions, injonctions, menaces, prison, argent. Le système des candidatures officielles est distancé de 100 kilomètres.

Une commission, la plus utile, celle où l'on peut adresser ses réclamations, a été créée et imposée d'office. Mais il faut dire à sa louange qu'elle ne fonctionne pas, parce qu'elle ne répond jamais ou qu'elle ne repond qu'aux membres de la majorité. Nous avons été libres de nommer les autres commissions, c'est-à-dire que la majorité fictive a pu les créer à l'aide de listes dressées et lithographiées.

Restait la parole ; mais à quelles conditions ? Défense de répliquer un mot, de discuter, d'éclairer. Si on voulait parler, il fallait se faire inscrire, et le lendemain, ou deux jours après, quand tout était refroidi, on pouvait

venir ennuyer l'assemblée par un discours. Défense
alors de sortir du thème donné aux écoliers (excepté
pour MM. de la majorité) et quand on a tenté de parler
de liberté, de règlement, de commission, d'acoustique, de
décentralisation, de désitalianisation, on a vu se produire
les scènes tumultueuses qui ont démoli les Cardinaux
Rauscher et Schwarzenberg, les Évêques de Colocza, de
Bosnie, d'Halifax, tandis qu'on trouvait bon que
Moulins, Belley et d'autres introduisissent de force la
grande question à propos de la vie des clercs.

La pauvre petite minorité est en butte aux injures,
aux calomnies, et traquée par la *Civiltà, l'Univers, le
Monde, l'Union, l'Osservatore* et *la Correspondance de
Rome.* Ces journaux sont autorisés et encouragés. Ils
soulèvent contre nous le clergé de nos diocèses, et ce
clergé applaudi. Un de nous a osé écrire contre son
collègue ; est il n'a pas reçu un blâme officiel.

Mais voici ce qui achève d'opprimer notre liberté :
elle est écrasée de tout le poids du respect que nous
portons à notre chef.

La question est pendante ; elle n'est pas même à
l'ordre du jour, les juges de droit divin sont réunis et
attendent pour la traiter. Or, en pleines assises, le chef
se sert de sa haute et divine autorité pour blâmer
devant les prêtres qui lui sont présentés *leurs* évêques
mineurs. Il fait l'éloge funèbre de M. de Montalembert
devant 400 personnes ; il écrit à Dom Guéranger, à
l'Abbé de Cabrières de Nîmes, qui s'est dressé devant
l'Évêque d'Orléans, aux diocèses dont les prêtres font
des Adresses pour forcer la main à *leurs mandataires ;*

et il fait tout cela en termes tels que *la Gazette du Midi* et *tutti quanti* déclarent qu'il n'est plus permis ni aux évêques ni à personne de soutenir le contraire ; et on appelle cela de la liberté !

On nous menace de passer par-dessus une minorité imposante, contrairement à toute la tradition, de fouler aux pieds la règle suprême de saint Vincent de Lerins : *Quod ubique, quod semper, quod ab omnibus.* On prêche que l'unanimité morale n'est pas nécessaire, que le chef est maître de tout, et que nous devons rendre des services et non point des sentences, faire de l'affection quand il s'agit de la foi. Voilà notre liberté ! Un Cardinal me disait pour conclusion : " Mon cher, nous allons aux abîmes."

Tout cela est capable d'ébranler les faibles, de désagréger ce qui tient à si peu.

Je crois vous avoir peint la position ce qu'elle est. Priez pour nous, faites valoir la chose, parce qu'elle est *vraie*, parce que je crois servir l'Église en vous la révélant.

Après mes souffrances de cet hiver, je ne pense pas pouvoir affronter les chaleurs. . . . D'ailleurs, Dieu seul peut nous sauver.

APPENDIX III.

Difficultés de la Situation a Rome.[1]

I.

La question de l'infaillibilité pontificale, devenue, contre l'attente universelle, l'objet capital du Concile du Vatican depuis son ouverture, ne semble pas toucher encore à une solution immédiate. Cette grave question qui devait, au dire de certains hommes, être définie par acclamation dès les premières séances du Concile, puis le jour de l'Epiphanie, puis, après de courts débats, pour la fête de Saint Joseph ou le 25 Mars jour de l'Annonciation ; différée de jour en jour à raison des énormes difficultés qu'elle rencontre, à la grande surprise des partisans de l'infaillibilité, doit enfin, nous dit-on, être, sans nouveau délai, résolue solennellement le 29 Juin, jour de la fête du Prince des Apôtres. Si telle est véritablement la pensée des Présidents du Concile, il semble difficile qu'elle puisse se réaliser. Quelques jours seulement nous séparent de cette solennité, et près de cent orateurs sont inscrits pour traiter cette question devant le Concile. Dans cette situation, il faut qu'on choisisse entre trois partis : ou supprimer

[1] From the *Gazette de France* of June 28. The Vicar-General of an eminent French Bishop, who had been at Rome, is the reputed author.

toute discussion, ou proroger le Concile, ou exiger qu'il poursuive ses travaux jusqu'à ce qu'enfin toutes les difficultés soient pleinement éclaircies, et que tous les Pères puissent donner leur suffrage en parfaite connaissance de cause.

Supprimer, ou du moins restreindre la discussion de telle sorte que la conscience d'un nombre considérable de Pères qui sentent vivement toute la gravité de la question et les difficultés de tout genre dont elle est hérissée, ne soit pas pleinement satisfaite, ce serait violer toutes les règles des délibérations conciliares que nous voyons de siècle en siècle pratiquées avec la liberté et la maturité la plus complète. Rien ne saurait dispenser d'un examen approfondi, lorsqu'il s'agit d'imposer un dogme nouveau à la croyance des fidèles ; et, au dire des théologiens, toute définition rendue sans une discussion préalable qui porte jusqu'à l'évidence le caractère de doctrine révélée dans le point mis en délibération, demeure par cela même frappée de nullité. Il suffit de parcourir rapidement les actes des Conciles Œcuméniques pour se convaincre des patientes recherches, de la sage lenteur qu'ils ont apportées à leurs délibérations ; et il est incontestable que les questions à résoudre dans ces grandes assemblées étaient loin de présenter les difficultés qui se rencontrent dans celle qui s'agite en ce moment. Le monde Chrétien n'ignore pas cela, et il ne verrait pas d'un œil indifférent un jugement solennel, en une matière qui touche à la constitution même de l'Eglise, prononcé à la hâte et par un coup de majorité.

Sans doute ceux qui tiennent dans leurs mains la direction du Concile, se persuadent que la question est depuis longtemps assez discutée pour qu'on sache à quoi s'en tenir sans de plus amples recherches ; et, parce qu'à leurs yeux l'infaillibilité du Pape est une vérité, ils regardent toute nouvelle discussion comme une pure formalité que rien ne commande impérieusement. Mais par cela même que la question est discutée depuis plusieurs siècles, et que l'on discute encore avec science, érudition et bonne foi, il faut conclure évidemment que la lumière n'est pas encore faite à ce point qu'on puisse dire que telle est incontestablement la tradition antique et universelle.

Si à leurs yeux l'infaillibilité du Pape est une vérité certainement révélée, et qu'ils tiennent à précipiter la définition par égard pour certaines impatiences, ils ont un moyen bien simple de les satisfaire, sans commettre une violation des lois conciliaires. Dans le système ultramontain, le Pape étant infaillible, et, du consentement de tous les catholiques, l'Église universelle ne pouvant jamais accepter l'erreur et y adhérer, toute définition *ex cathedrâ* sera immanquablement suivie de l'assentiment de tout le corps de l'Église. Pie IX., assure-t-on, est profondément convaincu de son infaillibilité comme Pontife suprême. Eh bien ! de deux choses l'une : ou il faut que le concile agisse en concile, et par conséquent avec circonspection, pesant avec une attention scrupuleuse les raisons graves, les faits, les textes allégués de part et d'autre ; ou le Pape, en vertu de son autorité apostolique, par un acte des plus solennels, doit trancher toutes les difficultés et définir lui-même le dogme de cette infaillibilité qu'il croit être un apanage essentiel de la dignité suprême dont il est revêtu. Pourquoi ne pas tenter cette expérience ? Si l'Église adhère à sa décision, son infaillibilité est très canoniquement établie : si elle n'adhère pas, il est évident qu'il ne peut prétendre à ce privilège. La question est alors définitivement établie, et toute dispute cesse. Jusqu'ici, aucune décision nette, précise et solennelle sur ce point n'a été donnée : hésiter sur l'emploi de ce moyen, ne serait-ce pas douter de cette infaillibilité ? Et si, en l'écartant on veut que le Concile prenne lui-même la responsabilité d'une définition dogmatique, il est alors de toute convenance, de toute justice, de toute nécessité qu'il ne prononce qu'après l'examen le plus approfondi.

L'état des esprits dans le Concile et hors du Concile, les discours prononcés, les écrits nombreux publiés de part et d'autre, prouvent évidemment, aux yeux de quiconque juge sans parti pris et avec une parfaite impartialité, que la question, depuis 1682, pour ne pas remonter plus haut, n'a pas encore fait un seul pas ; elle en est toujours au même point. L'étude la plus attentive de la Tradition n'a pas donné de nouvelles lumières à ceux qui sont capables de ces études, et sans doute l'état de la question dans cette sphère mérite une attention tout exceptionnelle, et bien différente de celle que prétend attirer sur soi un enthousiasme factice ou irréfléchi.

II.

La prorogation du Concile serait donc la mesure la plus rationelle et la plus prudente. Mais les impatiences provoquées, enflammées de plus en plus par toute sorte de manœuvres, comment les contenir ? Ces feuilles, ces écrits, cette propagande pieuse, qui les excitaient par la promesse d'une satisfaction prochaine, tout cela ne va-t-il pas devenir l'objet d'un mépris universel, pour avoir leurré si longtemps les âmes honnêtes et religieuses d'une espérance si lente à se réaliser ? Mais que faire ! Telle est la difficulté de la situation qu'on a si imprudemment créée. S'il faut que le Concile décide, il ne reste plus qu'à le proroger, pour qu'il puisse un peu plus tard reprendre ses travaux avec toute la patience et la liberté d'esprit qu'ils réclament : ou bien il faut qu'il les poursuive actuellement sans désemparer, jusqu'à ce qu'enfin tout soit mûr pour le jugement à prononcer.

Mais ici deux tristes réflexions se présentent à l'esprit. D'abord, quelle rigueur,—le mot n'est pas excessif, et on l'a entendu sortir de la bouche de bonnes femmes Romaines, au moment où les vénérables Pères faisaient cortège au Sauveur du monde porté en triomphe à la procession solennelle de la Fête-Dieu ;—quelle rigueur ne serait-ce pas de retenir plus longtemps, dans cette saison de chaleurs accablantes, sous un climat que les Romains eux-mêmes se hâtent de fuir à cette époque de l'année, des vieillards épuisés par l'âge, par les infirmités, par les fatigues de tout genre, fatigues du corps, fatigues de l'esprit, angoisses de l'âme en présence des plus terribles dangers pour leurs troupeaux particuliers, pour l'Église universelle, pour la société tout entière ; des vieillards qui sentent le poids énorme de cette responsabilité, qui entendent tous les jours la voix de l'opinion publique, et la voix plus puissante et plus pénétrante de la religion alarmée ; des vieillards, parmi lesquels plusieurs ont déjà succombé, plusieurs autres sont atteints de maladie, tous sont privés de l'air vivifiant du pays natal, des soins particuliers que ne sauraient donner des mains étrangères, des consolations qu'un pasteur fidèle trouve toujours au milieu d'un peuple qui l'aime.

Les séances en Congrégation Générale, continuées presque tous les jours sans interruption, durent, depuis huit heures et demie du matin jusqu'à une heure de l'après-midi. Le devoir de la prière, la récitation de l'office canonial, la méditation des matières à discuter, la préparation des discours à prononcer, rien de tout cela ne peut être suspendu. Des jeunes gens robustes ne résisteraient pas longtemps à ce travail si multiplié, si continu, à l'effort d'une attention soutenue pendant les longues heures des séances conciliaires sur des questions qui ne pèsent pas uniquement sur la pensée, mais aussi et plus encore sur la conscience, et enfin à l'action accablante des fortes chaleurs, dont l'intensité, par l'agglomération de six cents prélats, redouble sans mesure dans une salle d'ailleurs extrêmement incommode sous tous les rapports. On entend les plus vigoureux de corps et d'esprit déclarer qu'ils sont à bout de forces. Et l'on persisterait encore à les retenir !

Mais il y aurait encore là quelque chose de plus grave. Retenir les évêques jusqu'à ce qu'une définition de l'infaillibilité pontificale ait pu être rendue après une discussion parfaitement libre, et aussi longue qu'on doit l'augurer du nombre des orateurs inscrits et des questions graves et nombreuses qui se rattachent à cette définition, c'est leur dire : évêques, il faut vous résoudre à mourir ou à bâcler en toute hâte un jugement duquel dépendent les destinées de l'Église et du monde. Oui, mourez, accablées par l'ennui, la fatigue, le climat dévorant, l'âge et les infirmités ; ou, si vous tenez à vivre encore, foulez aux pieds les règles les plus sacrées des conciles, sacrifiez votre conscience, et avec la vôtre celle de plusieurs millions d'âmes !

Sous le rapport de la liberté de discussion, bien des choses dans le Concile du Vatican ne ressemblent pas aux anciens Conciles Généraux, toujours vénérés dans l'Église. Au dedans, au dehors, un parti a exercé sur les Pères une pression toujours croissante. Au dedans, des règlements mal faits, des interruptions sans cause, dont le résultat inévitable était de décourager les hommes les plus fermes, et d'empêcher ou d'affaiblir la manifestation de la vérité ; une certaine fraction de l'assemblée, turbulente, impétueuse, arrêtant par des murmures les prélats les plus vénérables dont la doctrine ne se pliait pas à ses idées ; les présidents fermant les yeux sur ces faits et n'ayant de sévérités que pour les adversaires de l'infaillibilité ; la discussion brusquement arrêtée au gré de ceux qu'elle déconcertait. Au dehors, des journalistes qui ne cessaient de prodiguer l'insulte aux évêques contraires à leurs opinions.

Rome est tout émue d'un fait récent concernant l'un des membres les plus éminents du Concile, le Cardinal Guidi, Archevêque de Bologne, précédemment religieux Dominicain, et très célèbre professeur de théologie dans la capitale du monde Chrétien. Il avait parlé dans le Concile sur la question de l'infaillibilité, exigeant pour celle des définitions pontificales le concours de l'épiscopat. Le jour même, il est mandé et admonesté du ton le plus sévère. "Saint-Père, a répondu le cardinal, j'ai dit aujourd'hui ce que j'ai enseigné au grand jour pendant plusieurs années à votre collège de la Minerve, sans que jamais personne ait trouvé cet enseignement repréhensible. L'orthodoxie de mon enseignement avait dû être attestée à votre Sainteté lorsqu'elle daigna me choisir pour aller à Vienne combattre certains docteurs allemands dont les principes ébranlaient les fondements de la foi catholique. Que mon discours d'aujourd'hui soit soumis à l'examen d'une commission de théologiens ; je ne redoute pas ce jugement." Des paroles menaçantes pour le cardinal ont terminé cet entretien. Le matin, après la séance, un prélat domestique disait dans la salle même du Concile : après un pareil discours, le cardinal devrait etre enfermé pendant dix jours dans un couvent pour y vaquer aux exercices spirituels.

La puissance absolue du Pape, son opinion visible, le pouvoir arbitraire qu'exercent les présidents, la pétulance de certains prélats, trop notoirement passionnés et violents ; tout cela pèse sensiblement sur les membres les plus sages de l'assemblée qui ne peuvent s'empêcher de s'en plaindre avec tristesse dans des entretiens intimes. Faut-il s'étonner que plusieurs, le fait est très certain, expriment le désir d'un vote secret, s'il était possible ?

C'est avec une douleur profonde que nous racontons toutes ces choses. Mais la situation de l'Église en ce moment est telle qu'on ne peut se dispenser de parler. Au Concile du Vatican se traite une question de l'ordre le plus élevé. Chacun a le droit de savoir comment est conduit ce grand procès, qui est le procès de tous. Il s'agit de la paix du monde, il s'agit aussi de choses qui sont au-dessus de tous les intérêts périssables, de la foi, de la conscience et du salut éternel des âmes.

APPENDIX IV.

LETTER OF A FRENCH BISHOP TO COUNT DARU.

On sait à Rome que vous aviez l'intention de rédiger une note ou un memorandum qui devrait être appuyé par les puissances.

Si vous agissez, vous serez appuyés. Ici les diplomates se plaignent de votre inaction.

Mais il faut agir immédiatement, on veut introduire l'infaillibilité après Pâques.

Vous ne pouvez rien faire par le M. de Banneville. Ses collègues ne le comptent pour rien, sinon pour un obstacle.

Il ne faut pas vous mettre exclusivement sur le terrain des canons des Ecclesia. On vous répondrait, soit en supprimant les Canons auxquels vous vous opposez; soit en disant que cela ne vous touche pas, à cause du concordat; soit, enfin, en les expliquant dans un sens qui vous paraîtra satisfaisant, quitte à décréter après tous les Canons, tous les Syllabus qu'ils voudront, et les plus formidables. Mais il y a un terrain où vous êtes invincibles, et sur lequel les puissances vous suivent. C'est celui de la liberté du

Concile et du droit publique de l'Église, sous la protection duquel vos évêques sont venus à Rome.

Cette liberté n'existe plus. Ce droit est violé sur un point que plus de 100 évêques ont déclaré de la dernière importance.

Leur protestation vous donne un point de départ et des arguments invincibles.

Ces évêques déclarent que le Règlement est contraire à la loi de l'Église sur le point décisif de la Majorité. Car ce droit, depuis Nicée jusqu'à Trente, déclare que la règle indisputable et certaine pour les définitions dogmatiques c'est l'unanimité morale, et non la majorité.

Un nombre immense de faits confirme leur protestation :

Les scènes de violence faites à Haynald et à Strossmayer.—Les Présidents n'ont pas cherché à protéger leur droit et liberté de parole, tout au contraire.

La précipitation de la discussion par les Présidents.

Le Schema de Fide, 4 chapitres, 20 pages, canons avec anathèmes, a été distribué 24 heures seulement avant l'ouverture de la discussion, on a voté sur 47 amendements en 5 quarts d'heure.

Le lendemain de là scène avec Strossmayer, on a lu un *Monitum*, non pas pour admonéter les interrupteurs, mais pour recommander aux orateurs de se presser, de peur qu'ils n'ennuyent l'assemblée, et n'en provoquent des manifestations.

Ce *Monitum* est une provocation aux interruptions. Quelquefois un évêque est reçu avec des murmures avant de commencer.

Les demandes de la Minorité :

D'une salle où on puisse les entendre.

De bureaux, pour les discussions préliminaires, qui enverraient des Commissaires à la Députation.

De la liberté d'imprimer leurs discours et mémoires pour les distribuer parmi les pères.

Que les auteurs d'amendements puissent les expliquer et les défendre dans la Commission, et puissent avoir le droit de répondre dans les discussions.

D'un procès-verbal des séances.

Sur la majorité et l'unanimité.

Toutes ces demandes sont restées sans réponse et sans effet.

La pression exercée sur les Orientaux.

La scène faite au Patriarche Chaldéen.

L'emprisonnement intimé à l'Archévêque d'Antioche et au chef de sa communauté.

L'arrestation et les coups donnés au prêtre, secrétaire de l'Arch. de Diarbelair.

Les menaces aux Melchites, Maronites, et Chaldéens.

Le langage tenu par le pape lui même. Les cas de Montalembert et de Falloux.

Les lettres du pape à Guéranger, Cabrières, etc., traitant les Évêques de l'Opposition en ennemis.

Les allocutions publiques roulant presque toutes sur l'Infaillibilité.

Les cadeaux faits aux Vicaires Apostoliques en les priant de ne pas l'abandonner.

Attitude de la presse approuvée par le Vatican, exploitant ces lettres, et appelant les évêques à se retracter, en les dénonçant à leur clergé.

Même le journal officiel de Rome traitant la minorité d'alliés des Franc-maçons. Après tout cela, il n'y a pas de liberté au Concile.

L'ambassadeur que vous enverrez en recevra des preuves péremptoires. Les autres puissances sont déjà plus avancées que la France : la Prusse, la Hongrie, même la Turquie.

A nom de l'ordre publique menacé par l'inévitable refus de reconnaître ce Concile. Au nom de votre droit, ayant rendu possible la réunion du Concile, de protéger la liberté de vos évêques.

Dire—

" Ce Concile ne peut pas continuer dans les conditions actuelles.

" Nous protestons dès à présent contre la Non-liberté manifeste du Concile.

" Achevez ce que vous avez déjà commencé.

" Il y a des points sur lesquels vous pouvez espérer l'unanimité morale, sans violation de liberté.

" Tenez une session publique sur les *Schema de Fide* et de Discipline assez pour sauver votre honneur.

" Et prorogez une assemblée qui, aux yeux des évêques et du monde, ne possède plus ces conditions d'ordre et de liberté sans lesquelles ce n'est pas un Concile.

" Nous désirons que nos évêques retournent dans leurs diocèses jusqu'à ce que les conditions soient plus favorables pour la célébration d'un Concile."

APPENDIX V.

(Presented early in May.)

Permettez, Monseigneur, que je proteste ici contre
un tel projet, s'il existe, et que je consigne entre vos
mains ma protestation. Saisir ainsi, irrégulièrement et
violemment, le Concile de cette question, c'est absolument impossible.

Cette discussion immédiate de l'Infaillibilité Pontificale, avant toutes les autres questions qui la doivent
nécessairement précéder, ce renversement de l'ordre et
de la marche régulière du Concile, cette précipitation
passionnée dans l'affaire la plus délicate, et qui par sa
nature et ses difficultés, exige le plus de maturité et de
calme, tout cela serait non seulement illogique et
absurde, inconcevable, mais encore trahirait trop ouver-
tement aux yeux du monde entier, chez ceux qui
imaginent de tels procédés, le dessein de peser sur le
Concile, et pour dire le vrai mot, serait absolument
contraire à la liberté des évêques.

Comment une telle question, sous-introduite tout à

coup dans un chapitre annexé à un grand *Schema*, le dessein de ceux qui nous ont été soumis, passerait avant tous les schemata déjà étudiés, avant toutes les autres questions déjà discutées, et non encore résolues par le Concile.

Des questions fondamentales, essentiellement préliminaires à toutes les autres : Dieu, sa personnalité, sa providence, Jésus-Christ, sa divinité, sa redemption, sa grâce, l'Église, on laisserait tout celà de coté pour se précipiter sur cette question, dont nous n'avions entendu parler avant le Concile presque qu'à des Journalistes, dont la bulle de convocation ne parlait pas, dont le *Schema* sur l'Église lui-même ne disait pas un seul mot.

Et l'examen de cette nouvelle question, si compliquée, cette discussion, si nécessaire, cette définition si grave, tout cela se ferait à la hâte, violemment, au pied levé. On ne nous laisserait ni le temps ni la liberté d'étudier un point si important de doctrine avec gravité et à fond, comme il doit l'être. Car aucun évêque ne peut, sans blesser gravement sa conscience, déclarer de foi, sous peine de damnation éternelle, un point de doctrine de la révélation duquel il n'est pas absolument certain. Ce serait, Monseigneur, dans le monde entier, une stupeur et un scandale. Ce serait de plus autoriser trop manifestement les calomnies de ceux qui disent que dans la convocation du Concile, il y a eu une arrière pensée, et que cette question qui n'était pas l'objet du Concile, au fond devait être tout le Concile. Ceux qui poussent à de tels excès oublient clairement toute prudence : il y a un bon sens et une bonne foi publique qu'on ne blesse pas impunément.

Sans doute on peut passer par dessus toutes les ré-criminations des ennemis de l'Église ; mais il y a des difficultés avec lesquelles il faut nécessairement comp-ter. Eh bien ! Éminence, si les choses venaient à se passer de la sorte, je le dis avec toute la conviction de mon âme, il y aurait lieu de craindre que des doutes graves ne s'élèvent touchant la vérité même et la liberté de ce Concile du Vatican.

Que les choses se passent ainsi, on le peut, si on le veut : on peut tout, contre la raison et le droit, avec la force du nombre.

Mais c'est lendemain, Éminence, que commenceraient pour vous et pour l'Église les difficultés.

Par un procédé aussi contraire à l'ordre régulier des choses, à la marche essentielle des assemblées d'évêques qui ont été de vrais Conciles, vous susciteriez incontest-ablement une lutte dans l'Église et les consciences sur la question de l'issue œcuménique de notre assemblée : c'est à dire, tout ce qu'on peut imaginer aujourd'hui de plus désastreux.

Ceux qui essayent d'engager le Pape dans cette voie, en l'abusant et le trompant, sont bien coupables. Mais je ne doute pas que la sagesse du Saint-Père ne déjoue toutes ces menées.

EDINBURGH : PRINTED BY THOMAS AND ARCHIBALD CONSTABLE,
PRINTERS TO THE QUEEN, AND TO THE UNIVERSITY.